BLACK NATIONALISM IN AMERICAN HISTORY

BAAS Paperbacks

Published titles

Black Nationalism in American History

From the Nineteenth Century to the Million Man March

MARK NEWMAN

EDINBURGH
University Press

Edinburgh University Press is one of the leading university presses in the UK. We publish academic books and journals in our selected subject areas across the humanities and social sciences, combining cutting-edge scholarship with high editorial and production values to produce academic works of lasting importance. For more information visit our website: edinburghuniversitypress.com

© Mark Newman, 2018

Edinburgh University Press Ltd
The Tun – Holyrood Road, 12(2f) Jackson's Entry, Edinburgh EH8 8PJ

Typeset in 10/12 Adobe Sabon by
IDSUK (DataConnection) Ltd, and
printed and bound in Great Britain by
CPI Group (UK) Ltd, Croydon CR0 4YY

A CIP record for this book is available from the British Library

ISBN 978 1 4744 0541 6 (hardback)
ISBN 978 1 4744 0543 0 (webready PDF)
ISBN 978 1 4744 0542 3 (paperback)
ISBN 978 1 4744 0544 7 (epub)

Contents

Abbreviations

AAPRP	All-African People's Revolutionary Party
ABB	African Blood Brotherhood for African Liberation and Redemption
ACS	American Colonization Society (founded as the American Society for Colonizing the Free People of Color in the United States)
ALD	African Liberation Day
ALSC	African Liberation Support Committee
AME	African Methodist Episcopal Church
ANA	American Negro Academy
AOC	African Orthodox Church
AUC	African Universal Church and Commercial League
BARTS	Black Arts Repertory Theater/School
BEDC	Black Economic Development Conference
BLA	Black Liberation Army
BOI	Bureau of Investigation
BPP	Black Panther Party for Self-Defense
BSL	Black Star Line
CAP	Congress of African People
CFUN	Committee for a Unified Newark
COINTELPRO	Federal Bureau of Investigation Counterintelligence Program
CORE	Congress of Racial Equality
DRUM	Dodge Revolutionary Union Movement
FBI	Federal Bureau of Investigation
FOI	Fruit of Islam
FPCC	Fair Play for Cuba Committee
GOAL	Group on Advanced Leadership
ILDP	International League of Darker Peoples
LCFO	Lowndes County Freedom Organization
MFDP	Mississippi Freedom Democratic Party

MGT-GCC	Muslim Girls' Training and General Civilization Class
MMI	Muslim Mosque, Inc.
MSTA	Moorish Science Temple of America
NAACP	National Association for the Advancement of Colored People
NBPA	National Black Political Assembly
NCBC	National Committee of Black Churchmen
NOI	Nation of Islam
NUL	National Urban League
OAAU	Organization of Afro-American Unity
OAU	Organization of African Unity
RAM	Revolutionary Action Movement
RNA	Republic of New Africa
SCLC	Southern Christian Leadership Conference
SNCC	Student Nonviolent Coordinating Committee
UNIA	Universal Negro Improvement Association
WCIW	World Community of Al-Islam in the West

Chronology

1773   Four Boston slaves petitioned the Massachusetts colonial legislature to allow them a day a week to work to support their return to Africa.

1787   A group of free blacks petitioned the General Court of Massachusetts for resettlement in Africa.

1791–1804   Successful Haitian revolution against French rule.

1811   Paul Cuffe's first voyage to Sierra Leone.

1815–1816   Paul Cuffe's second voyage resettled a small group of African Americans in Sierra Leone.

1816   ACS founded by white Americans.

1817   Paul Cuffe died.

1820   Congressional approval of the Missouri Compromise divided the nation between slave and free at the latitude 36° 30′.

1822   The ACS founded Liberia.

1829–1830   David Walker published *An Appeal in Four Articles; Together with a Preamble to the Colored Citizens of the World, but in Particular, and Very Expressly, to Those of the United States of America.*

1830   The first National Negro Convention met in Philadelphia.

1843   Henry Highland Garnet gave an *Address to the Slaves of the United States* at the National Negro Convention.

1847   Liberia became independent.

1850   Congress approved the Compromise of 1850, including the Fugitive Slave Act.

1852   Martin R. Delany published *The Condition, Elevation, Emigration and Destiny of the Colored People of the United States.*

1854   Congress passed the Kansas-Nebraska Act, which overturned the Missouri Compromise.

	National Emigration Convention of Colored Men met in Cleveland, Ohio.
1857	*Dred Scott v. Sanford* denied African Americans citizenship rights and prohibited Congress from barring slavery from a territory.
1858	African Civilization Society founded.
1859–1860	Niger Valley Exploring Party.
1877	'Exoduster' movement began in response to the demise of Reconstruction.
1900	Pan-African Conference met in London.
1914	Marcus Garvey organised the UNIA in Jamaica.
1916	Marcus Garvey began a thirty-eight state American speaking tour.
1917	New York UNIA branch organised.
1919	The First Pan-African Congress met in Paris. ABB founded by Cyril V. Briggs.
1920	The UNIA's first International Convention of the Negro Peoples of the World adopted a 'Declaration of Rights of the Negro Peoples of the World'.
1921	African Orthodox Church organised. The Second Pan-African Congress met in London, Paris and Brussels.
1922	Marcus Garvey met with the Ku Klux Klan in Atlanta.
1923	Marcus Garvey imprisoned for mail fraud and released on bail after three months. The Third Pan-African Congress met in London and Lisbon.
1925	Noble Drew Ali founded the MSTA in Chicago. Marcus Garvey imprisoned.
1927	The Fourth Pan-African Congress met in New York. Marcus Garvey deported from the United States.
1928	Laura Kofey organised the AUC in Miami and was subsequently murdered.
1930	W. D. Fard established the NOI in Detroit.
1935	Elijah Muhammad became NOI leader after a factional struggle.
1945	The Fifth Pan-African Congress met in Manchester, England.
1959	Television broadcast of the documentary *The Hate That Hate Produced* brought increased NOI membership.

1964	Malcolm X left the NOI.
1965	Malcolm X murdered.
1966	Stokely Carmichael called for Black Power during the Meredith March in Mississippi.
	BPP founded in Oakland, California.
1969	Congressional Black Caucus organised.
	James Forman presented the Black Manifesto.
1972	The National Black Political Convention met in Gary, Indiana.
	African Liberation Day first held.
1974	The Sixth Pan-African Congress met in Dar es Salaam, Tanzania.
1975	Elijah Muhammad died. His son and successor, Wallace, began reorienting the NOI towards Sunni orthodoxy and repeatedly renamed the organisation.
1978	Louis Farrakhan began to re-establish the NOI.
1982	The BPP became defunct.
1995	Louis Farrakhan organised the Million Man March in Washington, DC.

CHAPTER I

Black Nationalism before Marcus Garvey

Historians do not agree on what constituted black nationalism in America, when it began and the extent of its adherence among blacks, but they agree that it has been a recurrent theme in American history that has manifested itself in different forms and has enjoyed periodic peaks of popularity. Scholars have divided over the extent to which black nationalism possessed its own initiative and agency and how much it was influenced by and imitative of trends in white western society. This book presents an introduction to and overview of the development of black nationalism in America in the nineteenth and twentieth centuries without which it is not possible fully to understand the African American experience during that time. It places black nationalism in context and argues that its content and expression in any given era reflected the particular circumstances of that period.[1]

Chapter 1 begins by explaining and assessing contrasting definitions of black nationalism developed by its leading scholars. The chapter also analyses early manifestations of black nationalism in America, the growing popularity of black nationalism in the 1850s, its resurgence after Reconstruction and the condition of black nationalism in the 1890s and early 1900s. Chapter 2 examines the rise and fall of Marcus Garvey and the Universal Negro Improvement Association (UNIA) in the United States, investigates the nature of their appeal and support, and assesses contrasting interpretations by historians. Chapter 3 discusses the evolution of the Nation of Islam (NOI), with particular attention to change over time, the contribution of W. D. Fard, Elijah Muhammad and Malcolm X to the NOI, internal conflict and the extent to which

I

Malcolm X changed after leaving the NOI. Chapter 4 considers the origins of Black Power, addresses the relationship between Black Power and black nationalism and argues that Black Power was too diverse and contradictory to constitute a movement. Chapter 5 explores black nationalism in the early 1970s, the refounding of the NOI by Louis Farrakhan after the death of Elijah Muhammad, the development of Afrocentricity, and the appeal and popularity of black nationalism prior to and during the Million Man March in 1995. The conclusion offers analytical reflections on the origins, diversity and appeal of black nationalism across two centuries.

Defining Black Nationalism

There is no uniformly accepted scholarly definition of black nationalism. Wilson Jeremiah Moses, its most prolific historian, focuses on 'classical black nationalism', which he defines as 'the ideology that argued for the self-determination of African Americans within the framework of an independent nation-state, [that] came into existence at the end of the eighteenth century' and declined alongside the UNIA after its leader Marcus Garvey's imprisonment in 1925 for mail fraud.[2] Moses's definition fits within a generally accepted and widely applied understanding of nationalism in world history as, Daryl Michael Scott explains, 'fundamentally a political concept' entailing 'a people's pursuit, attainment, or maintenance of sovereignty, or at least self-rule in a multinational system'. However, as Moses observes, black nationalism, unusually among nationalist forms, was based on the idea of racial unity, rather than geographical habitation or a shared language.[3]

In an overview of black nationalism, Dean E. Robinson accepts Moses's conception and chronology of a 'classical black nationalism' that existed until the mid-1920s but argues that subsequent 'modern' black nationalism, especially after 1945, should be more broadly defined 'to include both those who favored separate statehood, as well as self-identified "nationalists" who supported the more modest goal of black administration of vital private and public institutions'. However, it is not clear why a broad definition would, as Robinson claims, obscure historical understanding of the 'classical' period but not of the 'modern' period that followed it, although he is also dismissive of much of what passed as 'nationalism' in the late 1960s as 'better described as a black version of ethnic pluralism', meaning the 'pursuit of racially solidaristic efforts in a pluralistic political system subsumed by a capitalistic economic one'. In practice, ethnic pluralism entailed blacks voting collectively in areas where they formed a majority to elect black officials and thereby gain control of public services, such as 'medical, educational, and social welfare services', and 'the police and fire departments'.[4]

Historian James Lance Taylor contends that Moses's conception of 'classical black nationalism' is inadequate because it ignores nineteenth century '"stay at home" black nationalism' that not 'necessarily entailing the acquisition of land' manifested itself in black jeremiadic nationalist thought with 'religious foundations'. The jeremiad, named after the Old Testament prophet Jeremiah who warned that God would bring forth his judgement against sinners, was adopted by whites to call people back to righteousness but adapted by black nationalists to apply to white sins in their enslavement and treatment of blacks.[5]

Taylor has a more inclusive conception of black nationalism than Moses, regarding it as 'an articulation of the desire for self-determination in relation to white structures of power in ideas, law, politics, culture, society, religion, and economy on black people's terms, facilitated most fundamentally in forms of group solidarity'. Focused in particular on articulations of 'black rage' and 'revolutionary anger', Taylor argues for continuity in black nationalism. He finds the black jeremiadic tradition expressed by figures such as David Walker and Maria W. Stewart in the nineteenth century, novelist Richard Wright and Malcolm X in the twentieth century, and Chicago pastor Jeremiah Wright, Jr, in the twenty-first century. Taylor contends that black nationalism had a vitality and longevity that was more than a reaction to, or a mirror reflection of, 'white nationalism' in America as Moses suggests. However, the black jeremiad was essentially a critique of white racist oppression and so reactive and shaped by the circumstances of its time. Taylor's inclusion of 'black rage' as a key characteristic of black nationalism renders the concept more vague and imprecise. His claim that 'Since its earliest articulation in social and political discourse, black nationalists have steadfastly insisted on *perpetual* as opposed to *utilitarian* racial solidarity as both a means and an end to realising self-determination in a hostile society and world' is too restrictive. As Moses observes, 'There were elements of assimilationist thought in the philosophies of pioneering black nationalists . . . just as there were elements of black nationalism in the philosophies of such assimilationists as Frederick Douglass.' By assimilation, Moses meant that Douglass wanted blacks to be absorbed into the wider society as equals.[6]

Taylor's book is in part a response to Moses, who conceded that 'classical black nationalism' also included efforts to 'formulate an ideological basis for a concept of a national culture', and could 'In a very loose sense ... refer simply to any feelings of pride in a distinct ethnic heritage.' However, Moses also contended that such '"cultural black nationalism" did not manifest itself strongly in the classical period'.[7]

Some historians include cultural nationalism in a much broader definition of black nationalism. John H. Bracey, Jr, August Meier and Elliott Rudwick argue for 'many varieties of black nationalism, of varying degrees of intensity' that include cultural, economic and political forms, each underpinned by the most basic form of black nationalism 'racial solidarity' meaning 'the desire that black people organize themselves on the basis of their common color and oppressed condition to move in some way to alleviate their situation'. However, under their conception of racial solidarity the twentieth-century civil rights movement, which sought equal rights for blacks and inclusion in the American mainstream, could paradoxically be viewed as black nationalist, even though movement leaders, such as Roy Wilkins of the National Association for the Advancement of Colored People (NAACP), rejected black nationalism and sought integration.[8]

Undoubtedly nationalist in orientation, the NOI rejected the civil rights movement. In a study of the NOI, E. U. Essien-Udom defined nationalism as

> the belief of a group that it possesses, or ought to possess, a country; that it shares, or ought to share, a common heritage of language, culture and religion; and that its heritage, way of life, and ethnic identity are distinct from those of other groups.

While this definition adhered to the widely accepted idea of nationalism entailing or aspiring to sovereignty over land, such a definition would exclude many of the groups that arose in the 1960s that many historians regard as black nationalist, such as the Black Panther Party for Self-Defense (BPP) and the United Brothers. Scott has rightly argued that a stateless definition of nationalism by scholars makes black nationalism, regarded by him as 'the peculiar labeling of Black solidarity and cultural consciousness as nationalism', unique, with the exception of 'Chicano solidarity in the 1960s, which gets treated as an expression of nationalism'.[9]

Introducing a collection of documents about 'modern black nationalism', dated between 1920 and 1992, William L. Van Deburg concedes that 'there is no foolproof litmus test for use in nationalist accreditation', but he regards 'self-definition and self-determination' as crucial criteria. He maintains that 'Whether their nationalism is expressed in demands for territorial cession, political empowerment, or increased cultural autonomy, confirmed nationalists believe that the ethnic, religious, or linguistic group to which they are most intimately attached is undervalued and oppressed by "outsiders".'[10] Van Deburg's conception of black nationalism could apply to its manifestations across the centuries. However, his claim that 'nationalists seek to strengthen in-group values while holding those promoted by the larger society at arm's length' is at odds with nineteenth-century emigrationist black nationalists who, as Moses argues, shared an Anglo-American elite conception that a benighted, backward Africa needed to be redeemed from barbarism by being 'civilised' and Christianised.[11] The same difficulty afflicts Tunde Adeleke's claim that black nationalists shared and acted upon

> the desire for freedom and liberation from oppressive conditions, emphasis on black people acquiring greater control over their destinies and resources, a conviction that blacks, regardless of geographical location, share identity, cultural and historical experiences, and emphasis on a distinct black worldview, culture, and heritage.

Moses notes that after Garvey, black nationalists tended to move from seeking to uplift, 'civilise' and remodel African Americans and African society to 'idealize African village life, sentimentalize the rural South, and romanticize the urban ghetto'. Adeleke's definition is also so broad that it could conceivably apply to civil rights leader Martin Luther King, Jr.[12]

Akinyele Umoja seeks to reconcile classical and modern black nationalism by contending that nationalists 'seek some form of self-determination, up to and including independent statehood'. Influenced by Van Deburg, he adds that 'Nationalists seek a separate national identity from the dominant society and self-determination' which may include establishing a nation state. Umoja also, like Van Deburg, distinguishes nationalists from assimilationists who protest their grievances in an effort to integrate and be included in the American mainstream, and pluralists who 'believe ethnic and interest groups should be able to participate in the political and economic mainstream of American society, while maintaining their cultural identity'.[13] The problem here is that just as there have been assimilationists, such as Frederick Douglass, who, at times, displayed nationalist thinking, there has also been what political philosopher Tommie Shelby terms 'pragmatic' nationalists, such as Martin R. Delany, who sometimes evidenced assimilationist inclinations by seeking to mobilise black politically to secure political and social inclusion and equality, and other apparent nationalists who advocated pluralism. Dean E. Robinson notes some Black Power advocates in the 1960s, such as Stokely Carmichael and Charles V. Hamilton in their book *Black Power*, accepted 'ethnic pluralism', in which ethnic groups in America competed for power and resources. Consequently, they sought to mobilise blacks on their basis of their ethnicity to achieve control of local institutions that served the community.[14]

Shelby suggests abandoning using classical and modern black nationalism as a means of periodisation and instead conceiving of black nationalism as comprising strong and weak components that have existed and often coexisted throughout its history. For him, strong nationalism, similar to Moses's classical black nationalism but shorn of necessarily seeking statehood,

> treats the establishment of an independent black republic or a separate self-determining community as an intrinsic goal of black liberation struggles. It advocates the development of a national identity, black self-reliance, and separatism, not only as a means to racial justice but as the political destiny of African Americans and perhaps of all those of African descent.

By contrast, 'pragmatic' or

> Weak nationalism . . . urges black solidarity and concerted action as a political strategy to life or resist oppression. This could . . . mean forming a self-governing black nation-state or a separate

self-determining community within a multinational state, but it could also mean working to create a racially integrated society.

Shelby's dual conceptions of black nationalism help explain shifts in approach by figures such as Delany, and to recognise that nationalists were not necessarily or always opposed to assimilation and pluralism.[15]

However, Shelby's weak nationalism is also akin to Bracey, Meier and Rudwick's conception of 'racial solidarity' and similarly vulnerable to being too open-ended. Focused on nationalism as a political programme, Shelby also neglects its cultural manifestations. Nevertheless, he ably justifies the inclusion of those who did not advocate statehood as nationalists. Shelby explains that

> when the idiom of nationhood is deployed to define a "people," to identify its collective interests and will, and to create bonds of political solidarity among those in this would-be community, the label of "nationalism" is appropriate, even if the political goal is not necessarily the creation of a separate self-determining corporate unit.

Moses also notes that black nationalism has often 'been "nationalism" only in the sense that it seeks to unite the entire black racial family, assuming that the entire race has a collective destiny and message for humanity comparable to that of a nation'.[16]

Defining black nationalism, then, is difficult and contentious, a problem compounded by the fact that the term itself did not gain usage until the twentieth century. In this study, black nationalism in America is conceived of as inclination or action by African Americans to improve their condition, whether political, economic, cultural or psychological, collectively as a people through an eth-noracially conceived identity and programme that seeks some measure of self-determination and autonomy that may, but does not necessarily, include statehood. Some African Americans, who are not generally considered nationalist at times exhibited aspects of nationalism as defined here, for example A. Philip Randolph's all-black March on Washington Movement in the 1940s, and some African Americans widely considered to be strong nationalists, such as Delany and Henry McNeal Turner, were often pragmatic and adaptable. Moses notes that 'most black leaders have occasionally shown black nationalist elements in their thinking'. Furthermore, as Robinson (and Moses before him) contends, black nationalism was not an unchanging phenomenon, rather its various manifestations were 'products of partly similar but largely unique eras of politics, thought, and culture'. Determining who were black nationalists at any given time has often been and remains disputed and is likely to remain so, but, as Van Deburg argues, 'if someone looks, speaks, writes, and acts like a nationalist, others may be justified in treating them as such', providing due attention is given to historical context.[17]

Although historians do not include an emphasis on masculinity or patriarchy in definitions of black nationalism, these notions have often been among its features. Nationalists such as Alexander Crummell in the nineteenth century and Marcus Garvey and Elijah Muhammad in the twentieth century expected black women primarily to focus on raising children and assuming a supportive and subordinate role to their husbands, who had a duty to protect them and provide for their families. Such ideas reflected the wider society in which they developed. They received added impetus by a need some black nationalists felt to counteract the effects of white efforts during slavery and subsequently to render black men powerless and exploit black women for sexual gratification and by a belief that slavery had left a legacy of licentiousness among the black masses that undermined the nuclear family. In the late 1960s, some Black Power leaders including Maulena Karenga and Amiri Baraka explicitly called for female submissiveness and Karenga's US organisation initially accepted polygamy. In a bid to reclaim manhood as they conceived it, some male Black Panther leaders including Huey Newton and Eldridge Cleaver initially advocated a masculinity which envisaged Panther men as heterosexual warriors who protected acquiescent black women and children and defended the black community.[18]

As their views were often unrecorded in the historical record even as recently as the early twentieth century, it is often difficult to know how black nationalist women responded to patriarchy. It is likely that some female nationalists, particularly before the 1960s, shared at least some of patriarchy's conceptions, but there were also examples of them challenging subordination in the UNIA, US and the BPP. Some black nationalist women had influential or prominent roles, among them Henrietta Vinton Davis of the UNIA and Erica

Huggins who led a Panther chapter in New Haven, Connecticut. Furthermore, some men associated with black nationalism including Martin R. Delany and W. E. B. Du Bois were sympathetic to female equality. Even Crummell claimed to believe in it, and he argued that intellectually able men and women should be educated together. A century later, Newton and Cleaver eventually endorsed sexual equality, although the party struggled to end patriarchy within its ranks. In the early 1970s, Karenga also repudiated patriarchy.[19]

The Emergence of Black Nationalism

Just as there is no commonly accepted definition of black nationalism, there is also no agreement about its first appearance. Like most nationalisms, black nationalism was a response to perceived, and in this case obvious, injustice from those holding power. Moses contends that insufficient written sources mean that its emergence cannot be determined with certainty. He regards slave revolts as 'opportunistic expressions of resentment', rather than indicative of 'plans for an alternative social order'. However, he notes that slave revolts in the colonial America and the early Republic were 'often linked to a desire for self-determination', and some escaped slaves formed self-governing maroon communities beyond the reach of whites in places such as Florida. For Taylor, slave revolts, conspiracies to revolt and maroon communities are evidence of nationalist consciousness. He contends that major slave uprisings and conspiracies, such as those associated with Gabriel in Richmond, Virginia (1800), Denmark Vesey in Charleston, South Carolina (1822), and Nat Turner in Southampton County, Virginia (1831) were 'deliberative, not simply opportunistic'. They were sometimes long in their planning and envisioned a 'new social order' of freedom and liberty. Historian Sterling Stuckey goes further, claiming that enslaved people, severed from their particular tribal cultures, forged a new identity in America, grounded in African culture, which produced and sustained their nationalism through the antebellum era.[20]

Scholars disagree about the extent and longevity of African survivals. However, as slavery continued, the likelihood of strong African survivals lessened with each generation and under the influence of a developing American culture, and their prospects of enduring varied greatly according to the size and often diverse nature of slave holdings, labour, location and management. As slaves were largely illiterate and there were few revolts, partly through a lack of opportunity and realistic prospects for success but also because of some degree of accommodation to slavery, it is difficult to determine the extent of nationalist feeling among them. The ways in which, and the extent to which, the enslaved accommodated to and resisted slavery remain contested by historians.[21]

That black nationalist sentiment was developing in the eighteenth century is suggested by the petition of four Boston slaves in 1773 to the Massachusetts colonial legislature to allow them a day a week to work for sufficient funds to enable their return to Africa. Moses characterises the petition as 'protonationalistic' because it 'did not articulate any sense of national destiny or any intention of creating a nation-state with a distinctive national culture'. Such thinking developed, he suggests, in 'unison with the American and French Revolutions' of 1776 and 1789 but was not a mere imitation of their nationalism because 'Black nationalism was an expression of the impulse toward self-determination among Africans transplanted to the New World by the slave trade.' Nevertheless, the ideology of the American Revolution and American institutions influenced black nationalism. In 1787, Prince Hall spoke on behalf of over seventy-five Boston blacks, some African-born, who unsuccessfully petitioned the General Court of Massachusetts to enable their 'return to Africa, our native country', where they planned to live under 'a political constitution', establish a black-run missionary Christian Church, and bring Christianity, 'civilisation' and commerce to the local populace. Black groups in Newport and Providence, Rhode Island, including many born in Africa, also wanted to emigrate to Africa and refashion it on the western model, but, without sufficient resources, they were unable to implement their plans. The Haitian Revolution (1791–1804) that overturned both French colonial rule and slavery also contributed to the development of black nationalism in the United States.[22]

Motivated by a desire to promote commerce, Christianity and encourage the abolition of slavery in the United States, Paul Cuffe, a free born black ship captain from Massachusetts, brought the first black settlers from America to Africa in 1816. He had undertaken a preliminary trading voyage in 1811 to Sierra Leone, a West African colony established in 1787 after American independence by British private interests, designed to absorb black American Loyalists in Britain and its territories. The colony had come under the British crown in 1808. After the War of 1812 between the United States and Britain had interrupted his plans, Cuffe returned to Sierra Leone with thirty-eight black migrants, at least of two of them African-born. Increasingly concerned to eliminate American slavery, he developed a dual colonisation plan that proposed establishing black settlements in an unoccupied part of the western United States and on the west coast of Africa. He also envisaged developing a black run shipping line to foster Africa's commercial growth.[23]

Sympathetic whites, including the New Jersey Presbyterian minister Robert Finley, contacted Cuffe about his plans for an African colony for black Americans. In 1816, Finley, who intended that colonisation should encourage emancipation, helped found the American Society for Colonizing the Free People of Color in the United States, generally known as the American Colonization Society (ACS). A white group, some of whose members opposed slavery's abolition and were only concerned with removing free blacks from the United States, the society sought federal aid to realise its ambitions. Cuffe encouraged Finley's efforts, but many black Americans, aware it seems, unlike Cuffe, of proslavers in the ACS, opposed the society, fearing that it sought to rid the United States of free blacks in order to strengthen slavery. Cuffe, who died in September 1817, was in historian Floyd J. Miller's view 'the first black of stature to connect colonization with emancipation', and his nationalistic advocacy of black American emigration to Africa to make it 'a black replica of Western society' anticipated 'the full-blown black nationalism of the 1850's', exemplified by Martin R. Delany. Miller regards Cuffe as a protonationalist. Moses and Taylor concur, but they consider Cuffe to have been less ideologically driven, arguing that his protonationalism was motivated as much, and for Taylor more, by commerce than it was by a concern for the resettlement of Africa.[24]

Although many blacks regarded the ACS as a proslavery deportation organisation, three or four hundred free blacks sailed on society chartered ships in the early 1820s to Sierra Leone and later to adjacent Liberia, the colony established by the society in 1822. They were motivated either by hope for better life away from white dominance or by a Christian missionary impulse. Suspicious of the ACS's motives, wary of Liberia's climate and bellicose neighbours, and responsive to offers of support from its government, a few thousand free blacks migrated from the northern United States to

Haiti in 1824 and 1825. However, many of them soon returned, unable to adjust to the climate and alien ways of Haitians, many of whom did not share the initially welcoming attitude of their government, which ended significant emigration in 1825 by withdrawing travel assistance and land grants.[25]

The failure of Haitian emigration gave added impetus to black Americans' hostility to emigration and colonisation which hardened in the late 1820s and also found expression after the early 1830s in national black conventions, although some blacks continued to emigrate to Liberia with ACS assistance. The conventions, which met between 1830 and 1835, provided black Americans with a vehicle for protest as did the spread of antislavery societies. At the same time, the switch of white abolitionists to advocating immediate rather than gradual emancipation, increasing white condemnation of slavery as evil, and growing black and white rejection of colonisation further solidified blacks' opposition to emigration and encouraged their hope for a better future in the United States.[26]

Although the emigrationist form of black nationalism was undoubtedly in decline, some historians contend that there was also a domestic stay-at-home black nationalism exemplified by David Walker's pamphlet, *An Appeal in Four Articles; Together with a Preamble to the Colored Citizens of the World, but in Particular, and Very Expressly, to Those of the United States of America*, issued between 1829 and 1830. In *The Golden Age of Black Nationalism*, Moses acknowledges that Walker 'was a fervent black nationalist, yet he opposed emigration under any auspices', and so was not part of 'classical black nationalism' since he had no aspiration for independent statehood for black Americans. Consequently, to consider 'classical black nationalism' as the totality of black nationalism before 1925 is to miss some of its other manifestations during that time. Stuckey considers Walker's *Appeal* 'the most all-embracing black nationalist formulation to appear in America during the nineteenth century'. Historian Bill McAdoo approvingly describes the *Appeal* as the beginning of revolutionary black nationalism which sought to destroy slavery and racial oppression in America by utilising 'the proven revolutionary potential of the enslaved black masses' to achieve 'the armed revolutionary overthrow of the oppressor'. Taylor also attests to Walker's significance, regarding him, alongside 'his intellectual and movement progeny' that included Maria

W. Stewart, Robert Alexander Young and Henry Highland Garnet, as epitomising a stay-at-home black nationalism that took the form of 'Afro-Christian jeremiadic agitation'.[27]

Little is known with certainty about Walker, who was born free to a free mother and to an enslaved father, who died before his birth, in North Carolina, in either 1785 or the 1790s. By the mid-1820s, Walker had moved to Boston. His *Appeal* rejected emigration and colonisation, stating that 'America is more our country, than it is the whites'. Walker vigorously condemned slavery for its inhumanity and barbarity and the denial of education to slaves and free blacks. He urged blacks to pursue self-improvement through education, work, temperance, morality and devotion to a Protestantism shorn of racism. Walker also called on them to challenge white religious defences of slavery and to work actively against slavery and discrimination. He rejected white conceptions of black inferiority and, affirming black pride, stated that 'we wish to be just as it pleased our Creator to have made us'. Walker called on whites to 'repent and reform, or you are ruined!!!!!!' Invoking a jeremiad, he warned that 'unless you speedily alter your course, *you* and your *Country are gone!!!!!!* For God Almighty will tear up the very face of the earth!!!!' Walker urged blacks to resist slavery and declared 'I ask you had you not rather be killed than to be a slave to a tyrant, who takes the life of your mother, wife, and dear little children?' Walker's nationalism was particularly evident in his assertion that after the end of slavery, 'we will want all the learning and talents among ourselves, and perhaps more, to govern ourselves'. Although the *Appeal* referred to whites as 'our natural enemies', Walker claimed that had not always been so and held out the prospect of reconciliation. He wrote:

> Treat us like men, and there is no danger but we will all live in peace and happiness together . . . [T]he whole of the past will be sunk into oblivion, and we yet, under God, will become a united and happy people.[28]

According to biographer Peter P. Hinks, Walker's views were shared by many other northern blacks. 'While an open appeal for slave revolt was surely rare', writes Hinks, Walker 'reflected the increased willingness of blacks by the late 1820s to avow publicly their outrage at the persistence of slavery and to consider new methods for fighting and ending it.' Although Walker called on slaves to resist their enslavement, he hoped reform would make violence unnecessary. Walker circulated the pamphlet through friends, acquaintances and the mail, particularly targeting the South, which alarmed southern whites, but Hinks notes that the *Appeal* did not 'generate slave resistance in the South. The slaves did not need Walker to tell them what they had been doing all along.' Walker died in 1830, probably of tuberculosis, although some suspected poison.[29]

Historians disagree about the *Appeal*'s relationship to black nationalism. In 1972, Stuckey found that 'there is scarcely an important aspect of Afro-American nationalist thought in the twentieth century which is not prefigured in that document', and he argued that Walker's 'conception regarding the need for Africans to rule themselves . . . mark his *Appeal* as unmistakably nationalist in ideology'. Fifteen years later in *Slave Culture*, Stuckey revised his earlier contention that Walker had called for a black nation, stating that 'There is no indication that he thought a separate nation desirable along or within the boundaries of white America.' Rather, Walker expressed the hope, although not the expectation, that whites would overcome their racism, and racial harmony and equality follow. Nevertheless, Walker's focus was primarily on black liberation and the 'indispensability of unified struggle by blacks for them to be free and to defend their freedom'. The *Appeal* was jeremiadic in that it castigated whites for their sins against blacks and warned them of retribution to come if they did not change. Stuckey writes of Walker:

> While he thought such [racial] harmony possible with God's intercession, he considered the vital destruction of white America more likely, which explains his not dwelling on a relationship of mutual respect between whites and blacks. The burden of the *Appeal* is essentially one of doom for whites.

For Stuckey, Walker 'is the father of black nationalist theory in America because much of the substance of that ideology is found in his writings'.[30]

In *Classical Black Nationalism*, Moses also views the *Appeal* as 'in the tradition of the "jeremiad"' which gave it a 'convincingly nationalistic ring', but, in a modification of his view in *The Golden*

Age of Black Nationalism, he argues that 'its ties to black national-ism are problematic' because Walker 'did not advocate a separate national destiny' and 'his ultimate objective was the social, politi-cal and cultural assimilation of black Americans into American society'. Whereas Stuckey connects the *Appeal* to later black nationalist formulations, Moses observes that, except for claim-ing 'an identity with ancient Egypt and Ethiopia, Walker's attitude toward Africa was negative'. Unlike late twentieth-century cul-tural black nationalism that 'romanticizes peasant and proletarian folkways', Walker admired the culture of white western society, except, of course, its racism. Stuckey recognises these caveats, but he sees in Walker's emphasis on racial unity, pride, common strug-gle and desire for self-determination much that anticipated later nationalist advocates. However, Stuckey unduly down plays Walk-er's hope for reform.[31]

Hinks rightly argues that 'Walker made his contributions to black nationalism broadly understood', but Stuckey 'overstated' Walker's 'stature as an architect of black nationalism' and under-played 'his commitment to a racially integrated society in which racial distinctiveness would play little role'. Walker's ideas fit within the definition of black nationalism advanced in this book. Black nationalism was not unchanging and was subject to the influence of the times in which its advocates lived. It did not necessarily or always advocate permanent separation. Walker regarded separate black organisations as a means to help end racial inequality, not as a permanent feature.[32]

Unlike Wilson Jeremiah Moses, fellow historian James Lance Taylor regards the black jeremiad as central to black nationalism, yet he is also sometimes unsure and imprecise in his treatment of its advocates in the 1820 and 1830s. He refers to 'first or "proto" – nationalist personalities such as' Walker, Stewart, Young and Garnet, but also claims that Stewart was not 'a nationalist per se', leaving her exact status in his interpretation unclear. Born to free black parents in Hartford, Connecticut, in 1803, Stewart became a friend of Walker's in Boston and, after his death, addressed public meetings in 1832 and 1833 in which she condemned slav-ery and discrimination, and called for black self-improvement. Unlike Walker, Stewart did not sanction violence, but she spoke in the same jeremiadic tradition and, like him, rejected colo-nisation. In an 1833 speech in Boston, Stewart lamented that

'America has become like the great city of Babylon'. She warned that

> many powerful sons and daughters of Africa will shortly arise, who will put down vice and immorality among us, and declare by Him that sitteth upon the throne, that they will have their rights; and, if refused, I am afraid they will spread horror and devastation around.

Stewart also invoked Psalms 68:31 'Princes shall come out of Egypt; Ethiopia shall soon stretch out her hands unto God', to claim that blacks would have God's blessing.[33]

Moses calls such invocations Ethiopianism and notes that they were a feature of much nineteenth-century black nationalism, in which Ethiopia referred to Africa and those of African descent. For its proponents, Ethiopianism might mean the Christianisation of African peoples, but it could mean the uplifting of Africa to the forefront of nations, 'God's judgment upon the Europeans' for their treatment of Africans and a belief that suffering had 'endowed the African with moral superiority and made him a seer'. Although David Walker's *Appeal* did not cite the biblical verse directly, Moses argues that Ethiopianism characterised it because Walker claimed that God would spare America only if it abolished slavery. Stewart's address, like the *Appeal*, appears in Moses's edited collection *Classical Black Nationalism* even though neither fit, as he acknowledges, within his definition of the term. For Moses, both documents were nationalist only insofar as they contained 'a biblically inspired perception of African Americans as a people with a special God-given mission and destiny'. Moses's other characterisations of Stewart suggest, but not to him, that she should be considered a black nationalist because 'She viewed black Americans as a captive nation with a distinct national destiny' which was 'separate . . . from that of other Americans'. Given that he characterises the black jeremiad as part of nineteenth-century nationalism, Taylor's ambivalence about Stewart's nationalism is also puzzling and even more so when he observes that she 'enjoyed unfettered public support from male nationalists *when it was patently impolitic for women to show interest outside of the domestic sphere*'.[34]

Taylor follows Moses in including Robert Alexander Young's *Ethiopian Manifesto* (1829) in the black jeremiadic tradition because

Young prophesied that God would send a liberator to free Africans, as blacks in America commonly referred to themselves in America in the 1830s until black opposition to ACS-sponsored African emigration caused many to abandon that designation. Even less is known about Young, who disappeared from the historical record after the manifesto, than Walker, who similarly predicted that God would send blacks a 'Hannibal' to deliver them from their 'deplorable and wretched condition under the christians of America'.[35]

Most historians detect the development of black nationalism in antebellum America, locating it largely among educated blacks in the North, who rejected African culture. By contrast, Stuckey regards African culture as a well-spring for nationalism among American slaves. In the 1830s and 1840s, most black leaders did not espouse nationalism, whether in the stay-at-home jeremiadic or emigrative form focused on leaving the United States. They worked through the Negro Convention Movement to oppose slavery and racial discrimination, and promote self-improvement, although some, in the convention's early years, supported emigration.

In 1830, forty blacks from seven states attended the first National Negro Convention, sparked by the imposition of prohibitive bonds on free blacks migrating to Cincinnati that caused blacks in the city to consider relocating to southern Canada, already a destination for escaped slaves. The convention met in Philadelphia at the invitation of Bishop Richard Allen, a former slave from Pennsylvania who had helped found a new denomination, the African Methodist Episcopal Church (AME) in the city in 1816. The AME fitted within a pattern of blacks creating their own Methodist and Baptist churches in the North in the early decades of the Republic in response to growing discrimination in white churches. While it rejected the ACS and emigration to Liberia, the convention supported those who felt compelled to go to Canada. Allen subsequently headed the American Society of Free Persons of Colour, for Improving their Condition in the United States; for Purchasing Lands; and for the Establishment of a Settlement in Upper Canada that emerged from the convention. In 1831, the second National Negro Convention announced that 2,000 blacks had gone to Canada, but, in subsequent years, the convention increasingly opposed all emigration, except for escaped slaves seeking refuge in Canada, and focused on self-improvement through education, work and temperance, alongside its support for abolition and racial equality.[36]

Bracey, Meier and Rudwick note that the conventions, which met annually between 1830 and 1835 in Philadelphia, with the exception of New York in 1834, 'did not themselves overtly express an ideology of nationalism'. White abolitionists, missionaries and colonisationists were also active participants in the 1831 and 1832 meetings. Nevertheless, such organised race-based efforts to improve black prospects through racial solidarity had a mildly nationalist tone. After the national conventions ceased to meet, free blacks in the North and West formed state conventions that focused on suffrage, increasingly restricted or denied to blacks, and self-improvement.[37]

During the late 1830s and early 1840s, the Reverend Lewis Woodson, an AME minister and participant in an 1841 black state convention in Pennsylvania, developed what historian Floyd J. Miller considers 'a fully-fledged nationalist-emigrationist philosophy' that influenced his student Martin R. Delany, who became the leading exponent of emigrationist nationalism in the 1850s. Born in Virginia in 1806, Woodson was a slave until he was nineteen when his father bought his liberty. After a period in Ohio, he relocated to Pittsburgh, Pennsylvania. Woodson rejected the ACS's programme of colonisation in Liberia, regarding it as the forced migration of the vulnerable. Instead, he called for a concentrated black-organised migration en masse to the western United States to create separate communities and later for mass emigration to Canada and the British West Indies, where the emigrants would develop economic power that he believed would undermine slavery in the United States. Woodson, who never became a national leader and often wrote under a pseudonym, later abandoned emigration, although he continued to advocate separate black organisations.[38]

By 1840, militancy was growing among northern blacks as moral suasion, meaning efforts to persuade white opinion, had not ended slavery. Following the crushing by a white militia of Nat Turner's slave rebellion in Virginia in 1831, southern states had sought to protect slavery by banning teaching enslaved people literacy and bolstering the militia and countryside patrols. Some southern states also prohibited membership in abolitionist groups. Proslavery arguments gained currency among southern white opinion makers and leaders. Such actions increased belligerency among northern blacks. The mood was apparent in Henry Highland Garnet's address to the

National Negro Convention when it met, for the first time in eight years, in Buffalo, New York, in 1843.[39]

Born in Maryland in 1815, Garnet had escaped from slavery with his family as a child, and later became the pastor of a black Presbyterian Church in Troy, New York. His address urged slaves to refuse to work without pay, challenge their enslavement and defend themselves until death if, as likely, they suffered retribution. He celebrated figures such as Vesey and Turner, who had resisted slavery. Opponents, including Frederick Douglass, protested that the address 'was war-like, and encouraged insurrection'. The convention rejected a modified version by nineteen votes to eighteen. Although this version bore slight changes, 'all of its original doctrine', Garnet claimed, remained intact. In it, his repeated calls for 'resistance', exhortations that it was better to die than remain a slave, and declaration that 'there is not much hope of Redemption without the shedding of blood' were tempered by advice not 'to attempt a revolution with the sword' because 'Your numbers are too small, and moreover the rising spirit of the age, and the spirit of the gospel, are opposed to war and bloodshed.' Instead, the address counselled that 'What kind of resistance you had better make, you must decide by circumstances that surround you, and according to the suggestion of expediency.' Douglass ensured that the convention continued on the path of moral suasion when it met next in 1847 at Troy, despite Garnet reiterating his ideas there. Garnet published his 1843 address a year later. Formerly an opponent of emigration, by 1849 he countenanced it, whether to Central America, California, Mexico or Liberia, and he claimed that the ACS had helped Africa.[40]

Black Nationalism in the 1850s

In the second half of the 1840s, emigration became increasingly attractive to some blacks, with Liberia, often previously scorned because of its ACS association, as well as Haiti and Canada, considered among the possibilities after Liberia, led by American-Liberians, declared independence from the United States in 1847. Worsening racial conditions in the United States contributed to this trend. In 1850, Congress passed the Fugitive Slave Act, part of the Compromise of 1850 which allowed California, acquired in the Mexican War of 1846–8, to join the Union as a free state. The act obliged citizens to help federal marshals recapture alleged fugitive slaves, or face imprisonment of up to six months and a $1000 fine, and denied fugitives a jury trial, thereby placing both escaped enslaved people and free blacks at risk, especially as slaveholders needed only to claim that a black person was an escaped slave. Federal commissioners who tried the suspects received a double fee for each conviction. The act thereby extended the reach of slaveholders into the North, and it prompted some blacks, among them Mary Ann Shadd, Henry Bibb and James Theodore Holly, to emigrate to Canada West (Ontario).[41]

Free born in Delaware in 1823, Shadd became an advocate of emigration and, in 1852, she published the pamphlet *Notes of Canada West* as a practical guide and inducement. Born in Kentucky in 1815, Bibb had finally escaped slavery in 1842 after being recaptured five times. He founded Canada's first black newspaper, *The Voice of the Fugitive* in 1851, which he edited until his death in 1854, and promoted Canada as a destination for black Americans. Holly, who was born free in Washington, DC in 1829, appealed in Bibb's newspaper for large-scale Canadian emigration, contending that emigration aided slavery's abolition. Bibb and Holly called for a North American convention of blacks, which met in Toronto in 1851, nine months before Holly himself moved to Canada. The convention called on slaves and free blacks to migrate to Canada and proposed forming an organisation that would include blacks in the British West Indies as well as North America.[42]

However, the organisation did not take root, and it was Delany, a delegate at Toronto, who became the best known voice for nationalist emigration. Delany, who prided himself on his dark appearance, had been born in Charleston, Virginia (later West Virginia), in 1812 to a free mother and an enslaved father. The family later moved to Chambersburg, Pennsylvania, and, in 1831, Delany relocated to Pittsburgh, his base for a quarter of a century. He became a 'cupper and leecher', who treated illness by extracting blood using leeches or inverted glass cups applied to the back from which the air was withdrawn to create vacuum, and later a doctor. An activist for abolition, temperance and black rights, and a gifted public speaker, Delany edited a black newspaper, *The Mystery*, in Pittsburgh before working between 1847 and 1849 with escaped slave Frederick Douglass's abolitionist paper, *The North Star*, published in Rochester, New York. In the 1840s, Delany advocated education, hard work, learning a trade, self-help, thrift and morality, believing that these would ensure black advancement in America and boost their practitioners' self-worth. He opposed the ACS and Liberia as a tool of white interests. Delany's belief that it was their condition and not their race that held blacks back, conflicted with his recognition that most northern states denied blacks the vote, whatever their economic and social circumstances. The Fugitive Slave Act provided confirmation that race determined blacks' treatment and status in the United States; a message reinforced for Delany personally when student opposition led Harvard Medical School to insist that he and two other black students withdraw in 1851, only months after their admission.[43]

Present at the Toronto Convention, Delany opposed black emigration to Canada and elsewhere, but he soon reconsidered and became a committed emigrationist. In a pamphlet he published privately in 1852, *The Condition, Elevation, Emigration and Destiny of the Colored People of the United States*, Delany called for emigration to Central and South America and the British West Indies, although he opposed Canadian emigration, except as a temporary refuge for fugitive slaves, claiming that Canada would likely become part of the United States. The pamphlet repeated his insistence that blacks should improve their condition through self-help by become economically independent and eschewing menial work. Delany maintained his opposition to the ACS and dismissed Liberia as its dependent, while also warning against reliance on white abolitionists, arguing that, like slaveholders, they relegated blacks to 'a mere secondary, underlying position'. If blacks migrated south of the United States, they could, he argued, forge a nation with the black peoples already there that could withstand American expansionism. In an appendix, Delany proposed sending an expedition to the eastern coast of Africa to assess its suitability for migration and claimed that 'We are a nation within a nation; as the Poles in Russia, the Hungarians in Austria, the Welsh, Irish, and Scotch in the British dominions.'[44]

The pamphlet drew the ire of white abolitionists. Delany responded that blacks had to devise their own solutions. He explained:

We have always adopted the policies that white men established for themselves without considering their applicability or adaptedness to us. No people can rise in the way. We must have a position, independently of anything pertaining to white men as nations.

Although considered to be the father of black nationalism by historian Theodore H. Draper, Delany was not its originator, and he was, compared to some of his contemporaries, late in embracing its emigrationist variant.[45]

In 1853, emigrationists held a second convention in Canada at Amherstburg, where they endorsed their host country as appropriate for emigration and recognised Haiti as a suitable alternative. Blacks opposed to emigration, including Frederick Douglass and Lewis Woodson, met at the Colored National Convention in Rochester, New York, where they established a National Council, envisaged the creation of separate racial organisations, such as a college, consumers' union and employment bureau, to serve black interests and condemned the ACS. In effect, they responded to emigrationist nationalism with a form of stay-at-home nationalism grounded in racial solidarity and distinct black institutions. Although he consistently opposed emigration to Africa, in 1853 even Douglass briefly toyed with the idea that blacks might need to emigrate to places within the western hemisphere that would enable them to maintain pressure on America slavery. He observed that blacks in the United States were 'becoming a nation, in the midst of a nation which disowns them' and speculated that North America's black inhabitants might 'mould them[selves] into one body, and into a powerful nation'.[46]

Moses explains that 'Douglass ... opposed colonization and the doctrine that the races should be perpetually separate.' He was pragmatic and, conscious of his mixed race as the son of a slave and a white slaveholder, had no time for racial pride or chauvinism. Nevertheless, he was, Moses writes with considerable hyperbole, 'as good a nationalist as most' and 'participated in and defended the right to institutional separatism', while remaining, for the most part, committed to staying in the United States to achieve abolition and racial equality. 'Douglass', Moses concludes, 'sought to use nationalistic means for integrationist and assimilationist ends.' However, internal disagreements saw the National Council fall apart after two years, and the convention's proposed separate institutions never developed.[47]

Within weeks of the Rochester meeting, Delany and others announced plans for a National Emigration Convention in 1854 to focus solely on possibilities in the Western Hemisphere. Both Bibb and Holly later joined the call for the convention, but Shadd, and others blacks in Canada, who published a new newspaper, the *Provincial Freeman*, remained committed to blacks migrating to Canada and becoming British subjects. The convention met in August, a few months after Congress had passed the Kansas-Nebraska Act that overturned the Missouri Compromise of 1820 which had permitted Missouri's admittance to the Union as a slave state but thereafter restricted slavery to latitudes below 36° 30', Missouri's southern border. By allowing new territories admitted into the Union to decide whether to be slave or free under the doctrine of popular sovereignty, the legislation made the spread of slavery possible, and consequently the appeal of black emigration greater. Unlike other antebellum black conventions which included few if any women, women, mostly from Delany's base in Allegheny County, Pennsylvania, made up nearly a third of the convention's delegates when it met in Cleveland, Ohio, reflecting Delany's desire for their inclusion. Reporting to the convention, Delany reiterated the arguments made in the main body of his pamphlet two years before for emigration to Central and South America and included Canada as a last resort, suggesting that blacks buy cheap land there. The convention passed a resolution recommending land purchase in Canada and, without being specific, authorised a survey of any countries it might choose for emigration. According to Delany, the convention also decided in 'Secret Sessions' to keep Africa 'in reserve'.[48]

James T. Holly, a delegate at the convention, had become an advocate of emigration to Haiti. Holly wanted to combine such emigration with Episcopalian missions to redeem Haiti from Catholicism and paganism. In 1855, with the approval of the convention's National Board of Commissioners, Holly visited Haiti between his ordination as deacon and then a priest. In 1856, he became rector of St. Luke's Episcopal Church in New Haven, Connecticut. A year later, Holly insisted that Haiti should become 'the lever that must be exerted, to regenerate and disenthrall the oppression and ignorance of the race, throughout the world'.[49]

The emigrationist movement, then, was not monolithic. With Holly returned to America and Bibb now deceased, Shadd, who remained in Canada, aligned herself with Delany, who became more open to emigration to Canada. In 1856, Delany himself relocated to Canada, residing in Chatham. The National Emigration Convention's headquarters followed him there.[50]

A year later, conditions for blacks in the United States worsened and emigration became more attractive when the United States Supreme Court ruled in *Dred Scott v. Sanford* that blacks were not citizens and Congress could not bar slavery in a territory. Chief Justice Roger B. Taney affirmed that blacks 'had no rights which the white man was bound to respect'.[51] Despite longstanding suspicion of Liberia and the ACS, Africa attracted increasing attention from nationalists. In 1858, Garnet, who had gone to Jamaica as a missionary in 1852 until ill health forced his return to the United States in 1855, became president of the newly organised African Civilization Society, which cited Psalms 68:31 in its constitution. The society called for 'the civilization and christianization of Africa, and of the descendants of African ancestors in any portion of the earth, wherever dispersed', 'the destruction of the African Slave-trade, by the introduction of lawful commerce and trade into Africa', and development of Africa's economy so that 'the natives may become industrious producers as well as consumers'. Although the organisation opposed the ACS, it included white ACS members and the two groups shared similar goals. Garnet's organisation disclaimed general black American emigration to Africa in favour of sending 'only such persons as may be practically qualified and suited to promote the development of Christianity, morality, education, mechanical arts, agriculture, commerce, and general improvement'. An emphasis on Christianity, 'civilisation' and commerce was common among black American nationalists who looked to Africa in the nineteenth century, which reflected their acculturation by and admiration for what they regarded as the best features of the white western society that had shaped them. Foremost perhaps among what Moses calls 'Anglo-African nationalism' was Alexander Crummell, Garnet's boyhood and lifelong friend.[52]

Free born in New York in 1819, Crummell was refused admission to the General Theological Seminary of the Protestant Episcopal Church because of his colour but, after mission work in Rhode Island, was ordained a priest in 1844. He later went to England, where, in 1853, he obtained a degree from Queen's College, Cambridge. After graduation, he became an Episcopal missionary in Liberia, where he stayed for twenty years, becoming a teacher after resigning his appointment in 1857 following disagreements with his superiors. According to Miller, 'Crummell was committed to the creation of a commercially viable black nation.' Crummell, who often referenced the Ethiopian prophecy in Psalms, argued that God intended that blacks from the New World would uplift Africans from a benighted condition by spreading Christianity and 'civilisation' and developing commerce, centred on the exploitation of Africa's natural resources. '[F]rom Liberia, as a fountainhead', Crummel explained in a visit to the United States, 'shall flow culture, learning, science and enlightenment to many of the tribes of Africa', facilitating the end of the African slave trade. Crummell, like Cuffe many years earlier, envisaged a black-owned shipping line carrying African exports abroad, especially cotton in an attempt to undermine southern slavery, and to transport black American emigrants to Africa.[53]

There were some parallels between Crummell and Edward Wilmot Blyden, whose arrival in Liberia preceded Crummell's own by three years. Born in 1832, Blyden was a native of St. Thomas in the Danish West Indies (present day United States Virgin Islands). He went to Liberia in 1850 at the behest of the New York Colonization Society, an ACS auxiliary, after Rutgers Theological College and two other colleges had refused him admission for ministerial training. In a long and varied career in Liberia, Blyden was a Presbyterian minister, a newspaper editor, a college professor and a government minister. In 1861, Blyden and Crummell, who both championed racial pride and were seemingly of pure African descent, went to the United States in an unsuccessful joint effort to promote emigration to Liberia. Moses finds a common thread in Blyden, Crummell and Holly. He explains that

> Crummell and Blyden spoke of the duty of Africans of the diaspora to support the work of civilizing the blacks of West Africa and elevating them to self-governing status; James T. Holly adapted the rhetoric of Christian expansionism to the black Caribbean.[54]

Frederick Douglass shared the desire of emigrationist nationalists to see Africa Christianised and 'civilised'. Like them, Douglass admired western culture, and he welcomed the efforts of missionaries in Africa and the promotion of commerce there, but he prioritised abolition and racial uplift at home. Douglass argued that blacks should remain in the United States to abolish slavery and its internal trade, and he dismissed the African Civilization Society for perpetuating, like the ACS, the 'bitter and persecuting idea, that Africa, not America, is the Negro's true home'. Regarded as a black nationalist, but not a classical black nationalist, by Moses, and as a non-nationalist by Robinson, Douglass undoubtedly sometimes displayed a nationalist sensibility, contending that 'our people should be let alone, and given a fair chance to work out their own destiny where they are'.[55]

Douglass's former co-worker Delany returned to the idea of an exploratory African expedition that he had mooted in 1852, but this time with the Niger Valley in West Africa the target for a survey to determine its fitness for the selective emigration of skilled black Americans. Looking for support, in 1858 Delany arranged a third meeting of the now wilting National Emigration Convention in Chatham. However, the disinterested convention merely affirmed its rejection of general emigration and, concerned to widen its support base, renamed itself the 'Association for the Promotion of the Interests of the Colored People of Canada and the United States'. Its board subsequently commissioned Delany and four others to explore the Niger Valley but offered no material support. Eventually, Delany obtained financial backing from white colonisationists, associated with the African Civilization Society, and agreed at their insistence to visit Liberia, a place he had once scorned, first. In 1859, Delany arrived in Liberia on board a Liberian ship mainly carrying emigrants sent by the ACS. He visited Crummell, but Delany's secular approach and focus on the Niger Valley was at odds with Crummell's desire to redeem Africa by first Christianising and 'civilising' Liberia, regarding its indigenous people, according to biographer Wilson Jeremiah Moses, 'either as children or as victims of depravity and degradation'. Delany spent nine months in Africa, eventually meeting up with Robert Campbell, who claimed to have the African Civilization Society's direct support to explore the Niger Valley. The two men signed a treaty with the Alake of Abeokuta and his chiefs granting them land for black American settlement. Both men eventually returned to North America and gave separate reports promoting the Niger Valley, after first seeking support from white sympathisers and commercial interests in Britain.[56]

During Delany's time away from America, Haitian emigration re-emerged as an attractive opportunity for some blacks in the United

States and Canada, where thousands of blacks, perhaps as many as 40,000, sought refuge between 1850 and 1861. In 1859, the Haitian government, in need of labour, offered to support and finance black immigration. Several hundred black Louisianans responded and emigrated. More blacks followed them from northern ports in the first months of 1861. In January, Frederick Douglass, a long-time opponent of emigration, declared that he did not object to Haitian emigration because it offered emigrants a better life and the 'inducements offered to the colored man to remain here are few, feeble, and very uncertain'.[57]

In April, Douglass agreed to join James T. Holly and a group of emigrants bound for Haiti to explore its possibilities. Like other blacks in America, Douglass was influenced by deteriorating conditions in the country. White proslavers and their opponents had fought for control of Kansas, white abolitionist John Brown had been executed after a failed effort to spark a slave uprising, and president-elect Abraham Lincoln was anxious to conciliate the white South after six southern states had followed South Carolina in seceding. However, following the outbreak of the Civil War in April, Douglass cancelled his trip to Haiti, hoping that the war would aid black freedom. Holly emigrated with several hundred blacks from the United States and Canada West. By the summer, Douglass and other black leaders, including Mary Ann Shadd Cary in Canada, publicly opposed Haitian emigration, which began to unravel as returning emigrants reported disease, death and inadequate Haitian government support. Holly lost several family members but remained in Haiti and became the Episcopal bishop of the independent Orthodox Apostolic Church.[58]

During 1861 and the first months of 1862, Delany and the African Civilization Society continued their advocacy of selective emigration to West Africa. However, the Alake of Abeokuta and his chiefs repudiated the treaty made with Delany and Campbell, and a war in the interior also deterred North America blacks. Delany moved to New York and worked with the African Civilization Society, but the Civil War gave blacks hope that slavery would cease and their prospects improve without recourse to emigration. Emigrationist nationalists also felt drawn to the Union, especially when, in September 1862, President Lincoln announced a preliminary Emancipation Proclamation declaring that all slaves within Confederate lines on 1 January 1863 would be accorded their freedom if the Confederacy had not surrendered. With the war continuing, Lincoln issued the Emancipation Proclamation on 1 January and announced that the Union army would enlist black soldiers. Garnet and Mary Ann Shadd Cary, who returned to the United States, recruited blacks, and Delany, who joined the army as a major in February 1865, also did so.[59]

More than any other emigrationist nationalist, Delany has drawn criticism from some historians. Bill McAdoo dismisses him as 'one of the chief spokesmen and prime movers of black zionism', which McAdoo describes as the 'dominant form of reactionary black nationalism' in the antebellum era. McAdoo claims that those emigrationist nationalists who, like Delany, supported establishing a black capitalist nation in Africa, whether in Liberia or elsewhere, in effect abandoned the struggle against American slavery. Furthermore, they oppressed Africans by supporting Liberia's African-American rulers, who exploited Africans, and colluded with European powers by seeking their military support.[60]

Historian Tunde Adeleke is particularly critical of emigrationist nationalists for seeking to impose western culture on Africans and calling on western powers to intervene militarily. Delany, he notes, urged the British to stamp out indigenous conflict in the African interior. Adelele argues, like Draper before him, that Delany had a superficial commitment to Africa and black nationalism. It accounted for Delany's willingness to abandon both when the Civil War presented an opportunity for blacks to pursue equality within the United States, which, for Adeleke, was the driving force for many black nationalists, whether emigrationist or part of the far larger stay-at-home contingent. Adeleke argues that Delany was a black nationalist only between 1852 and 1862 and was otherwise an integrationist.[61]

Paradoxically, he refuses to recognise Delany as a nationalist when he pursued equality through racial solidarity in the United States, while recognising that approach as being a legitimate part of black nationalism when undertaken by many others. Adeleke rightly contends that Delany was pragmatic but, unlike Tommie Shelby, he does not appreciate that although, at times, Delany's nationalism included the classical variant centred on territory, he was 'most deeply committed to pragmatic black nationalism'. For Delany, like other pragmatic black nationalists, Shelby explains 'Black solidarity and separatism were never ends in themselves but merely strategies for realizing his most cherished values – equality, citizenship, self-government, and "manhood".' Shortly after the publication of his 1852 pamphlet advocating emigration, Delany had explained to white abolitionist leader William Lloyd Garrison, 'I would as willingly live among white men as black, if I had an equal possession and enjoyment of privileges.' Miller rightly discerns a 'common "nationalist" tendency' within 'emigrationism and anti-emigrationism' that 'often intersected and overlapped (as their adherents moved nimbly from one position to another or combined elements of each ideological strain)' in search of ways to alleviate and end black subordination in America, which explains Delany and others' shifts to and from emigration.[62]

Emigrationists, such as Delany and Crummell, did not advocate the wholesale emigration of North American blacks to Africa, and they believed that the creation of an economically successful black African nation would help undermine slavery within the United States by providing effective competition to slave produced goods, primarily cotton, that would make American slavery uneconomic. While their plans were overly optimistic and long term, their advocates did not simply abandon American slaves to their fate but recognised the seemingly entrenched nature of slavery in 1850s and early 1860s America. Emigrationist nationalists, like other black American leaders of their time, subscribed to what they regarded as the best of western culture, and they wanted to emulate it in Africa with little or no appreciation of contemporary African culture. However, European imperialists did not need black American encouragement to intervene or legitimise their intervention in Africa, and nineteenth-century emigrationist black nationalists were not, with Europeans, 'equally responsible for the interruption of Africa's development and the loss of its independence' as Adeleke supposes.[63]

The Post-Reconstruction Resurgence of Black Nationalism

Black prospects seemed to improve with the onset of the Civil War, and emancipation, citizenship and male suffrage, under the thirteenth (1865) fourteenth (1868) and fifteenth (1870) constitutional amendments during Reconstruction after the war. As a result, interest in emigration declined, even among many of its former champions.

Between 1865 and 1868, Delany worked for the federal Freedmen's Bureau in South Carolina, designed to facilitate and manage the transition from slavery to freedom. He subsequently pursued an unsuccessful political career, first with the Republicans, the party of Reconstruction, and later with the Democrats, when he contended that black interests were best served by seeking reconciliation with white southern Democrats, their long-time oppressors. Increasingly concerned about Reconstruction's uncertain prospects, in January 1868 Delany called on blacks to board an ACS ship to Liberia. In the 1870s, white violence and intimidation helped Democrats regain power in the South. Reconstruction finally ended in 1877 with the collapse of the last remaining Republican governments in Louisiana and South Carolina. As southern Democrats enforced black subordination, Delany again expressed support for emigration. In 1878, he endorsed the short-lived Liberian Exodus Joint Stock Steamship Company, which aimed to transport blacks from South Carolina and Georgia to Liberia and thereby spread 'civilisation' and Christianity. The company made one voyage, sailing with 206 emigrants on board the *Azor*, before succumbing to debt. Delany twice sought appointment as American minister to Liberia, losing out on the second occasion in 1881 to Garnet, who died in 1882.[64]

Emigrationist nationalism had always had limited appeal for most black Americans and had largely been championed by elements of the northern black educated elite who advocated the selective emigration of the most able. The collapse of Reconstruction led some often uneducated and poorer blacks to seek out opportunity and a life free from discrimination by forming all-black towns and communities and, especially, by migrating west. Few of those who migrated, mostly in response to poverty and racial oppression, articulated a black nationalist ideology, but such race-specific efforts, which entailed solidarity, organisation and a desire for self-determination, had a black nationalist tinge.[65]

The first half of the nineteenth century had seen efforts by a few white planters and philanthropists to create very small communities of freed slaves typically controlled by white trustees, mostly in free states, such as Ohio and Pennsylvania. Some communities thrived but others were short-lived because of mismanagement and local white opposition. Wartime confiscation of Confederate supporters' plantations and their redistribution to former slaves saw freedpeople seize the opportunity for self-determination and exhibit a desire to be left to themselves. Although some freedpeople were able to keep the land, its former owners largely managed to regain ownership through the courts and by appealing to fellow southerner President Andrew Johnson, the assassinated Lincoln's successor, who was anxious to restore the Union and had little interest in black rights and aspirations. Across the Reconstruction South, many blacks, lacking land and tools, became sharecroppers, working for a half share of the cotton crop they produced for white landowners. Dependent on often unscrupulous white planters and merchants for their supplies during the year and the proceeds of falling prices for cotton, sharecroppers became highly in debt. Their bleak economic situation, the demise of Republican Reconstruction governments, and white racial violence by the Ku Klux Klan and other whites encouraged southern blacks to look for alternatives, with Kansas the favoured destination for many in the 1870s.[66]

Benjamin 'Pap' Singleton, an illiterate former slave born in Nashville, Tennessee, in 1809, emerged as a leading figure in Kansas migration. Unable to find suitable affordable land for black settlement in Tennessee, Singleton took 300 blacks to Kansas in 1873 and returned annually with more from the South, locating them around the state with his associates. By the close of 1878, Singleton claimed to have brought 7,432 blacks to Kansas. His and others' advocacy, alongside worsening southern economic and political conditions, helped spur mass migration of at least 20,000 blacks to Kansas between 1879 and 1881. According to historian Steven Hahn, 'fewer than half' of these southern migrants came from Arkansas, Texas and the Deep South states of Alabama, Louisiana and Mississippi. Some migrants were poor, but they also included others, especially from Texas, with some resources. Migration aroused opposition from some whites and blacks already in Kansas. Some white Kansans feared that black migration would deter white migration to the state, and they regarded blacks as immoral. White labourers felt aggrieved by lower wages resulting from black migration, and they resented the willingness of black migrants to work for less pay than themselves. Some Kansans of both races were concerned that migration brought the destitute to the state. As opposition grew in Kansas, Singleton, who had appealed for aid for poverty-stricken arrivals, urged paupers not to come and warned there would be no jobs or further aid for them. Migration declined and, unable to establish themselves as farmers, most, perhaps two thirds, of the migrants eventually left to return home or move to other states. Singleton urged the remaining migrants to 'consolidate the race as a brethren' through mutual aid and self-help, and he recruited blacks to his United Links organisation, designed to engage politically with whites. He was disappointed that many blacks moved to the towns, rather than becoming independent farmers. As black prospects diminished in Kansas and the South, Singleton instead advocated emigration abroad, suggesting Canada, Cyprus and Liberia. He called for a separate 'nation' away from whites but remained in Kansas until his death in 1892.[67]

Edwin P. McCabe had migrated to Nicodemus, Kansas, in 1878, but when the federal government opened up Indian territory to settlement in the late 1880s, he relocated again. McCabe established Langston, an all-black town in Oklahoma, which soon attracted 2,000 settlers. He envisaged Oklahoma developing into an all-black state. However, white migrants were also attracted by cheap land, so making his goal unobtainable. Nevertheless, McCabe and others' efforts saw the territory's black population increase from 22,000 (8.4 per cent) to 56,000 (7 per cent) between 1890 and 1900, and led to the establishment of over twenty-five all-black towns. McCabe held political appointments for a decade, but, in 1910, Oklahoma, now a state, followed the South in adopting a literacy test and a grandfather clause, limiting the vote to those whose male forebears had been eligible to vote before Reconstruction, to disenfranchise most black voters. Another veteran of Kansas migration, Isaiah T. Montgomery, founded the all-black town of Mound Bayou, Mississippi, in 1887, which developed a farmers' cooperative and a cottonseed mill. Beyond Oklahoma, most black towns developed in the Deep South.[68]

Deteriorating conditions in the South characterised by disenfranchisement, segregation, lynching and falling cotton prices brought a revival of interest in African migration in the 1890s. Born poor but free in Newberry Court House, South Carolina, in 1834, Henry McNeal Turner became its best known advocate. According to historian Edwin S. Redkey, Turner 'more than any other factor, gave direction and enthusiasm to black nationalism in the 1890s'. A Union Army recruiter and chaplain during the Civil War, Turner organised AME churches in Georgia afterwards. Elected as a Republican during Reconstruction in 1868, the Georgia legislature expelled him and other black members, although they later secured reinstatement. Turner claimed a Crummell sermon in 1862 had convinced him that black Americans should immigrate to Africa, but the withering of Reconstruction made the attraction more immediate. In 1876, Turner became a lifetime honorary ACS vice-president, while largely operating independently. He also gave a benediction for the *Azor*. Like Crummell, Turner advocated the Christianisation, 'civilisation' and economic development of Africa, and the selective emigration of the talented and resourceful, envisaging the development of an African nation that would bolster blacks' self-respect and identity everywhere. Black-owned shipping companies would facilitate trade and emigration. Turner used the denominational press and his travels in the South as an AME minister and, from 1880, bishop to disseminate his message. Although committed to equal rights for blacks within the United States, he sometimes suggested that all blacks should go to Africa.[69]

In 1883, the United States Supreme Court overturned the 1875 Civil Rights Act by stating that federal law did not apply to racial discrimination by individuals, leading Turner to claim that 'If the decision is correct, the United States Constitution is a dirty rag, a cheat, a libel, and ought to be spit upon by every negro in the land.' He argued that the federal government should finance black emigration as reparations for slavery. Turner emphasised racial pride and contended that blacks should worship a black deity, just as other races saw themselves as created in God's image. As racial violence increased in the South, he advised blacks to arm themselves to fight lynch mobs. Turner visited Africa four times in the 1890s ostensibly to organise for the AME Church and returned with glowing reports of Africa's possibilities for emigrants. Turner remained an emigrationist nationalist and fervent critic of the United States, but he, like the poor southern blacks he attracted, lacked the means to fulfil his vision. In 1889, Senator Matthew Butler of South Carolina proposed a $5 million federal appropriation for black emigration to another country. His bill, which Turner supported, died in committee in 1890. Most black leaders opposed emigration, a position that its middle class, and mostly northern delegates reiterated in 1893 at a convention Turner called in Cincinnati.[70]

The ACS had sent around 100 black emigrants annually during the late 1880s, but, as American racial and economic conditions worsened still further, it saw an opportunity to recruit more and, in 1889, brought Edward Wilmot Blyden to the United States to promote Liberia. Like Turner, Blyden supported the Butler bill, aware that the society lacked the resources to facilitate mass emigration. Between 1872 and 1890, the ACS sent only 1,130 black Americans to Liberia. The Butler bill helped revive black interest in emigration, but the ACS could not meet the demand when blacks from Oklahoma and Arkansas arrived in New York City in 1892 expecting a ship. Consequently, the society decided on a policy of sending only professionals and the highly skilled to Liberia, but, as Turner found, such people generally did not seek emigration. Thereafter, the ACS sent at most three or four emigrants annually, before abandoning emigration altogether in 1910 and focusing instead on aiding Liberia.[71]

Other emigration agents and organisations appeared. They attracted interest primarily from impoverished rural southern blacks, despite opposition from middle class blacks. The Reverend Benjamin Gaston, a Baptist pastor from Georgia, recruited southern blacks for Liberia, where he had spent twenty years, and, despite his sometimes fraudulent conduct, sent eighty-nine blacks there between 1893 and 1894. African emigration remained prohibitively expensive for many interested southern blacks. Consequently, several hundred blacks from Alabama and Georgia went to neighbouring Mexico in the mid-1890s to join a farming venture organised by black American H. Ellis and a Mexican land company, although many returned because of poor conditions and a smallpox outbreak. In 1894, four white men in Birmingham, Alabama organised the International Migration Society with Turner's support. The society sent thirteen southern blacks to Liberia that year, followed by 197 in 1895 and 321 in 1896. All but a few in the last group, some so poor that even Turner had urged them not to go, died or left Liberia. Returning emigrants' dire warnings and an economic depression in the United States that made even the society's subsequently reduced fees beyond the reach of many led to its collapse in 1899. There were many other attempts in the 1890s and early 1900s to send blacks to Liberia, which were often small scale and sometimes fraudulent. Lack of funding doomed many of these efforts, and reports of hardships in Liberia from those who had emigrated or returned increasingly diminished emigration's appeal.[72]

Black Nationalism at the Turn of the Century

Booker T. Washington, who emerged as the nation's premier black leader in the second half of the 1890s, consistently opposed black emigration. Born a slave in Franklin County, Virginia, in 1856, Washington's enslavement deprived him of education. After emancipation, he attended school in Malden, West Virginia, and then Hampton Normal and Agricultural Institute in Virginia. In 1881, he became the first head of the Tuskegee Institute, an all-black school initiated with funding from the Alabama legislature, which Washington gradually enlarged by vigorous solicitation of white philanthropy. The institute's entirely black staff taught literacy and industrial education. Its more academic students entered higher education or the professions.[73]

A few months after Frederick Douglass died, Washington's address to the Atlanta Cotton States and Industrial Exposition in September 1895 met with widespread white approval that made him a national black leader by providing him with much greater access to white charity and also patronage in black federal appointments. Washington declared that 'In all things that are purely social we can be as separate as the fingers, yet one as the hand in all things essential to mutual progress.' He argued that blacks should avoid protest and politics, and instead work hard to earn money and develop 'friendly relations with the Southern white man'. According to historian Louis R. Harlan, Washington wanted to engender 'independent small businessmen, farmers, and teachers rather than wage-earners or servants of white employers'. In private, Washington raised funds for court cases challenging disenfranchisement, railroad segregation and peonage, and maintained that social separation referred to family and friendship networks. He condemned lynching and the inferior condition of black train cars and waiting rooms. Washington also supported all-black towns and, in 1900, founded the National Negro Business League to promote black commerce.[74]

'If black separatism in the form of local control and black-owned business enterprise is to be regarded as an expression of black nationalism', historian Rodney Carlisle observes, 'then clearly Washington worked within the tradition and made contributions to its institutional development.' Carlisle also notes that even undoubted black nationalists 'Crummell and Blyden . . . cooperated with white supporters such as the ACS, white clergy, and conservative and openly racist politicians.' Bracey, Meier and Rudwick characterise Washington as belonging to 'bourgeois economic nationalism', and historian Manning Marable draws attention to Washington's 'racial pride and black nationalist tendencies'. However, Washington's ingratiating and accommodationist approach to whites from whom he derived his power and influence, and his oft declared optimism in their goodwill, despite mounting segregation, disenfranchisement and lynching, differentiated him from leading late nineteenth-century black nationalists.[75]

Washington and Crummell shared a commitment to racial pride, Christian morality and black institutional development, but whereas Washington focused on uplifting the South's black masses, Crummell, in his last years, concentrated on developing a cadre of elite black leaders to bring about racial uplift. Disappointed with the American-Liberian ruling elite, which he criticised for failing to develop the country's economy and infrastructure and spread 'civilisation' to 'the heathen tribes around us', and disturbed by escalating violence in Liberia, Crummell returned to the United States in 1873, after making a forlorn plea for an American-Liberian protectorate. He took a pastorate in Washington, DC until retiring in 1895. Like Washington, Crummell argued that blacks could improve their condition through self-help, character development and moral rectitude, rather than agitation, but he dismissed relying only on economic advancement and also emphasised developing the mind.[76]

In 1897, the year before his death, Crummell founded the American Negro Academy (ANA) to achieve 'the civilization of the Negro race in the United States, by the scientific processes of literature, art, and philosophy', disseminated by the black intellectual and artistic elite. 'This was a plan for domestic nationalism', Moses explains, 'which would somehow perform many of the cultural and economic functions of a nation, while lacking both land, and the political apparatus of a state.' The academy published occasional papers but struggled to maintain the interest of its small membership.[77]

The ANA prohibited females from joining, but black women also gave black nationalism organisational form by establishing the National Association of Colored Women in 1896, which combined various national and local groups. The association, which had 18,000, primarily middle class, members in 300 clubs by 1900, sought to uplift the poor and improve family life, adopting the slogan 'Lifting As We Climb'. It promoted conventional sexual morality and self-improvement, provided job training, day care, health care and other social services, and regularly denounced segregation, disenfranchisement, peonage and lynching. However, it lacked the resources to have much impact on the poor and became increasingly beset by leadership rivalries, factionalism and internal social climbing.[78]

Although the ANA also struggled, founding member and Crummell devotee W. E. B. Du Bois rose to prominence. Born in 1868, Du Bois grew up mostly free from racial discrimination in the largely white Massachusetts town of Great Barrington. Academically gifted, he gained a doctorate from Harvard University after studying at the University of Berlin and taught for twelve years at Atlanta University. Du Bois became an ardent critic of Washington's public accommodation to white dominance and, influenced by Crummell, envisaged a talented tenth of highly educated blacks leading racial progress.[79]

In 1905, a small number of blacks, who were committed to equal rights and opportunities and the removal of discriminatory legislation through the courts, formed the Niagara Movement under Du Bois and William Monroe Trotter's leadership, but, within a few years, it fell apart without accomplishment. However, in 1909, some white northerners and blacks initiated the NAACP, dedicated to achieving these same goals using litigation, education and lobbying. Du Bois and most of the Niagara Movement joined the association, which remained largely white led during its first twenty years, despite an overwhelmingly black membership. In 1910, Du Bois founded and then edited and controlled the NAACP's magazine *The Crisis*, which campaigned against injustice but also, historian Adam Fairclough observes, 'instilled pride of race, extolling blacks' accomplishments, showcasing black history, art, scholarship, and literature'.[80]

Du Bois's interests also extended to the black diaspora. In 1900, he and eleven other black Americans had attended a small Pan-African Conference in London, organised by West Indian H. Sylvester Williams to establish a network among people of African descent that would seek to secure 'to all African races living in civilized countries their full rights, and to promote their business interests'. It yielded little immediate result. The conference's vice-president for the United States, Du Bois wrote the meeting's 'Address to the Nations of the World', which called for self-government in Africa and the Caribbean. He would later play an important role in developing Pan-Africanism, which stressed the commonality and unity of Africans and people of African descent and opposed colonialism. In *The Souls of Black Folk* (1903), Du Bois expressed anguish that 'One ever feels this twoness, – an American, a Negro; two souls, two thoughts, two unreconciled strivings; two warring ideals in one dark body, whose dogged strength alone keeps it from being torn asunder.' In Moses's view, 'This ambivalence makes it impossible to neatly pigeonhole Du Bois into either the black nationalist or the radical assimilationist tradition.' Du Bois briefly joined the Socialist Party in 1910 and became increasingly interested in Marxism. Carlisle justifiably concludes that although he made a 'significant' contribution 'to the black nationalist tradition within the United States', primarily through his Pan-Africanism, cultural nationalism and 'interest in separate black institutions', Du Bois engaged in 'more energetic advocacy of civil rights and socialism'.[81]

While Du Bois and the NAACP embarked on a long-term programme of challenging discrimination, some blacks continued to seek emigration. In 1913, Chief Alfred Charles Sam, a native of the British Gold Coast, sold shares in his Akim Trading Company Ltd mainly to Oklahoma blacks eager to escape white domination and economic hardship by migrating to Africa. Sam purchased a ship with the proceeds and, in August 1914, set sail from Galveston, Texas, for the Gold Coast with a black crew and 60 male and female emigrants from among thousands who had bought stock and about 600 who had arrived hoping for passage. Sam claimed that the emigrants would settle on land arranged for them. Hostile British authorities impounded the ship in Sierra Leone, which delayed the emigrants' arrival in the Gold Coast until January 1915 and depleted their resources. The tribal chiefs who controlled the land also restricted the newcomers. Their goods were stolen and some fell ill from disease or died. Most of the emigrants did not stay, unable to adjust to an alien lifestyle and climate. Some moved to other areas of the West African coast and others eventually returned to America. Sam eventually went to Liberia; hundreds of shareholders in Oklahoma lost their money.[82]

However, the outbreak of World War One in August 1914 provided blacks in America (which did not enter the war until April 1917) with new opportunities for domestic migration. By increasing demand for American exports and cutting off European immigration, the war created a labour shortage in northern industry that began hiring black workers, who migrated in their thousands from the South in search of a better life only to find themselves confined to ghettoes and facing discrimination and white hostility. Ruination of cotton crops by boll weevil infestation and declining cotton prices also drove southern blacks away from the land in search of employment. The Great Migration, as it became known, continued after the war ended and made African Americans into an increasingly urban people with a significant presence in many of the nation's cities. In 1915, as migration gathered pace, Washington and Turner died, leaving a leadership vacuum that would soon be filled by an unlikely Jamaican immigrant, Marcus Garvey. Partly influenced by Washington's economic ideas, Garvey advocated a wide-ranging black nationalism.

Notes

1. The terms 'black' and 'African American' are used in this book because at the time of writing they are self-adopted and widely accepted, although not uniformly so, by many members of the communities they seek to describe. Historically, community self-naming has often changed over time and may do so again in the future. In this study, black is an inclusive term that may encompass Caribbean migrants, enslaved and free Africans in America and African Americans born in America.

2. Wilson Jeremiah Moses, *The Golden Age of Black Nationalism 1850–1925* (1978; New York and Oxford: Oxford University Press, 1988), p. 9; Wilson Jeremiah Moses (ed.), *Classical Black Nationalism: From the American Revolution to Marcus Garvey* (New York and London: New York University Press, 1996), p. 6.

3. Daryl Michael Scott, 'How Black Nationalism Became Sui Generis', *Fire!!!* 1 (Summer–Winter 2012), p. 6; Moses, *Golden Age of Black Nationalism*, p. 17.

4. Dean E. Robinson, *Black Nationalism in American Politics and Thought* (Cambridge: Cambridge University Press, 2001), pp. 2, 6–7, 89–93, 96, 100–2, 111–12.

5. James Lance Taylor, *Black Nationalism in the United States: From Malcolm X to Barack Obama* (Boulder and London: Lynne Rienner, 2011), pp. 2, 7, 13–14, 111, 136–9.

6. Taylor, *Black Nationalism in the United States*, pp. 2–4, 6–7, 111–14, 120, 157–9; Moses, *Golden Age of Black Nationalism*, p. 43.

7. Moses (ed.), *Classical Black Nationalism*, pp. 2, 20.

8. John H. Bracey, Jr, August Meier and Elliott Rudwick (eds), *Black Nationalism in America* (Indianapolis and New York: Bobbs-Merrill, 1970), p. xxvi.

9. E. U. Essien-Udom, *Black Nationalism: A Search for an Identity in America* (Chicago: University of Chicago Press, 1962), p. 6; Scott, 'How Black Nationalism Became Sui Generis', p. 8.

10. William L. Van Deburg (ed.), *Modern Black Nationalism: From Marcus Garvey to Louis Farrakhan* (New York and London: New York University Press, 1997), pp. 2, 4.

11. Ibid., p. 3.

12. Tunde Adeleke, *UnAfrican Americans: Nineteenth-Century Black Nationalists and the Civilizing Mission* (Lexington: University Press of Kentucky, 1998), pp. 10–11; Moses (ed.), *Classical Black Nationalism*, p. 3.

13. Akinyele Umoja, 'Searching for Place: Nationalism, Separatism, and Pan-Africanism', in Alton Hornsby, Jr (ed.), *A Companion to African American History* (Malden, MA: Blackwell, 2005), pp. 530–1.

14. Tommie Shelby, 'Two Conceptions of Black Nationalism: Martin Delany on the Meaning of Black Political Solidarity', *Political Theory* 31 (October 2003), pp. 667–8; Robinson, *Black Nationalism in American Politics and Thought*, pp. 6–7, 88–103; Stokely Carmichael and Charles V. Hamilton, *Black Power: The Politics of Liberation in America* (New York: Vintage, 1967).

15. Shelby, 'Two Conceptions of Black Nationalism', p. 667.

16. Shelby, 'Two Conceptions of Black Nationalism', p. 688; Moses, *Golden Age of Black Nationalism*, p. 17.

17. Moses, *Golden Age of Black Nationalism*, p. 6; Robinson, *Black Nationalism in American Politics and Thought*, pp. 5–6; Van Deburg (ed.), *Modern Black Nationalism*, p. 4. The definition of black nationalism expounded here draws on Alphonso Pinkney, *Red, Black, and Green: Black Nationalism in the United States* (Cambridge: Cambridge University Press, 1976), pp. 2–3 and William W. Sales, Jr, *From Civil Rights to Black Liberation: Malcolm X and the Organization of Afro-American Unity* (Boston: South End Press, 1994), p. 59.

18. Wilson Jeremiah Moses, *Alexander Crummell: A Study of Civilization and Discontent* (New York and Oxford: Oxford University Press, 1989), pp. 4, 217–20, 293, 298–9; Beryl Satter, 'Marcus Garvey, Father

Divine and the Gender Politics of Race Difference and Race Neutrality', *American Quarterly* 48 (March 1996), pp. 48–51; Ula Taylor, 'As-Salaam Alaikum, My Sister, Peace Be Unto You: The Honorable Elijah Muhammad and the Women Who followed Him', *Race and Society* 1 (1998), pp. 177, 182–8, 192, 194; Ula Taylor, 'Elijah Muhammad's Nation of Islam: Separatism, Regendering, and a Secular Approach to Black Power after Malcolm X (1965–1995)', in Jeanne Theoharis and Komozi Woodard (eds), *Freedom North: Black Freedom Struggles Outside the South, 1940–1980* (New York: Palgrave Macmillan, 2003), pp. 190–2, 194; Scot Brown, *Fighting for US: Maulana Karenga, the US Organization, and Black Cultural Nationalism*, with a foreword by Clayborne Carson (New York and London: New York University Press, 2003), pp. 31–3, 35, 56–7, 62–5, 178 n. 118; Daniel Matlin, '"Lift Up Yr Self!" Reinterpreting Amiri Baraka (LeRoi Jones), Black Power, and the Uplift Tradition', *Journal of American History* 93 (June 2006), pp. 91–4, 99–103, 106–10, 115–16.

19. Brown, *Fighting for US*, pp. 57–8, 157; Moses, *Alexander Crummell*, pp. 151, 159, 219; Robert S. Levine (ed.), Martin Delany, *Martin R. Delany: A Documentary Reader* (Chapel Hill and London: University of North Carolina, 2003), pp. 18–19; Garth E. Pauley, 'W. E. B. Du Bois on Woman Suffrage: A Critical Analysis of His *Crisis* Writings', *Journal of Black Studies* 30 (January 2000), pp. 383–410; Barbara Bair, '"Ethiopia Shall Stretch Forth Her Hands Unto God": Laura Kofey and the Gendered Vision of Redemption in the Garvey Movement', in Susan Juster and Lisa MacFarlane (eds), *A Mighty Baptism: Race, Gender, and the Creation of American Protestantism* (Ithaca, NY and London: Cornell University Press, 1996), pp. 39–40, 44–53; Tracye Matthews, '"No One Evers Asks, What a Man's Place in the Revolution is": Gender and the Politics of The Black Panther Party 1966–1971', in Charles E. Jones (ed.), *The Black Panther Party Reconsidered* (Baltimore: Black Classic Press, 1998), pp. 267–304; Angela D. LeBlanc-Ernest, '"The Most Qualified Person to Handle the Job": Black Panther Party Women, 1966–1982', in Jones (ed.), *The Black Panther Party Reconsidered*, pp. 305–34; Taylor, 'As-Salaam Alaikum, My Sister, Peace Be Unto You', pp. 183–4, 194; Taylor, 'Elijah Muhammad's Nation of Islam', pp. 192, 194.

20. Moses (ed.), *Classical Black Nationalism*, pp. 6–7; Taylor, *Black Nationalism in the United States*, pp. 43–4, 179–80; Sterling Stuckey, *Slave Culture: Nationalist Theory and the Foundations of Black America* (New York and Oxford: Oxford University Press, 1987), pp. ix, 3.

21. Robinson, *Black Nationalism in American Politics and Thought*, pp. 16–17; Eugene D. Genovese, *In Red and Black: Marxian Explorations*

in Southern and Afro-American History (Knoxville: University of Tennessee Press, 1984), pp. 130–8; Peter J. Parish, *Slavery: History and Historians* (New York: Harper and Row, 1989), pp. 67–85, 88–9; Peter Kolchin, *American Slavery, 1619–1877* (1993; London: Penguin, 1995), pp. 40–61.

22. Moses (ed.), *Classical Black Nationalism*, pp. 6–10; Floyd J. Miller, *The Search for a Black Nationality: Black Emigration and Colonization, 1787–1863* (Urbana, Chicago and London: University of Illinois Press, 1975), pp. 3–15, 21; Bill McAdoo, *Pre-Civil War Black Nationalism* (New York: David Walker Press, 1983), pp. 35–6, 38–9, 43, 51, 62; Taylor, *Black Nationalism in the United States*, p. 159; David Walker and Henry Highland Garnet, *Walker's Appeal in Four Articles: An Address to the Slaves of the United States of America* (1848; New York: Cosimo, 2005), pp. 30–1.

23. Miller, *Search for a Black Nationality*, pp. 21–47; Rodney Carlisle, *The Roots of Black Nationalism* (Port Washington, NY and London: Kennikat Press, 1975), pp. 7, 12–20, 43.

24. Miller, *Search for a Black Nationality*, pp. 44–53, 55; Moses (ed.), *Classical Black Nationalism*, pp. 12–13, 48; Taylor, *Black Nationalism in the United States*, p. 142; Carlisle, *Roots of Black Nationalism*, pp. 20–3.

25. Miller, *Search for a Black Nationality*, pp. 54–82.

26. Ibid., pp. 55, 89–90.

27. Moses, *Golden Age of Black Nationalism*, pp. 38–9; Sterling Stuckey (ed.), *The Ideological Origins of Black Nationalism* (Boston: Beacon Press, 1972), pp. 8–9; McAdoo, *Pre-Civil War Black Nationalism*, pp. 1, 35, 46, 77–8; Taylor, *Black Nationalism in the United States*, pp. 157–8.

28. Peter P. Hinks, *To Awaken My Afflicted Brethren: David Walker and the Problem of Antebellum Slave Resistance* (University Park: Pennsylvania State University Press, 1997), pp. 9–13, 64, 66; Taylor, *Black Nationalism in the United States*, pp. 159, 190, 203–4 n. 10; Walker and Garnet, *Walker's Appeal in Four Articles*, pp. 22, 26, 30, 33, 37, 51, 52, 76, 80–1. Taylor notes that Walker 'made a last-minute shift in the third edition of his writing to a tempered support for emigration'. Taylor, *Black Nationalism in the United States*, p. 190.

29. Hinks, *To Awaken My Afflicted Brethren*, pp. 108–11, 172, 269–70.

30. Stuckey (ed.), *Ideological Origins of Black Nationalism*, p. 9; Stuckey, *Slave Culture*, pp. 120–1, 123, 130; Thabiti Asukile, 'The All-Embracing Black Nationalist Theories of David Walker's Appeal', *Black Scholar* 29 (Winter 1999), pp. 16–24.

31. Moses (ed.), *Classical Black Nationalism*, pp. 15–17. However, Moses also concedes that Walker, Stewart and Young adopted a 'messianic

nationalism' expressed through the black jeremiad. Moses (ed.), *Classical Black Nationalism*, p. 18.

32. Hinks, *To Awaken My Afflicted Brethren*, pp. 249–50.
33. Taylor, *Black Nationalism in the United States*, pp. 136–9, 157–8, 203 n. 6, 249; Maria Stewart, 'Address at the African Masonic Hall (1833)', in Moses (ed.), *Classical Black Nationalism*, pp. 90, 92, 97.
34. Moses, *Golden Age of Black Nationalism*, pp. 156–61; Moses (ed.), *Classical Black Nationalism*, pp. 16, 18, 90; Taylor, *Black Nationalism in the United States*, p. 249; Gayraud S. Wilmore, *Black Religion and Black Radicalism: An Interpretation of the Religious History of African Americans*, 3rd edn (Maryknoll, NY: Orbis, 1998), p. 148.
35. Taylor, *Black Nationalism in the United States*, p. 158; Robert Alexander Young, 'The Ethiopian Manifesto (1829)', in Moses (ed.), *Classical Black Nationalism*, pp. 60–67; Walker and Garnet, *Walker's Appeal in Four Articles*, p. 30.
36. Howard H. Bell, 'Free Negroes of the North 1830–1835: A Study in National Cooperation', *Journal of Negro Education* 26 (Autumn 1957), pp. 447–55; Bella Gross, 'The First National Negro Convention', *Journal of Negro History* 31 (October 1946), pp. 435–8; Bracey, Meier and Rudwick (eds), *Black Nationalism in America*, p. xxxi.
37. Bella Gross, *Clarion Call: The History and Development of the Negro People's Convention Movement in the United States From 1817 to 1840* (New York: Bella Gross, 1947); Bell, 'Free Negroes of the North', p. 449; Bracey, Meier and Rudwick (eds), *Black Nationalism in America*, p. xxxiii; Howard H. Bell, 'Some Reform Interests of the Negro During the 1850's as Reflected in State Conventions', *Phylon* 21 (2nd Qtr., 1960), pp. 173–81.
38. Miller, *Search for a Black Nationality*, pp. 93–105.
39. Steven Hahn, *A Nation under Our Feet: Black Political Struggles in the Rural South from Slavery to the Great Migration* (Cambridge, MA and London: Belknap Press of Harvard University Press, 2003), pp. 55–6; Eric Foner, *Give Me Liberty!: An American History*, 2nd Seagull edn (New York and London: W. W. Norton, 2009), pp. 406–7.
40. Walker and Garnet, *Walker's Appeal in Four Articles*, pp. 89–96; W. H. Brewer, 'Henry Highland Garnet', *Journal of Negro History* 13 (January 1928), pp. 36–46, 52; Howard H. Bell, 'National Negro Conventions of the Middle 1840's: Moral Suasion vs. Political Action', *Journal of Negro History* 42 (October 1957), pp. 247–56, 259–60; Howard H. Bell, 'Expressions of Negro Militancy in the North, 1840–1860', *Journal of Negro History* 45 (January 1960), pp. 11–13; Howard H. Bell, 'The Negro Emigration Movement, 1849–1854: A Phase of Negro Nationalism', *Phylon* 20 (2nd Qtr., 1959), pp. 133–4;

Miller, *Search for a Black Nationality*, pp. 187–90; Carlisle, *Roots of Black Nationalism*, pp. 62–5.

41. Moses (ed.), *Classical Black Nationalism*, pp. 19, 101.
42. Bell, 'Negro Emigration Movement', pp. 134, 139; Miller, *Search for a Black Nationality*, pp. 94, 105–15.
43. Miller, *Search for a Black Nationality*, pp. 115–25.
44. Martin R. Delany 'The Condition, Elevation, Emigration and Destiny of the Colored People of the United States (1852)', in Moses (ed.), *Classical Black Nationalism*, pp. 101–24; Miller, *Search for a Black Nationality*, pp. 125–9.
45. Miller, *Search for a Black Nationality*, pp. 130–2; Theodore H. Draper, 'The Father of American Black Nationalism', *New York Review of Books* 14 (March 12, 1970), pp. 33–41.
46. Bell, 'Negro Emigration Movement', pp. 139–40; Carlisle, *Roots of Black Nationalism*, pp. 68–9; Miller, *Search for a Black Nationality*, pp. 135–6, 239, 270 n. 5.
47. Moses, *Golden Age of Black Nationalism*, pp. 39–41; Miller, *Search for a Black Nationality*, pp. 136–7. More convincingly, Moses also writes that 'Douglass, like most black Americans, occasionally displayed nationalistic sentiment.' Moses, *Golden Age of Black Nationalism*, pp. 84–5.
48. Miller, *Search for a Black Nationality*, pp. 137, 142–6, 148–50, 152–3; 'Proceedings of the National Emigration Convention of Colored People; Held at Cleveland, Ohio, on Thursday, Friday and Saturday, the 24th, 25th and 26th of August, 1854', available at <http://coloredconventions.org/files/original/feff770283ff4b2cd95cd8f8aa9be5f8.pdf> (last accessed 30 December 2016); Martin R. Delany, 'Official Report of the Niger Valley Exploring Party (1861)', in Moses (ed.), *Classical Black Nationalism*, pp. 145–9.
49. Miller, *Search for a Black Nationality*, pp. 144, 146, 162–3, 161–9; James T. Holly, 'A Vindication of the Capacity of the Negro Race for Self-Government and Civilized Progress (1857)', in Moses (ed.), *Classical Black Nationalism*, pp. 131–4.
50. Miller, *Search for a Black Nationality*, pp. 157–60, 166.
51. Roger B. Taney, 'Obiter Dictum on the Dred Scott Case (1857)', in Moses (ed.), *Classical Black Nationalism*, pp. 125–30.
52. Brewer, 'Henry Highland Garnet', pp. 41, 48; Moses, *Golden Age of Black Nationalism*, pp. 18, 37, 48, 157; Robinson, *Black Nationalism in American Politics and Thought*, pp. 19–20.
53. Kathleen O'Mara Wahle, 'Alexander Crummell: Black Evangelist and Pan-Negro Nationalist', *Phylon* 29 (4th Qtr., 1968), p. 389; Alexander Crummell, 'The Progress of Civilization along the West Coast of Africa (1861)', in Moses (ed.), *Classical Black Nationalism*, pp.

169–87; Miller, *Search for a Black Nationality*, p. 204; Moses, *Golden Age of Black Nationalism*, pp. 41–2, 62–5, 157; Carlisle, *Roots of Black Nationalism*, pp. 83–6, 102–3.

54. Carlisle, *Roots of Black Nationalism*, pp. 80–3; Edwin S. Redkey, *Black Exodus: Black Nationalist and Back-to-Africa Movements, 1890–1910* (New Haven and London: Yale University Press, 1969), pp. 48–9; Moses, *Golden Age of Black Nationalism*, pp. 49–50, 62. Historian Kathleen O'Mara Wahle claims that Crummell took pride in 'his pure African ancestry', whereas Wilson Jeremiah Moses notes that although Crummell seems to have had an African-born father, 'very little is known' about Crummell's mother who was free born on Long Island. Wahle, 'Alexander Crummell', p. 388; Moses, *Alexander Crummell*, p. 11.

55. Frederick Douglass, 'African Civilization Society (1859)', in Moses (ed.), *Classical Black Nationalism*, pp. 135–41; Moses, *Golden Age of Black Nationalism*, pp. 38, 84–5; Robinson, *Black Nationalism in American Politics and Thought*, pp. 20–1.

56. Miller, *Search for a Black Nationality*, pp. 170–83, 192–231; Moses, *Alexander Crummell*, pp. 278–9, 289.

57. Miller, *Search for a Black Nationality*, pp. 232–40; Carlisle, *Roots of Black Nationalism*, pp. 61, 66.

58. Miller, *Search for a Black Nationality*, pp. 239–49; Howard H. Bell, 'Negro Nationalism: A Factor in Emigration Projects, 1858–1861', *Journal of Negro History* 47 (January 1962), pp. 49–53. Shadd had married in 1856.

59. Miller, *Search for a Black Nationality*, pp. 250–65.

60. McAdoo, *Pre-Civil War Black Nationalism*, pp. 23, 26–30.

61. Adeleke, *UnAfrican Americans*, pp. 2, 7–8, 57–9, 61–8, 140–1, 144–5, 150–2; Tunde Adeleke, *Without Regard to Race: The Other Martin Robison Delany* (Jackson: University Press of Mississippi, 2003), pp. xxii–xxiii, xxxi–xxxii, 3–5, 38, 66, 70–6.

62. Adeleke, *UnAfrican Americans*, pp. 6–8, 11; Miller, *Search for a Black Nationality*, pp. 131, 270–1; Shelby, 'Two Conceptions of Black Nationalism', pp. 668, 682.

63. Adeleke, *UnAfrican Americans*, pp. 125, 143.

64. Miller, *Search for a Black Nationality*, pp. 264–6; Carlisle, *Roots of Black Nationalism*, pp. 103–4. Historian Steven Hahn notes that 'Between 1865 and 1868, 2,232 blacks actually emigrated, for an annual average of 558, more than twice the average for the entire period 1820 to 1861', but the number of emigrants fell sharply thereafter as Reconstruction conferred citizenship rights. Hahn, *A Nation under Our Feet*, pp. 321–3.

65. Hahn, *A Nation under Our Feet*, pp. 333–5.

Nationalism, pp. 113–14; Moses, *Golden Age of Black National-ism*, p. 102; John White, *Black Leadership in America: From Booker T. Washington to Jesse Jackson*, 2nd edn (London and New York: Longman, 1990), pp. 36–7.

75. Carlisle, *Roots of Black Nationalism*, pp. 112–16; Bracey, Meier and Rudwick (eds), *Black Nationalism in America*, p. 235; W. Manning Marable, 'Booker T. Washington and African Nationalism', *Phylon* 35 (4th Qtr., 1974), pp. 403–4.

76. Moses, *Golden Age of Black Nationalism*, pp. 42, 69–70; Wahle, 'Alexander Crummell', pp. 392–5; Wilmore, *Black Religion and Black Radicalism*, p. 140.

77. Moses, *Golden Age of Black Nationalism*, pp. 71–4.

78. Moses, *Golden Age of Black Nationalism*, pp. 103–31; Fairclough, *Better Day Coming*, pp. 33–7.

79. Fairclough, *Better Day Coming*, pp. 55–7, 70, 74–6; Moses, *Golden Age of Black Nationalism*, p. 81; Carlisle, *Roots of Black Nationalism*, p. 116.

80. Fairclough, *Better Day Coming*, pp. 55–6, 68–73, 77–82.

81. Thomas H. Henriksen, 'African Intellectual Influences on Black Americans: The Role of Edward W. Blyden', *Phylon* 36 (3rd Qtr., 1975), p. 286; Bracey, Meier and Rudwick (eds), *Black Nationalism in America*, p. xlii; Milfred C. Fierce, *The Pan-African Idea in the United States, 1900–1919: African-American Interest in Africa and Interaction with West Africa* (New York: Garland, 1993), pp. 199–204; Moses, *Golden Age of Black Nationalism*, pp. 136, 140–1; Carlisle, *Roots of Black Nationalism*, pp. 118, 120; W. E. B. Du Bois, *The Souls of Black Folk*, with introductions by Nathan Hare and Alvin F. Poussaint (1903; New York and Scarborough, Ontario: Signet Classic, 1982), p. 45. Although scholars do not agree on a definition of Pan-Africanism, historian Tunde Adeleke notes that 'The notion of shared identity between blacks in dias-pora and Africans, efforts towards mutual upliftment, development, and defense of mutual interest are at the heart of Pan-Africanism.' Tunde Adeleke, 'Black Americans and Africa: A Critique of the Pan-African and Identity Paradigms', *International Journal of African Historical Studies* 31 (October 1998), pp. 505, 510–11.

82. Fierce, *Pan-African Idea in the United States*, pp. 125–6, 128–31; William E. Bittle and Gilbert L. Geis, 'Alfred Charles Sam and an African Return: A Case Study in Negro Despair', *Phylon* 23 (2nd Qtr., 1962), pp. 178–94; J. Ayo Langley, 'Chief Sam's African Movement and Race Consciousness in West Africa', *Phylon* 32 (2nd Qtr., 1971), pp. 164–78; Kendra Field and Ebony Coletu, 'The Chief Sam Move-ment: A Century Later', *Transition* 114 (2014), pp, 108–30; Redkey, *Black Exodus*, p. 292.

CHAPTER 2

Marcus Garvey and the Universal Negro Improvement Association

Within a few years of his arrival from Jamaica in 1916, Marcus Garvey quickly established a popular black nationalist organisation, which attracted support from blacks in the urban industrial North, the rural and urban South, and parts of the Midwest and West. Garvey's Universal Negro Improvement Association (UNIA) won adherence from African Americans and West Indian immigrants, despite some tension between them inside and outside the organisation, and from among agricultural and industrial workers, elements of the middle class and some intellectuals. His emphasis on racial pride, Christianity, commerce, the redemption of Africa and selective emigration of skilled African Americans to the continent reflected ideas long established among black nationalists in America during the nineteenth and early twentieth centuries. However, Garvey harnessed the support of the black masses unlike any black nationalist leader before him, even Turner. Like many of his nationalist predecessors, he was also hierarchical and authoritarian. Garvey's UNIA evinced a form of black civil religion; both clergy and religious ritual played an important role in many of its branches, known as divisions. Garvey created structures and organisations within the UNIA that paralleled those of the wider society and gave his supporters a sense of mission, belonging and pride. An effective orator, Garvey also used his and others' journalism skills in the UNIA's newspaper, the *Negro World*, to disseminate his message, and by encouraging pride in African history and blacks' appearance he foreshadowed some of the direction of late twentieth-century black nationalism.

The Formation of the Universal Negro Improvement Association

Marcus Garvey was born in St Ann's Bay, Jamaica, in 1887. His stonemason father claimed descent from Jamaica's maroons who had escaped from slavery. Jamaica was a British colony, but, unlike the American South, it did not have legal segregation or lynching and permitted racial intermarriage. Blacks formed a majority in a comparatively racially tolerant society, although they also suffered discrimination and occupied the lowest rungs of employment. Unlike most of the American South, Jamaica had a distinct tri-racial order with a small minority of whites at the top, a large minority of 'coloured' mixed-race 'mulattoes' in the middle, and blacks, like Garvey, at the bottom. Whites exploited racial divisions and Garvey lamented that coloureds aligned with whites, rather than with leaderless blacks. Like many nineteenth-century African American nationalists, Garvey argued that blacks were largely responsible for their benighted condition and needed to uplift themselves by emulating white civilisation, which he admired, through hard work and dedication.[1]

After completing an apprenticeship as a printer, Garvey moved to Kingston. Between 1910 and 1912, he worked and travelled widely in South and Central America and urged West Indian banana plantation workers in Costa Rica to seek improved conditions. Between 1912 and 1914, Garvey travelled in Europe, basing himself in London, where he worked for and became influenced by Duse Mohammad Ali, a Sudanese-Egyptian nationalist, whose *African Times and Orient Review* lambasted racism and published material about prominent blacks. Garvey learned about Egyptian history, Pan-Africanism and anticolonial efforts around the world, and he unfavourably contrasted Britain's espousal of democracy with its maintenance of an autocratic empire. Garvey also read Booker T. Washington's autobiography *Up from Slavery* and admired its message of self-help and the black-run Tuskegee Institute. The book, he recalled, inspired him to become a 'race leader'.[2]

Within days of his return to Jamaica in July 1914, Garvey founded the Universal Negro Improvement and Conservation Association and African Communities (Imperial) League, a title subsequently shortened. Appealing to 'all people of Negro or African parentage', the UNIA sought 'To establish a Universal Confraternity among the race; to promote the spirit of race pride and love . . . to assist in civilizing the backward tribes of Africa . . . to promote a conscientious Christian worship among the native tribes of Africa', strengthen the independence of African states, establish educational institutions from schools through to universities and promote worldwide commerce. The manifesto's emphasis on 'civilisation', Christianity and commerce were ideas common among nineteenth-century black nationalists in the United States. The UNIA proclaimed 'One God! One Aim! One Destiny!' as its motto. Garvey served as UNIA president and, his later wife, Amy Ashwood as associate secretary.[3]

Garvey's immediate aim was to create 'educational and industrial colleges' in Jamaica modelled on Tuskegee, but he failed to generate black Jamaican interest. Coloureds, who rejected categorisation as 'Negro' that would identify them with the black population, opposed the UNIA, which struggled to recruit members. Garvey corresponded with Washington, who invited him to visit Tuskegee but declined to make a contribution. Garvey decided to visit the United States on a fundraising tour to inaugurate an industrial institute at home and to meet Washington. Although Washington died in December 1915, Garvey proceeded with his planned American visit and arrived in New York in March 1916 for what he envisioned would be a five-month lecture tour focused on the South. Garvey lodged in the Harlem section of the city, which had recently become black following large-scale migration of southern blacks and West Indian immigrants, and found work to fund his tour. He lectured in thirty-eight states and developed his public speaking ability but raised little more money than he needed for expenses. In 1917, Garvey founded the New York division of the UNIA and attracted several hundred members, but it broke up among acrimony as he resisted black politicians' attempts to exploit the group. He started again, recruited 1,500 members for the reincorporated UNIA and withstood further takeover attempts. Encouraged by such initial progress, he decided to remain in the United States, where the UNIA grew rapidly in 1919 and 1920.[4]

The UNIA's newspaper, the *Negro World* founded in New York by Garvey in 1918, was an important factor in his growing success in the United States and abroad. The paper was particularly significant in generating support in the South where Garvey made few visits, and in gaining UNIA adherents in the Caribbean and Central America, assisted by the addition of French and Spanish language sections. Affordably priced for low-income earners and soon earning a reputation as one of the best black weekly newspapers in America, the *Negro World* achieved a circulation of almost 50,000 by 1919 and was likely read by four times as many people. Although the front page always carried a Garvey editorial, the paper was run by a series of gifted editorial staff, W. A. Domingo,

William H. Ferris, Hubert H. Harrison, T. Thomas Fortune and, until his death in 1924, columnist John Edward Bruce, known as 'Bruce Grit'. Apart from disseminating the UNIA's message and reporting its activities, the *Negro World* published stories about black history and gloried in the African past. At a time when the black press often accepted well-paid advertisements for skin lighteners and hair-straightening treatments, the *Negro World*, which emphasised black pride and beauty, refused them. Although Garvey was not the first black nationalist to advocate racial pride or to publish a newspaper, he did both at a time when many black Americans were particularly receptive to his message. The United States was to have nearly 80 per cent of the UNIA's divisions that spread to the Caribbean, Central America, Africa and Europe.[5]

The Appeal of Marcus Garvey and the Universal Negro Improvement Association

When Garvey arrived in the United States, there was both an opportunity and a need for new black leadership following the deaths in 1915 of Booker T. Washington, America's most prominent and influential black leader, and Henry McNeal Turner, the nation's most outspoken black nationalist. Garvey's message combined ideas and strategies adopted by both men. Like Washington, Garvey, historian Mary G. Rolinson observes, 'emphasised the solidarity and separation of the black race and . . . believed that blacks could succeed economically through their own thrift and diligence'. However, Garvey, unlike Washington, regarded white philanthropic support as inimical to those goals. Like Turner, Garvey emphasised racial pride, argued that blacks should worship a black Christian God in whose image they had been created, advocated the selective emigration of blacks to Africa, and castigated those blacks he believed lacked energy, ambition, drive and determination. Such messages, Rolinson contends, appealed to many blacks in the South and to the many black southerners who began in 1915 to migrate in significant numbers to other parts of the country away from overt racial discrimination and lynching in the South. The boll weevil also pushed them off the land by devastating much of southern cotton especially in 1915 and 1916. At the same time, better paying industrial employment opportunities arose in the North as World War One cut off the immigrant labour supply from Europe and increased demand for industrial output to supply the western powers and later to sustain America's participation in the war after it entered the conflict in 1917.[6]

The war raised African American expectations of a better life but saw these rising expectations thwarted, eventually creating a sense of frustration and disillusionment. In April 1917, President Woodrow Wilson successfully asked Congress to declare war on Germany and announced that 'The world must be made safe for democracy.' He later championed the principle of national self-determination and the rights of national minorities but, in practice, applied them only to the peoples of Central and Eastern Europe, regarding non-whites as first in need of prolonged preparation and guidance. Although it appointed black advisers, the Wilson administration did nothing of significance against racial discrimination at home. In June, Hubert H. Harrison, who had immigrated to New York from St Croix in the Danish West Indies in 1900, held the first meeting of the Liberty League, which demanded racial equality, called for loyalty to race over country, advocated black armed self-defence and opposed colonial rule throughout the world. Garvey, who spoke by invitation, adopted many of Harrison and the Liberty League's ideas and eventually transformed the small UNIA into the mass organisation that Harrison had envisaged for the League. Most African Americans, like nearly all of the black press, patriotically supported the war, with 367,000 serving in the army and many black civilians buying Liberty Bonds to support the war effort. In July 1918, W. E. B. Du Bois wrote an editorial in *The Crisis* urging blacks to 'Close Ranks' and support the war. Many African Americans, like Du Bois, hoped that service to their country would also help bring recognition of their rights at home after the war.[7]

Although some African Americans eventually went into combat, reservations in the War Department delayed and restricted such opportunities. Black soldiers often acquitted themselves well in combat, but racial discrimination remained commonplace in the military. The army used 80 per cent of African American conscripts as labourers. Initially, few African Americans could obtain officer commissions, and white officers often commanded black troops. The Marine Corps refused blacks admittance, and the Navy confined them to service roles, such as messmen. Despite maintaining colonial empires in Africa and Asia, Britain and France largely welcomed African American servicemen as contributors to the Allied cause and, for the most part, without the discrimination blacks were subject to at home and in America's armed forces. Black servicemen favourably contrasted their experiences abroad with their treatment by their white compatriots, which, in consequence, seemed even harder to bear.[8]

Racial tensions in America increased during the war. Around 330,000 African Americans moved north during the conflict and some also migrated from the rural South to work in southern dockyards. African American migrants in northern cities competed for scarce housing and for jobs with often resentful whites. In July 1917, white mobs, with little hindrance from the police, ran riot in East St. Louis, Illinois, after African Americans had killed two white detectives a day earlier believing them to have fired on black homes. The mobs killed at least thirty-nine African Americans. Thirty-four people, twenty of them white, were later convicted. They included Leroy N. Bundy, a black dentist, businessman and Republican, who was found guilty in 1919 of being the ring leader in a conspiracy to murder the two detectives. Fiercely independent, Bundy clashed with the National Association for the Advancement of Colored People (NAACP), which had initially supported his case, and successfully appealed his conviction in 1921 without its help. He subsequently joined the UNIA, which, by then, had entered into an increasingly quarrelsome and competitive rivalry with the NAACP.[9]

Conflicts arose between black soldiers and white civilians in the South, notably in Houston, Texas, when 100 black soldiers from Camp Logan sought revenge for the humiliations of segregation and discrimination. In August 1917, they marched downtown and attacked local police in response to earlier police brutality against Corporal Charles W. Baltimore, who led the avenging soldiers. Five policemen and twelve other whites died in the attack, along with two black soldiers. In response, the army hanged nineteen black soldiers and gave fifty others life sentences.[10]

The lynching of African Americans, which had decreased to thirty-six in 1917, the lowest total since the Tuskegee Institute began recording them in 1882, increased to seventy-six across the United States in 1919. Determined to maintain black subordination, whites sometimes attacked returning black veterans. Some whites, taking their cue from the federal government's crackdown on leftist political radicals in the developing Red Scare (fear of communist subversion), justified antiblack violence on the spurious grounds that communists were stirring black discontent as part of their revolutionary designs to spread Bolshevism. In June 1919, the first of twenty-six race riots in the nation's cities began, marking the start of Red Summer. African Americans, particularly in the North, often defended themselves in these conflicts, which occurred in many parts of the country. The greatest tumult of the summer broke out in Chicago, where the black population had doubled since 1916. In July, a white man stoned a black teenager near a beach contested by the two races. The teenager drowned. Fighting broke out on the beach and spread, inaugurating five days of violence, largely orchestrated by whites. African Americans organised their own defence and sometimes engaged in retaliatory violence. White violence also produced greater militancy in other black communities and a willingness to adopt armed self-defence. In the Elaine, Arkansas, riot of October 1919, black farmers, some of whom were preparing a legal challenge against exploitative landlords, also fought back. However, they were no match for the firepower of local whites who, aided by 600 federal troops, killed an unknown number of blacks, and a white-controlled judicial system that condemned twelve African Americans to death, although the United States Supreme Court later overturned their convictions.[11]

The worsening racial climate also saw the rebirth of the Ku Klux Klan. Refounded in Atlanta, Georgia, in 1915, the Klan, which combined xenophobia, anti-Semitism, opposition to Asians and anti-Catholicism with its traditional opposition to blacks, soon spread beyond its southern strongholds to over twenty-seven states by late 1920, including many cities to which African Americans had migrated.[12]

The NAACP increased its membership significantly during World War One, especially in the South where most blacks continued to live. The association campaigned against racial injustice, maintained that blacks had a right to self-defence and won United States Supreme rulings that outlawed the grandfather clause and residential segregation ordinances. However, these early efforts and victories had virtually no effect on the everyday lives of African Americans as whites devised alternative stratagems. Furthermore, litigation was a slow, time-consuming process subject to appeals and delays in implementation that could take years to resolve. By contrast, Garvey responded to growing militancy among blacks. Whereas the NAACP was interracial and, in its early years, dominated by whites at the national level, Garvey appealed to racial chauvinism.[13]

After the East St. Louis riot of July 1917, Garvey became increasingly combative in his speeches, denouncing whites for their treatment of blacks and calling on blacks to unite through the UNIA. Garvey advocated a right to self-defence, which blacks had increasingly adopted from necessity, and, reportedly, the retaliatory lynching of whites in the North or Africa whenever southern blacks suffered that fate. Whereas the UNIA's founding manifesto had adopted the nineteenth-century black nationalist goals of 'civilising' and Christianising Africa, Garvey now celebrated the continent as the origin of civilisation and learning at a time when Europe had been beset by barbarism. Yet, he also regarded western educated blacks as central to its redemption from colonial rule and material progress. Both his audiences and UNIA membership increased as he adjusted his message to changing American and world conditions.[14]

In January 1919, Garvey and several prominent African Americans, including socialist A. Philip Randolph and New York clergyman Adam Clayton Powell, Sr, formed the International League of Darker Peoples (ILDP), designed to foster collaboration and pave the way for a council that would unite the world's non-whites in defending their interests. The ILDP did not endure, but the UNIA nominated Randolph, along with Ida B. Wells-Barnett and Eliezer Cadet, a translator, to represent the association at the Paris peace conference and present its demands for Germany's former African colonies to be given over to educated, western-ised blacks. After the French government refused the others visas, Cadet, a Haitian, attended without them. The British and French allocated the colonies to themselves, South Africa and Belgium as mandates under the newly formed League of Nations. Garvey dis-missed their action as a reaffirmation of European colonialism at the expense of Africans.[15]

Garvey's address in Newport News, Virginia, in October 1919 typified much of what historian Adam Ewing describes as a newly emergent 'radical Garveyism', reflecting the UNIA leader's belief that the recent world war presented an opportunity for significant change. Garvey refashioned Wilsonian rhetoric and appealed to black militancy, asserting that 'We are in a very great war, a great con-flict, and we will never get liberty, we will never capture democracy, until we ... shed our sacred blood.' Recognising that blacks were massively outnumbered by whites in the United States, he declared that the fight would not be in America, but 'one day on the African battlefield', a vague assertion that provided emotional release for, but no commitment from, his audience. Adapting Patrick Henry's rousing call against the British in the American Revolution that was well known to his audience, Garvey proclaimed to cheers that 'We new Negroes of America declare that we desire liberty or we will take death.' Blacks had recently fought in Europe 'to give liberty and democracy to the other peoples of the world', now 'in the very near future' they would fight for it 'in the African plains' against unnamed enemies, meaning white colonial powers.[16]

Garvey castigated whites as murderers, who were 'unfit . . . to rule' and condemned their enslavement of Africans. Believing that many blacks had internalised feelings of inferiority, he maintained that 'There is not a white man so educated that you cannot find a Negro to equal him' in Britain, France or the United States. Inverting white claims of African savagery and backwardness, Garvey declared that Africa had 'given civilization to mankind' and whites 'science and art and literature'. Indeed 'The Negro has been the savior of all that has been good for mankind.' Garvey predicted that 'in the Negroes' rule there will be mercy, love and charity to all', and he asserted that the establishment of 'a black republic of Africa' would ensure the protection of blacks everywhere.[17]

Whereas Crummell and Turner had argued that under American slavery Africans had been evangelised and 'civilised' and predicted that their free descendants would become agents for Christianising and 'civilising' Africa, Garvey declared dismissively, 'The white man never schooled us for the 250 years. He hid the book from us, even the very Bible, and never taught the Negro anything.' Like many of his black nationalist predecessors, Garvey invoked Psalms 68:31, arguing that its prediction was being realised because 'we are stretching forth our hands unto God in New York, in Pennsylvania, in the West Indies, in Central America and in Africa and throughout the world'. He claimed that 'With Jesus as our standard bearer the Negro will march to victory.'[18]

Garvey's address was also designed to elicit further support for the Black Star Line (BSL), named in imitation of the British shipping company the White Star Line, which he had organised earlier in the year. Like earlier black nationalist proponents of independent shipping, Garvey envisaged the BSL as a black-owned and black-crewed shipping line that would promote trade, connect the black peoples of North America, Central America, the Caribbean and Africa, and transport emigrants to Africa. The BSL sold its five dollar shares, heavily promoted in the *Negro World*, only to blacks and capped individual holdings at 200 shares, making them affordable even to poorer blacks and a significant source of the UNIA's appeal and funds. Ownership offered stockholders participation in a collective racial enterprise that generated feeling of pride and the prospect of making a profit, reflecting the booming trade in the stock market of this era. The BSL bought its first ship, the S.S. *Yarmouth* in September 1919 and renamed it the SS *Frederick Douglass*.[19]

In 1920, the UNIA initiated another commercial enterprise designed to generate and keep money within the black community. Like the BSL, the Negro Factories Corporation offered blacks shares for five dollars. It aimed, according to the *Negro World*, 'to build and operate factories in the big industrial centers of the United States, Central America, the West Indies, and Africa to manufacture every marketable commodity'. Such enterprises would provide employment for blacks and profits for stockholders. UNIA businesses included a cooperative grocery store chain, restaurants, tailoring and millinery, laundries, a doll factory, a hotel and printing. Within a year, UNIA businesses employed 300 people.[20]

Membership in the UNIA's branches required 35 cents in monthly dues, with ten cents of that amount designated for the organisation's headquarters established in Harlem. To attract members, Garvey based the UNIA on black American fraternal organisations and offered members sickness and death benefits. However, in practice the headquarters lacked funds to provide benefits, and Garvey often called for the headquarters to be given its share of dues.[21]

In August 1920, Garvey staged the First International Convention of the Negro Peoples of the World, a month-long gathering that brought delegates who claimed to represent twenty-five countries to Harlem. Colourful parades of uniformed UNIA auxiliaries gave participants a sense of belonging, pride and identity as part of the world's large black community that Garvey often referenced in speeches. Men staffed the African Legion, a paramilitary unit that was in practice largely ceremonial, and women the Black Cross Nurses, who mostly lacked formal medical qualifications but knew first aid and nutrition and offered health care to local communities. Further maintaining the idea of a government in waiting were the

Black Flying Eagle Corps and the Universal African Motor Corps, a female auxiliary which taught driving and mechanics.[22]

On 2 August, 25,000 people gathered at Madison Square Garden to hear Garvey. They sang a new anthem, 'Ethiopia, Thou Land of Our Fathers', and waved what the convention subsequently approved as the UNIA's official colours: red for the 'color of the blood which men must shed for their redemption and liberty', black for the colour of the skin and green for 'the luxuriant vegetation of our Motherland'. Garvey told his audience it was time to organise the world's black population 'into a vast organization to plant the banner of freedom on the great continent of Africa'.[23]

In a speech later that month, Garvey seemed to threaten war against the colonial powers in Africa, declaring that if they did not withdraw from the continent 'we are coming 400,000,000 strong, and we mean to retake every square inch of the 12,000,000 square miles of African territory belonging to us by right Divine'. However, Garvey and the UNIA did not formulate any military plans to underpin the rhetoric. Nevertheless, the convention proclaimed Garvey the Provisional President of the African Republic. It also issued a 'Declaration of the Rights of the Negro Peoples of the World' that proclaimed 'our most solemn determination' to reclaim Africa 'for the Africans at home and abroad' and condemned the League of Nations, which had given Germany's former colonies in Africa to Allied powers. The declaration demanded that blacks be accorded equal rights under the law and condemned segregated transport, disenfranchisement, employment discrimination and lynching. It called for 'Negro' to be spelt with a capital 'N' as a matter of respect and for black history to be taught in schools. The declaration also advocated the right to self-defence and self-determination, and pledged protection of 'the honor and virtue of our women and children'.[24]

In keeping with the UNIA's desire to promote black dignity and self-worth, as well as to display some features of an embryonic nation state, the convention created titles of nobility for the association's most distinguished members, borrowing European terms, such as baron, duke and knight. On formal occasions, Garvey often wore uniforms modelled on those of European monarchies. Titles, uniforms and parades were part of the UNIA's appeal, and the UNIA shared the militarism of the age. Accordingly, it named its local branches divisions and UNIA recruiters used footage of marching African Legions at convention parades to project an appearance of strength and pride. Historian Tony Martin observes that by 1921, 'Garvey was unquestionably the leader of the largest organization of its type in the history of the race.' Although Garvey exaggerated the UNIA's size by including sympathisers as members, by August 1921, the association had a total of 418 chartered and 422 unchartered divisions worldwide (with a minimum of seven people required to form a branch and pay dues for a charter) and nineteen chapters, the name for additional branches formed in cities that already had a division.[25]

The Nature of the Universal Negro Improvement Association

Historians disagree about the UNIA's appeal and the nature of its membership. In 1955, historian E. David Cronon produced the first full-length study of Garvey and the UNIA, finding the core of its American support in northern industrial cities. However, twenty years later Emory J. Tolbert challenged that approach in a study of the Los Angeles UNIA division, established in January 1921. There, Tolbert argues, the UNIA's 'leadership and members were . . . trades-men and laborers who, along with a few professionals, attempted to use the UNIA to secure more prosperous lives'. They were 'person-ally intent on local achievement and status', rather than attracted by 'Garvey's stress on building an African nation', and were mostly migrants from the South. The Los Angeles UNIA resisted Garvey's attempts to control it and, as a consequence, created a rival organi-sation, the Pacific Coast Negro Improvement Association.[26]

In 1986, Judith M. Stein offered a similar argument in a wider study of the UNIA. Stein contends that Garveyism was stamped by the needs and aspirations of the black middle class which sought entrepreneurial opportunities in the association's business enter-prises. Accordingly, the UNIA had vigour in the cities of the north-ern United States but was weak elsewhere, whether in the American South, the Caribbean or Africa. In Stein's view, 'The nearly four hundred UNIA divisions and chapters of the South testified that Garvey had been there but not much else.' Seeking to identify the UNIA's core support, she writes that 'Garvey's appeal received a hearing wherever economic development had destroyed old cul-tures and dangled the prospects of new prosperity.' She claims that

'UNIA members viewed the local chapter as an instrument for their own economic self-improvement' and that the UNIA's local leaders were 'an upwardly mobile petite bourgeoisie'.[27]

Stein's willingness to look beyond the figure of Garvey and to consider the UNIA's high-level officials, and, to some extent, its local leaders and divisions is a strength of her work. However, while there were, as Stein demonstrates, those who saw in the UNIA an opportunity to further their personal ambitions, and who moved on when they were not fulfilled, and divisions that largely comprised such people, she fails to examine the UNIA's widespread support in the South. She neglects its appeal to blue-collar, agricultural and household workers who formed the bulk of UNIA membership, and the attraction of race-based approaches that focused on pride, solidarity, identity and Africa. Her claim that 'UNIA divisions did not and could not provide services for impoverished blacks' ignores their provision of charitable, relief and service programmes for local communities.[28]

Stein's class-based analysis also neglects the importance of religion in the UNIA, which historian Randall K. Burkett had explored earlier. Burkett demonstrates that the UNIA received significant support from clergy and laity from a broad swathe of mainly black Protestant denominations and from black Jews. UNIA organisers were often clergymen. He argues that although not ordained, Garvey was 'the foremost Black theologian of the early 20th Century' who created a civil religion focused on the uplift of black people and 'the Redemption of Africa'. Each UNIA division had a chaplain. Divisional, chapter and convention meetings 'reflected the tone of a religious service' with 'hymn singing, prayers, and sermons'. The UNIA elected Episcopalian George Alexander McGuire, a native of Antigua, as its second chaplain general in 1920. When McGuire created the nondenominational, but strongly Episcopalian influenced, African Orthodox Church (AOC) in 1921 and sought to make it the UNIA's official church, Garvey blocked the move and soon forced McGuire to resign his chaplaincy. Garvey refused to identify the UNIA with the AOC, or with any one denomination or religious belief, anxious not to alienate any of his followers or black church leaders, and he never joined the AOC. McGuire later reconciled with the UNIA, but the AOC remained a separate organisation, although several prominent association figures held significant positions. It advocated racial pride and made its governance

a black preserve but permitted whites at its services and in its con-
gregations.[29]
Like Turner before him, Garvey contended that God was not
white and had no specific colour, but, as they were created in
God's image, blacks could worship Him 'through the spectacles of
Ethiopia'. Less often, Garvey articulated the jeremiadic belief that
God would punish those who had so unjustly made blacks suffer.
Burkett argues that 'Garvey's speeches and editorials were sermonic
in style, containing extensive use of Biblical references and religious
imagery' that his audience readily understood, and they helped
ensure Garveyism's widespread popularity and acceptability among
clergy and laity.[30]
Much of the laity was female, and many women joined the
UNIA, forming a majority in some divisions. According to historian
Beryl Satter, the UNIA 'offered women a wide variety of participa-
tory roles and was one of the few organizations offering leadership
positions to black women in the 1920s'. Amy Ashwood Garvey,
whom Garvey divorced in 1922, had been appointed UNIA general
secretary in 1919 and also served as an early BSL director. Garvey's
second wife, Amy Jacques Garvey, was office manager in the UNIA's
New York headquarters and secretary of the Negro Factories Corporation. An associate editor of the *Negro World*, she introduced a
women's page in 1924. Henrietta Vinton Davis held several UNIA
posts and worked closely with Marcus Garvey. She was the UNIA's
International Organizer, a director of the BSL, first and fourth assistant president-general of the UNIA, and, in 1924, the only female
member of a UNIA delegation to Liberia. Davis travelled widely in
Central and South America and the West Indies recruiting for the
association and frequently addressed audiences in the United States.
The UNIA had three female auxiliaries: the Black Cross Nurses, the
Universal African Motor Corps and Juvenile Divisions. Each UNIA
division had a 'Lady President'. Some women served as regional and
national organisers, as well as local officers. Nicaraguan immigrant
Alaida Robertson organised UNIA divisions in Georgia, Louisiana,
Mississippi and the Midwest. Mamie Reason was treasurer of the
New Orleans UNIA. As delegates from local divisions, women par-
ticipated in the UNIA's international conventions.[31]
However, the UNIA largely ascribed women roles and responsibilities subordinate to men. Women undertook much of the UNIA's
benevolence and community service work but were rarely among

the association's top officials and policy makers. The *Negro World* emphasised the role of men as leaders and rulers and protectors of women who were to occupy supportive, private roles and to produce the strong and healthy children on whom the future of the race depended. Moreover, at a time when white men denigrated black manhood and some used their power and wealth to seek or engage in sexual liaisons with black women, many black women wished to support black manhood, and they welcomed protection from exploitative white men. The UNIA's emphasis on black women's natural beauty helped instil racial pride and counter negative self-images absorbed from white portrayals. However, the fostering of black manhood and female protection in the UNIA often involved male control. Divisional lady presidents presided over women's sections, but male presidents oversaw the entire division, although some divisions observed equality between them. Although headed by a female brigadier general, the Universal African Motor Corps' officers and commanders were men. Supported by a majority of female delegates at the UNIA's International Convention in 1922, Victoria Turner of St. Louis presented resolutions calling for women to be included on all committees, given additional 'important offices', and allowed to initiate policy. Although Garvey responded that the UNIA's constitution addressed their concerns and modified the resolutions, they were adopted largely intact.[32]

Garvey contended that black women should be race mothers. He frequently attacked his critics, such as W. E. B. Du Bois and others in the NAACP, for their mixed racial heritage and argued that they wanted to be white, were ashamed of their black ancestry and sought racial mixing with whites. Garvey's hostility to mixed-race 'mulattoes' came from his West Indian background. West Indian immigrants constituted around half of the UNIA's top leadership but only a minority of its American membership, which was mostly African American. There were sometimes tensions between African American and Caribbean immigrant members. West Indian members were often more prone to militancy, notably in New York. However, 'mulattoes' were represented among the UNIA's leadership and, given the mixed race ancestry of most African Americans, formed a large part of its United States membership. Despite his rhetoric, Garvey seems to have had no more difficulty working with 'mulattoes', such as Henrietta Vinton Davis, than he did with darker skinned blacks whom he perceived as more similar to himself.[33]

Like many black nationalists, Garvey sometimes accused blacks of shiftlessness and lacking sophistication in terms more usually associated with white racists. Garvey's rhetorical attacks also on occasion extended to whites. He used but did not invent the term 'white devils' to characterise whites and popularised the idea, claiming that 'There isn't a greater devil in the world than the white man.' However, his usage of the devils theme was intended to characterise white oppression of blacks metaphorically and not literally. Before some audiences, Garvey threatened warfare and retribution against whites but, more often, he made vague predictions that blacks would reclaim Africa, using force if necessary. Some Garveyites physically attacked white men in New York.[34]

Opponents and critics sometimes characterised the UNIA as a utopian back to Africa movement, but, with some exceptions, Garvey generally did not advocate the large-scale return of diaspora blacks to Africa. Usually, he called for the selective migration of skilled blacks to the continent that would help its progress and development on the western model. Garvey explained that 'The majority of us may remain here, but we must send our scientists, our mechanics, and our artisans, and . . . let them build the great educational and other institutions necessary.' He believed that if Africa became a single country ruled by Africans, it would be able to represent and defend the interests of black people around the world, all of whom would be eligible for African citizenship. Just as other countries used their power and prestige to defend and protect the rights of their nationals abroad, so would Africa.[35]

However, Garvey and the UNIA became dismissive of the Pan-African congresses chiefly organised by his rival W. E. B. Du Bois of the NAACP. In Paris to represent the UNIA at the peace conference, Eliezer Cadet attended the Pan-African Congress there in 1919, but once rivalry and disagreements between Garvey and Du Bois developed, Garvey, the UNIA and the *Negro World* denounced later congresses. Du Bois organised three more interwar congresses, held in London, Paris and Brussels in 1921, London and Lisbon in 1923, and New York in 1927. Small gatherings of intellectuals and upper-class blacks from the diaspora in the United States, the Caribbean and Africa, the congresses passed resolutions that increasingly called on European colonial powers to allow Africans local self-government and address abuses in colonial rule. Although these efforts had no immediate effect, in the long-run the congresses, like the UNIA, helped pave the way for the Pan-African movement that emerged in an era of decolonisation after World War Two.[36]

Unlike Du Bois, Garvey hoped to use emigration to Liberia as a beachhead for the eventual restoration of African independence. The UNIA's emphasis on race pride, self-defence, emigration to Africa and African redemption through a 'civilising' and Christianising mission (subsequently amended to 'promote a conscientious Spiritual worship among the native tribes') had also been popular among Bishop Henry McNeal Turner's largely southern following. Speculatively, Rolinson attributes the UNIA's appeal in southwest Georgia, the Arkansas Delta and the Yazoo–Mississippi Delta in part to Turner's legacy. Although Garvey did not visit the rural South, he made several southern tours that, along with the efforts of UNIA recruiters, built support in the region's cities. Largely industrial workers, southern urban Garveyites welcomed the prospect of employment and investment in black businesses. Many bought BSL shares which promised to achieve both and also appealed to racial pride. The *Negro World* was the main means of UNIA recruitment in the rural South. According to Rolinson, 'rural southern Garveyites were mostly married, literate, Black Belt tenant farmers and sharecroppers with wives and daughters in their households', but 'women [also] played a significant role in sustaining the small, local divisions'. Most of the UNIA's urban and rural southern divisions and chapters were formed between 1919 and 1921, and 'ministers and their churches formed a crucial part of the UNIA infrastructure' in the region. White racial violence, economic dominance and licentiousness toward black females made the UNIA's message particularly appealing to rural Garveyites. The UNIA retained its strength in the rural South throughout most of the 1920s, and the conservative direction that Garvey took in 1921 and 1922, if anything, reinforced his appeal there.[37]

Historian Robert A. Hill attributes what he describes as Garvey's 'retreat from radicalism' to federal pressure. In 1918, the federal Bureau of Investigation (BOI) began investigating Garvey and the UNIA, concerned by their racial militancy. Garvey had predicted that the next war would be a racial war between white countries and an alliance of the Japanese and black peoples. Amid the Red Scare, the BOI's J. Edgar Hoover believed that the *Negro World* advocated Bolshevism and began planting black BOI agents and informants in the UNIA. The Military Intelligence Division and the United States State Department also investigated it.[38]

Socialist W. A. Domingo, the *Negro World*'s first editor, was, Martin observes, 'responsible for some at least of the Bolshevik propaganda appearing in the paper which alarmed authorities in 1919'. Garvey later claimed that he dismissed Domingo, a fellow Jamaican and boyhood friend who had introduced him to Hubert H. Harrison, as editor in September 1919 for holding communist views. Garvey avoided Communists in the United States and had no interest in working with whites in a class struggle, or in surrendering control of the UNIA. Domingo never became a member of the Communist Party, but, like a few other UNIA members who fell out with Garvey, he joined the African Blood Brotherhood for African Liberation and Redemption (ABB).[39]

A partly clandestine radical nationalist group of somewhere between 1,000 and 3,000 members, the ABB tried unsuccessfully to infiltrate the UNIA. Founded in 1919 by Cyril V. Briggs, a West Indian immigrant from Nevis, the ABB called for self-determination for southern blacks, equal rights, the end of disenfranchisement and segregation laws, and self-defence. By 1921, the ABB's leadership, including Briggs, began siding with the Communists in favour of an interracial class struggle. Briggs and other ABB members appeared as delegates at the UNIA International Convention that year and tried without success to align the convention with communism. Although he admired Russian Bolsheviks for ending Czarist oppression, committed to a race first policy Garvey condemned the ABB for its Bolshevism and held aloof from American communists. In 1923, the Communist Party absorbed the ABB, which discontinued in 1924.[40]

Unable to find evidence that Garvey was a communist, Hoover, a racist, increasingly targeted him for his racial agitation and pressured the State Department and the Commissioner General of Immigration to prevent Garvey from returning to the United States after a tour of Central America and the Caribbean in 1921. After repeatedly denying Garvey a visa, State Department officials relented, and, after several weeks delay, he re-entered the country but only after an interrogation by immigration staff could not find sufficient cause to exclude him. According to Hill, immediately after his return, Garvey, in a move soon followed by other UNIA officials, adopted a more patriotic tone toward the United States and abandoned his criticisms of white America.[41]

Garvey also began calling for racial purity. He endorsed President Warren G. Harding's condemnation of miscegenation (interracial sexual relationships) and urged blacks to oppose 'social equality'. Garvey asked, 'Why should I waste time in a place where I am out-numbered and where if I make a physical fight I will lose out and ultimately die?' although, prudently after his recent visa problems, he had submitted an application for American citizenship that month. Garvey also denigrated black achievements. He declared that in the past 500 years, blacks 'have made no political, educational, indus-trial, independent contribution to civilization for which they can be respected by other races, thus making themselves unfit subjects for free companionship and association with races which achieved greatness on their own initiative'.[42]

Hill convincingly attributes Garvey's increasing emphasis on racial purity and social separation, and his parallel attack on W. E. B. Du Bois and the NAACP for seeking social equality, to his 'decision to seek a resolution of his conflict with the American state' by accepting white domination in America. Rolinson agrees that the visa problem was 'an important factor' in Garvey's 'conservative turn'. However, she also argues that in southern states African American UNIA organisers had already begun to use 'moderate language' to defuse white opposition. Less plausible is her conten-tion that advised in 1918 by Emmet J. Scott, secretary-treasurer of the Tuskegee Institute, to temper his rhetoric, Garvey had taken note, although 'It took him two years to complete the toning-down process.'[43]

Garvey and his black critics, such as Du Bois and Cyril V. Briggs, engaged in increasingly vitriolic exchanges and traded personal insults as they competed for the allegiance of African Americans. Socialists A. Philip Randolph and Chandler Owen attacked Garvey in their newspaper, *The Messenger*, and helped form the Friends of Negro Freedom to oppose him. The UNIA used strong-arm tactics against opponents, for example in December 1921, its members forcibly broke up anti-UNIA meetings orchestrated by Briggs.[44]

The Decline and Fall of Marcus Garvey and the Universal Negro Improvement Association

If Garvey had hoped to mollify federal authorities by toning down his rhetoric, he was soon disappointed. In January 1922, Garvey and three BSL board members were arrested, for fraudulently using the mails to sell BSL stock. Although he did not sell shares for personal enrichment, Garvey was a poor businessman who routinely used money raised through stock sales to fund other UNIA activities and casually diverted ships from agreed trading routes to other ports to generate publicity, support and more stock sales, regardless of the commercial consequences. Ignorant of the shipping business and delinquent in record keeping, he selected associates for their supposed loyalty, rather than the business experience or acumen that might have offset his own deficiencies. Although undoubtedly headstrong, Garvey was also badly advised and taken advantage of by the unscrupulous within and outside the UNIA. Consequently, the BSL bought ships that were overpriced and unseaworthy and was unable to compete in a shipping market that already had excess capacity. None of the BSL's three ships made a profit, and the company was unable even to take possession of a fourth. In poor condition, its ships soon languished after ill-fated voyages, which led Garvey's opponents and a few disgruntled shareholders to call for an investigation by federal agencies that had long been seeking grounds to pursue him. While federal authorities gathered more evidence for Garvey's trial and opponents continued to condemn him, Garvey, still a free man, faced growing internal problems.[45]

Touring the South in June 1922, Garvey met with Edward Young Clarke, the acting imperial wizard of the Ku Klux Klan, in Atlanta. During the two-hour meeting, the two men agreed on their mutual commitment to racial separation and opposition to miscegenation. Garvey later recalled that he had explained the UNIA's programme in order to prevent conflict between their organisations. The meeting brought down a wave of criticism on both men. After strong condemnation by some Klansman, Clarke lost his leadership position. William Pickens, a field secretary for the NAACP, who had nearly joined the UNIA and had hitherto remained sympathetic, made a blistering condemnation of Garvey and joined a Garvey Must Go campaign, organised by Owen and Randolph. However, the UNIA retained and even increased its support in southern rural areas that had a strong Klan presence. Garvey's southern rural supporters favoured separation as way to prevent white sexual exploitation of females and hoped the meeting might stem Klan violence.[46]

Nevertheless, pressure on Garvey from within and outside the UNIA mounted. Garvey warned Pickens and Owen that 'The Universal Negro Improvement Association has no fear of anybody, and when you interfere . . . you will take the consequences.' Encouraged by his words, in some cities Garvey supporters attacked opposition meetings, and some leading opponents received death threats. Garvey also faced bitter criticism from within his organisation, especially from James W. H. Eason, an American Methodist Episcopal Zion minister in Philadelphia and the UNIA's Leader of American Negroes since 1920. Garvey charged Eason with financial misdeeds, disloyalty and poor conduct, while Eason accused Garvey of 'incompetence, forming an alliance with a discreditable organization and creating an unfriendly feeling among American Negroes'. Garvey retained sufficient hold on the UNIA's delegates to ensure Eason's expulsion, the impeachment of critics Adrian Johnson and J. D. Gibson who sat on the central office's executive council, and, in a constitutional revision, the replacement of the elected executive council with one appointed by himself. Garvey thereby ensured his control of the association, although his retreat from militant rhetoric cost him the support of more radical members, including some West Indians.[47]

In a reversal of policy, the UNIA convention announced it would send a delegation to the League of Nations in Geneva. In September, the delegation delivered a petition asking for German's former African colonies to be given to blacks. Seated in the assembly hall, the delegation persuaded the Persian delegation to submit the petition before taking seats among official delegates. Submitted too late for consideration, the petition was filed away. In 1923, the UNIA tried again, only to be told, most likely at the prompting of the British and French who had taken over many of Germany's colonies, that grievances should be submitted through national governments.[48]

By the time the UNIA returned to Geneva, Eason, who had opposed the move, formed the rival Universal Negro Alliance and agreed to testify against Garvey in the mail fraud case, had been assassinated in New Orleans, probably by Garvey loyalists. Convicted of Eason's manslaughter, two local Garveyite residents, Constantine F. Dyer and William Shakespeare, were acquitted after a retrial. A third Garveyite suspect, John Jeffries (also known as Esau Ramus), sent by Garvey to organise UNIA security, returned to Detroit. Although indicted in New Orleans, southern police did not seek his extradition for trial. However, there was no direct evidence linking Garvey to the crime, other than a self-interested confession by Jeffries intended to ease his sentence for another crime and an accusation by William Ferris that his leader had sent Jeffries to murder Eason.[49]

Within days of Eason's shooting in January 1923, eight leading African Americans, among them Owen, Pickens and Robert W.
Bagnall, director of the NAACP's branches, wrote a public letter
to the United States Attorney General Harry M. Daugherty. They
called on him to end the delay, caused by attempts to gather more
evidence, in holding Garvey's mail fraud trial and to 'use his full
influence completely to disband and extirpate this vicious movement'. The trial finally began in May 1923.[50]

Unlike his three co-defendants who retained counsel, Garvey
rather unwisely dismissed his lawyer and defended himself in a bel-
ligerent, argumentative manner. The case against the four men was
weak. In June, Garvey was convicted and his associates acquitted.
Fined $1,000 and sentenced to five years, the maximum permitted
but rarely imposed, he languished in jail until September when he
was freed for a very high bail of $25,000, pending appeal. Cronon
contends that the BSL's collapse was chiefly attributable 'to poor
judgment in the purchase and maintenance of the decrepit Black
Star fleet, and here the real criminals were the white culprits who
had unloaded the rusty hulks on unsuspecting and inexperienced'
African Americans. However, as Ewing notes, 'inexperience, poor
business management, bad luck, and widespread graft by Garvey's
subordinates' also made a significant contribution. Garvey believed
that he was convicted not for any crime but because he represented
'a movement for the real emancipation of my race'. His racial agitation had undoubtedly motivated federal authorities to seek, and
other black leaders to encourage, ways to undo him through the
courts. Martin attributes 'a major portion of the responsibility' for
Garvey's conviction to campaigns by Du Bois and the NAACP, and
Owen and Randolph, but federal efforts against Garvey had com-
menced long before those campaigns, which were not a decisive
factor in his incarceration.[51]

In 1924, Garvey used his freedom on bail to launch the Black
Cross Navigation and Trading Company, which sold bonds, rather
than stock, to UNIA members and proposed to sell more on its voyages. Garvey secured a ship, renamed the *Booker T. Washington*,
which was superior to any of the old line. However, the ship was
beset by the crew indiscipline and lack of funds that had also dogged
BSL vessels. It made only one voyage to the Caribbean and Central
America before being sold to pay debts as the company went
bankrupt.[52]

Garvey also pressed ahead with plans to establish a UNIA foot-hold in Liberia, where, in 1920, he had dispatched Elie Garcia to negotiate moving the association's headquarters, discuss emigra-tion and offer the prospect of UNIA financial assistance. The cash-strapped Liberian government promised to cooperate with UNIA 'industrial, agricultural and business projects'. Later that year, Garvey launched an appeal to raise a $2 million construction loan, and, in 1921, he sent a team of UNIA experts to Liberia. However, the appeal generated only $137,458, much of which Garvey used for the faltering BSL and other UNIA endeavours, and the UNIA's Liberian team lacked funds and cohesion. In December 1923, Garvey sent another UNIA group to Liberia to prepare the way for sending emigrants.[53]

The Liberian government became divided about the prospect of thousands arriving under UNIA auspices. When another contingent of UNIA experts arrived in the summer to begin the final prepara-tions for the first immigrants to arrive in October, the government deported them, declared its opposition to the UNIA and banned UNIA emigration. The Liberian volte-face was motivated by the opposition of Liberia's neighbouring British and French colonies to the UNIA's goal of ending colonialism in Africa and a fear that they might divide Liberia between them; justifiable concerns that the UNIA had political ambitions in Liberia; awareness that the coun-try's disenfranchised indigenous tribes, dominated by the country's governing American-Liberian elite, favoured Garvey; and a realisa-tion that the UNIA could offer little economic support. Although Garvey did not abandon the goal of sending emigrants to Africa, there was no longer any realistic prospect of doing so. A few of his supporters settled in Liberia but at the price of publicly denouncing him.[54]

Shortly after the Liberians expelled the UNIA, the association's convention met in New York. In a departure from his tendency to leave domestic American politics to whites, Garvey announced the formation of the Universal Negro Political Union to 'consolidate the political forces of the Negro through which the race will express its political opinion'. In the November 1924 election, Garvey endorsed candidates across the land and backed Republican Calvin Cool-idge for the presidency. However, for some years before the union's formation, some UNIA divisions had engaged in local politics in northern cities. Stein notes that 'UNIA locals endorsed a variety of candidates – white and black, Republican and Democratic . . . mostly seeking small favors – tax breaks, parade permits, and so forth.'⁵⁵

In February 1925, Garvey lost his court appeal and began his sentence in Atlanta penitentiary. From prison, Garvey issued instructions, largely through Amy Jacques Garvey, who had issued a compilation of her husband's less militant writings and speeches in 1923 as she took a more prominent public role in the UNIA. Despite Garvey's confinement, the association's membership continued to grow, numbering around 900 divisions and chapters in the United States by 1926, 423 of them in the South. From jail, Garvey forged links with the Anglo-Saxon Clubs of America, a white supremacist organisation in Virginia that called for federal financing of Liberian emigration.⁵⁶

Impatient to emigrate to Africa, thousands of Garvey supporters were attracted to a colonisation scheme advocated by Laura Adorkor Kofey (Kofi), an immigrant from the Gold Coast, who claimed to have been sent by her father, King Knesipi, to promote emigration. A gifted speaker who purported to be a Garvey representative and friend, Kofey toured New Orleans, Alabama and Florida in 1927 recruiting for the UNIA, collecting funds ostensibly for a sawmill and ships for emigration, and gaining prominence in the Miami UNIA. When informed, an imprisoned Garvey denied authorising Kofey, accused her of fraud and ordered UNIA divisions to break with her. In an effort to discredit her, the *Negro World* reported that she was an African American from Georgia. However, over half of the Miami UNIA stayed loyal to Kofey who established a new organisation, the African Universal Church and Commercial League (AUC) with aims akin to the UNIA's. Rivalry between the Miami UNIA and the AUC became violent when Kofey was shot dead at a rally in Miami in 1928, and, in revenge, the crowd beat Maxwell Crook, a captain in the UNIA African Legion, to death. By the time of Kofey's death, Garvey was no longer in the United States.⁵⁷

President Coolidge commuted Garvey's sentence in late November 1927. Deported in December for being an alien convicted of a felony, he then returned to Jamaica and soon toured the West Indies and Central America, before setting up UNIA offices in London and Paris. Garvey also presented a UNIA petition to the League of Nations in Geneva, modelled on that submitted in 1922, but, once more, the

League took no action. In August 1929, Garvey held the sixth UNIA convention in Kingston, Jamaica. When he refused the demand of American UNIA leaders to keep the association's headquarters in New York, rather than have it follow him, the Americans withdrew. The result was two UNIA organisations, one headed by Garvey, the UNIA, August 1929, of the World, and another, the UNIA Inc., by the Americans who had left. Some American divisions nevertheless remained loyal to Garvey. As the UNIA declined, women formed a growing proportion of delegates to its conventions, 39.5 per cent in 1929 compared to 19.4 per cent in 1924, and they gained more access to leadership roles. In 1930, Garvey appointed Maymie Leona Turpeau De Mena as his personal representative in the United States, and Ethel M. Collins served as secretary general of Garvey's UNIA between 1937 and 1942. However, the Depression of the 1930s effectively ended what remained of either UNIA as a mass organisation, although some divisions continued. Formerly of the UNIA, Mittie Maude Lena Gordon from Chicago founded the small Peace Movement of Ethiopia in 1932, which advocated emigration to Africa. With dwindling support and resources, Garvey continued his activism and advocacy but with little impact in the United States. In 1938, he held a much depleted UNIA convention in Toronto. Two years later, he died in London, where he had lived since 1935.[58]

After Garvey's deportation, Du Bois took an increasingly nationalist direction as he became disillusioned with the prospects for integration in America, and, eventually, he expressed appreciation for Garvey's sincerity of purpose, despite the vehemence of their earlier clashes. In 1934, Du Bois left the NAACP when it criticised his advocacy of voluntary separate cooperatives designed to promote black economic development. He later briefly returned to the NAACP, attended the fifth Pan-African Congress in Manchester, England, in 1945, and joined the Communist Party in 1961 before immigrating to Ghana where he died in 1963, celebrated, like Garvey, for his contribution to Pan-Africanism.[59]

Garvey and the UNIA have received conflicting historiographical assessments. Stein argues that Garveyism was a temporary phenomenon, dominated by the interests of an aspiring black middle class, that was ended by the Depression. Cronon contends that Garvey's success was 'ephemeral' and the UNIA 'only a transient, if extremely colorful, phenomenon' which brought no 'tangible gain'.

Furthermore, 'Garvey asked his followers to abdicate their hard-won, admittedly incomplete rights in the United States and to turn the country over to white supremacists of the Ku Klux Klan variety' in favour of 'an unrealistic escapist program of racial chauvinism'. In 1937, he notes, Garvey proudly declared that 'We were the first Fascists.' Cronon maintains that the UNIA 'with its fierce chauvinistic nationalism and strongly centralised leadership, had fascist characteristics'. Moses regards the UNIA as 'a stridently militaristic organization of black fascists' and also, like Cronon, characterises it as authoritarian and 'a movement of the extreme right'. Garvey, he notes, combined the nineteenth-century black nationalist ideas of Christianising and 'civilising' Africa, but, unlike nineteenth nationalists, he appealed to and celebrated the black masses. While noting 'reactionary elements in Garveyism', such as opposition to miscegenation, Moses also considers it 'somewhat radical'.[60]

Conversely, Martin contends that Garvey was a 'revolutionary' nationalist. However, he also notes that Garvey claimed Mussolini had copied his ideas and that Garvey took pride that 'he had preached raced purity before Hitler', while also opposing the two dictators' 'theories [that] could spell only ruin for Africa'. Rather than being ephemeral, as Cronon contends, Rolinson claims that Garvey left a legacy of separatism among 'many rural southern African Americans', which was 'represented later by the Black Power movement and the Nation of Islam', yet these were largely urban and strongest outside the South. While Rolinson notes that Garvey's appeal in the rural South was partly rooted in his advocacy of African redemption, Ewing regards the restoration of Africa as central to the UNIA's appeal across the United States and in Africa itself, where adherents adapted and reinterpreted Garveyism according to their own circumstances and ends to popularise 'colored internationalism' and anticolonialism.[61]

Undoubtedly, as Cronon, observes, Garvey was egotistical and autocratic. He contributed to his own downfall by forcing out the independently minded and relying on the loyal and obsequious but often incompetent, as well as falling victim to the unscrupulous. Garvey advocated the selective emigration of the skilled to Africa as a path toward the eventual restoration of the continent under African rule, but he did not present his followers with an escapist fantasy. Most of his supporters neither expected nor wanted to immigrate to Africa, but they shared and took pride in his vision of an independent Africa. The Universal Negro Political Union and its endorsement of political candidates in 1924 also demonstrated that Garvey did not simply abandon the United States to whites, despite his earlier rhetoric and flirtation with the Klan, which may have been a sincere, if misguided, attempt to protect his followers.

European colonialism in Africa was sufficiently entrenched that Garvey was a generation too early in anticipating its end. He, like his rival Du Bois, inspired Pan-Africanists on the continent, some of whom became leaders of independent African states in the 1950s and 1960s. Perhaps Garvey should have foreseen that his plans for Liberia would be thwarted by the Liberian elite, anxious to maintain its hold on the country, and by hostile colonial powers, but he had to operate within the unfavourable constraints of his time. Garvey was not a revolutionary nationalist. He did not plan or attempt to overturn white rule in America or Africa militarily, despite rhetorical flourishes about evicting colonial powers. Garvey's greatest contribution to black nationalism in America was his emphasis on racial pride and on black history, dignity and beauty. Although Rolinson lacks convincing evidence for her claim that Garveyism was 'the seedbed of modern black ideology', some former Garveyites joined subsequent black nationalist groups, such as the NOI, and in some ways Black Power's celebration of blackness in the 1960s and 1970s echoed that of Garvey, although he did not embrace African culture or dress.[62]

Notes

1. E. David Cronon, *Black Moses: The Story of Marcus Garvey and the Universal Negro Improvement Association*, with a foreword by John Hope Franklin (1955; Madison: University of Wisconsin Press, 1969), pp. 4–5, 9–11; Adam Fairclough, *Better Day Coming: Blacks and Equality, 1890–2000* (2001; New York: Penguin, 2002), pp. 113–14.

2. Colin Grant, *Negro with a Hat: The Rise and Fall of Marcus Garvey* (Oxford and New York: Oxford University Press, 2008), pp. 37–44, 49; Tony Martin, *Race First: The Ideological and Organizational Struggles of Marcus Garvey and the Universal Negro Improvement Association* (Dover, MA: Majority Press, 1976), pp. 4–6; Cronon, *Black Moses*, pp. 11–16.

3. Cronon, *Black Moses*, pp. 16–18.

4. Cronon, *Black Moses*, pp. 18–20, 42–4; Martin, *Race First*, pp. 7–9, 281; Judith Stein, *The World of Marcus Garvey: Race and Class in*

Modern Society (Baton Rouge and London: Louisiana State University Press, 1986), pp. 30, 32–6.

5. Cronon, *Black Moses*, pp. 45–8; Mary G. Rolinson, *Grassroots Garveyism: The Universal Negro Improvement Association in the Rural South, 1920–1927* (Chapel Hill: University of North Carolina Press, 2007), pp. 3, 15, 17, 19, 73–85. Financial pressures probably led the *Negro World* to accept bleaching cream advertisements after Garvey's imprisonment. Martin, *Race First*, p. 38 n. 8.

6. Rolinson, *Grassroots Garveyism*, pp. 41, 43, 47; Cronon, *Black Moses*, pp. 21–6.

7. Fairclough, *Better Day Coming*, pp. 91–3; Adam Ewing, *The Age of Garvey: How a Jamaican Activist Created a Mass Movement and Changed Global Black Politics* (Princeton and Oxford: Princeton University Press, 2014), pp. 56–7, 60, 71–2.

8. Cronon, *Black Moses*, pp. 28–30; Fairclough, *Better Day Coming*, pp. 95–7.

9. Fairclough, *Better Day Coming*, p. 89; *Chicago Tribune*, 29 March 1919; Elliott M. Rudwick, *Race Riot at East St. Louis, July 2, 1917* (Carbondale: Southern Illinois University Press, 1964), pp. 10, 37, 54, 111–31, 186, 261 n. 108.

10. Fairclough, *Better Day Coming*, pp. 94–5

11. Fairclough, *Better Day Coming*, pp. 102–5; Ewing, *Age of Garvey*, pp. 78–80; William M. Tuttle, Jr, *Race Riot: Chicago in the Red Summer of 1919* (New York: Atheneum, 1972), pp. 3–10, 29–30, 32–4, 40, 64, 159, 210–11, 215, 261.

12. Cronon, *Black Moses*, pp. 33–4

13. Fairclough, *Better Day Coming*, pp. 82–4, 100, 117; Martin, *Race First*, p. 274.

14. Fairclough, *Better Day Coming*, pp. 99, 117; Martin, *Race First*, p. 276; Theodore Kornweibel, Jr, *'Seeing Red': Federal Campaigns Against Black Militancy, 1919–1925* (Bloomington and Indianapolis: Indiana University Press, 1998), p. 101; Emory J. Tolbert, 'Federal Surveillance of Marcus Garvey and the U.N.I.A.', *Journal of Ethnic Studies* 14 (Winter 1987), pp. 29–30.

15. Ewing, *Age of Garvey*, pp. 80–1, 111.

16. Ewing, *Age of Garvey*, p. 80; Marcus Garvey, 'Address at Newport News (1919)', in Wilson Jeremiah Moses (ed.), *Classical Black Nationalism: From the American Revolution to Marcus Garvey* (New York and London: New York University Press, 1996), pp. 242–3, 246.

17. Garvey, 'Address at Newport News (1919)', pp. 243–4, 247, 249–50.

18. Ibid., pp. 244–5, 247.

19. Cronon, *Black Moses*, pp. 50–6; Rolinson, *Grassroots Garveyism*, p. 2.

20. Cronon, *Black Moses*, p. 60; Martin, *Race First*, pp. 13, 33–5.

21. Cronon, *Black Moses*, p. 61.
22. Ibid., pp. 62–4.
23. Cronon, *Black Moses*, pp. 64–5, 67; Martin, *Race First*, p. 44.
24. Cronon, *Black Moses*, pp. 65–7; Martin, *Race First*, pp. 43–4; Theodore G. Vincent, *Black Power and the Garvey Movement* (San Francisco: Ramparts Press, 1972), pp. 257–65.
25. Rolinson, *Grassroots Garveyism*, pp. 95, 134, 218 n. 6; Martin, *Race First*, pp. 11–13; Stein, *World of Marcus Garvey*, p. 223.
26. Cronon, *Black Moses*, pp. 204–7; Emory Tolbert, 'Outpost Garveyism and the UNIA Rank and File', *Journal of Black Studies* 5 (March 1975), pp. 233–53; Emory J. Tolbert, *The UNIA and Black Los Angeles: Ideology and Community in the American Garvey Movement* (Los Angeles: Center for Afro-American Studies, 1980).
27. Stein, *World of Marcus Garvey*, pp. 64, 160–1, 246, 273–8.
28. Stein, *World of Marcus Garvey*, p. 227; Rolinson, *Grassroots Garveyism*, p. 103; Ewing, *Age of Garvey*, p. 149.
29. Randall K. Burkett, *Garveyism as a Religious Movement: The Institutionalization of a Black Civil Religion* (Metuchen, NJ: Scarecrow/American Theological Library Association, 1978), pp. xviii, 5–8, 18–23, 29, 37, 40 n. 20, 66–7, 71–99, 112–49, 165–86; Warren C. Platt, 'The African Orthodox Church: An Analysis of Its First Decade', *Church History* 58 (December 1989), pp. 474–88; Byron Rushing, 'A Note on the Origin of the African Orthodox Church', *Journal of Negro History* 57 (January 1972), pp. 37–9; Martin, *Race First*, pp. 71–4.
30. Burkett, *Garveyism as a Religious Movement*, pp. 7, 25, 34, 46–77, 196; Martin, *Race First*, p. 77.
31. Satter, 'Marcus Garvey, Father Divine and the Gender Politics of Race Difference and Race Neutrality', p. 46; Barbara Bair, 'True Women, Real Men: Gender, Ideology, and Social Roles in the Garvey Movement', in Dorothy O. Helly and Susan M. Reverby (eds), *Gendered Domains: Rethinking Public and Private in Women's History* (Ithaca, NY and London: Cornell University Press, 1992), pp. 161–6; William Seraille, 'Henrietta Vinton Davis and the Garvey Movement', available at <https://henriettavintondavis.wordpress.com/henrietta-vinton-davis-and-the-garvey-movement-by-professor-william-seraille/> (last accessed 23 May 2016); 'Constitution of the Universal Negro Improvement Association, 1918', available at <http://www.blackpast.org/primary/constitution-universal-negro-improvement-association-1918#sthash.snpjMKJZ.dpuf> (last accessed 23 May 2016); Claudrena N. Harold, *The Rise and Fall of the Garvey Movement in the Urban South, 1918–1942* (New York and London: Routledge, 2007), pp. 21–2, 30–1, 135 n. 39; Rolinson, *Grassroots Garveyism*, pp. 121–2, 136.

32. Satter, 'Marcus Garvey, Father Divine and the Gender Politics of Race Difference and Race Neutrality', pp. 45–50; Bair, 'True Women, Real Men', pp. 155–61; Martin, *Race First*, pp. 23–4; Winston James, *Holding Aloft the Banner of Ethiopia: Caribbean Radicalism in Early Twentieth-Century America* (New York: Verso, 1998), pp. 137–41; 'People & Events: Women in the Garvey Movement', available at <http://www.pbs.org/wgbh/amex/garvey/peopleevents/index.html> (last accessed 23 May 2016).

33. Fairclough, *Better Day Coming*, p. 122; Martin, *Race First*, pp. 22, 27–9, 273–5; Harold, *Rise and Fall of the Garvey Movement in the Urban South*, pp. 51, 62; Rolinson, *Grassroots Garveyism*, pp. 6, 60; Nicholas Patsides, 'Allies, Constituents or Myopic Investors: Marcus Garvey and Black Americans', *Journal of American Studies* 41 (August 2007), pp. 282–305.

34. Fairclough, *Better Day Coming*, p. 118; Wilson Jeremiah Moses, *The Golden Age of Black Nationalism, 1850–1925* (1978; New York and Oxford: Oxford University Press, 1988), p. 266; Jeffrey O. G. Ogbar, *Black Power: Radical Politics and African American Identity* (Baltimore and London: Johns Hopkins University Press, 2004), p. 213 n. 13; Maxwell C. Stanford, 'Revolutionary Action Movement (RAM): A Case Study of an Urban Revolutionary Movement in Western Capitalist Society' (MA thesis, Atlanta University, 1986), pp. 29–30.

35. Martin, *Race First*, pp. 41, 121; Harold, *Rise and Fall of the Garvey Movement in the Urban South*, p. 134 n. 28.

36. Ben F. Rogers, 'William E. B. Du Bois, Marcus Garvey, and Pan-Africa', *Journal of Negro History* 40 (April 1955), pp. 156–8; Milfred C. Fierce, *The Pan-African Idea in the United States, 1900–1919: African-American Interest in Africa and Interaction with West Africa* (New York: Garland, 1993), pp. 208–14; Martin, *Race First*, pp. 289–92, 301; H. F. Worley and C. G. Contee, 'The Worley Report on the Pan-African Congress of 1919', *Journal of Negro History* 55 (April 1970), p. 141; Moses, *Golden Age of Black Nationalism*, pp. 142–3; Tamba E. M'Bayo, 'W. E. B. Du Bois, Marcus Garvey, and Pan-Africanism in Liberia, 1919–1924', *Historian* 66 (Spring 2004), pp. 33–4.

37. Rolinson, *Grassroots Garveyism*, pp. 8, 18–22, 29, 32–7, 47–51, 55, 86, 93, 100, 103, 105–6, 116–19, 130–2, 140–1, 149–59, 162, 180; Harold, *Rise and Fall of the Garvey Movement in the Urban South*, pp. 20–2, 27.

38. Robert A. Hill (ed.), *The Marcus Garvey and the Universal Negro Improvement Association Papers*, vol. 1 *1826-August 1919* (Berkeley, Los Angeles and London: University of California Press, 1983), pp. lxxviii–lxxxiv; Kornweibel, *Seeing Red*, pp. 100–7.

39. Martin, *Race First*, pp. 236, 238; Ewing, *Age of Garvey*, pp. 71, 80.

40. Kornweibel, *Seeing Red*, pp. 120–1, 132–54; Martin, *Race First*, pp. 221, 237–40; James, *Holding Aloft the Banner of Ethiopia*, pp. 155–80, 183; Robin D. G. Kelley, *Race Rebels: Culture, Politics, and the Black Working Class* (New York: Free Press, 1996), p. 106.

41. Hill (ed.), *Marcus Garvey and the Universal Negro Improvement Association Papers, vol. 1*, pp. lxxix–lxxxi; Kornweibel, *Seeing Red*, pp. 115–18.

42. Hill (ed.), *Marcus Garvey and the Universal Negro Improvement Association Papers, vol. 1*, pp. lxxx–lxxxii'; Martin, *Race First*, pp. 196–7.

43. Hill (ed.), *Marcus Garvey and the Universal Negro Improvement Association Papers, vol. 1*, p. lxxxiv; Rolinson, *Grassroots Garveyism*, pp. 6, 62, 150, 228 n. 60.

44. Kornweibel, *Seeing Red*, p. 122; Martin, *Race First*, pp. 58–9, 288–97, 319–20.

45. Martin, *Race First*, pp. 151–67; Stein, *World of Marcus Garvey*, pp. 74, 91–7.

46. Rolinson, *Grassroots Garveyism*, pp. 45, 143–50, 170; Grant, *Negro with a Hat*, pp. 333–6.

47. Cronon, *Black Moses*, pp. 108–9; Grant, *Negro with a Hat*, pp. 342–8; Harold, *Rise and Fall of the Garvey Movement in the Urban South*, pp. 38–9; Rolinson, *Grassroots Garveyism*, pp. 6, 63–5.

48. Martin, *Race First*, pp. 45–7.

49. Harold, *Rise and Fall of the Garvey Movement in the Urban South*, pp. 38–45; Stein, *World of Marcus Garvey*, pp. 171–3; Ewing, *Age of Garvey*, p. 120; Kornweibel, *Seeing Red*, pp. 124–5.

50. Cronon, *Black Moses*, pp. 110–11; Martin, *Race First*, pp. 325–7.

51. Cronon, *Black Moses*, pp. 112–20; Ewing, *Age of Garvey*, p. 115; Martin, *Race First*, p. 333.

52. Cronon, *Black Moses*, pp. 121–4; Martin, *Race First*, pp. 163–4.

53. Cronon, *Black Moses*, pp. 124–6.

54. Cronon, *Black Moses*, pp. 126–32; Martin, *Race First*, pp. 127–38; Stein, *World of Marcus Garvey*, pp. 209–15, 217–18; M'Bayo, 'W. E. B. Du Bois, Marcus Garvey, and Pan-Africanism in Liberia', pp. 36, 40–2.

55. Cronon, *Black Moses*, p. 132; Stein, *World of Marcus Garvey*, pp. 147–8.

56. Cronon, *Black Moses*, pp. 134–9; Martin, *Race First*, pp. 14–16; Rolinson, *Grassroots Garveyism*, pp. 3–4, 6, 11, 35, 103–11, 197–9.

57. Harold, *Rise and Fall of the Garvey Movement in the Urban South*, pp. 77–9, 149 n. 76; Grant, *Negro with a Hat*, pp. 419–20; Richard Newman, '"Warrior Mother of Africa's Warriors of the Most High God"; Laura Adorkor Kofey and the African Universal Church', in

Judith Weisenfeld and Richard Newman (eds), *This Far by Faith: Readings in African-American Women's Religious Biography* (New York: Routledge, 1996), pp. 110–23; Barbara Bair, '"Ethiopia Shall Stretch Forth Her Hands Unto God": Laura Kofey and the Gendered Vision of Redemption in the Garvey Movement', in Susan Juster and Lisa MacFarlane (eds), *A Mighty Baptism: Race, Gender, and the Creation of American Protestantism* (Ithaca, NY and London: Cornell University Press, 1996), pp. 54–61.

58. Cronon, *Black Moses*, pp. 142–8, 150, 154, 160–1, 167–8; Martin, *Race First*, pp. 18–19, 349–50; James, *Holding Aloft the Banner of Ethiopia*, p. 154; Erik S. McDuffie, 'Garveyism in Cleveland, Ohio and the History of the Diasporic Midwest, 1930–1975', *African Identities* 9 (2011), pp. 173, 176–7; Ewing, *Age of Garvey*, pp. 156–8, 240.

59. Martin, *Race First*, pp. 309–10; *New York Times*, 28 August 1963; Cronon, *Black Moses*, p. 204; James, *Holding Aloft the Banner of Ethiopia*, pp. 136–7; John White, *Black Leadership in America: From Booker T. Washington to Jesse Jackson* 2nd edn (London and New York: Longman, 1990), pp. 60–2, 64–5, 100–1.

60. Stein, *World of Marcus Garvey*, pp. 6, 275–8; Cronon, *Black Moses*, pp. 198–9, 203, 220, 222–3; Moses, *Golden Age of Black Nationalism*, pp. 198, 262, 265–7, 295 n. 41.

61. Martin, *Race First*, pp. ix, 60–1, 360; Rolinson, *Grassroots Garveyism*, p. 23; Ewing, *Age of Garvey*, pp. 6–7, 11, 108, 125–6, 130–1, 135.

62. Rolinson, *Grassroots Garveyism*, pp. 22–3, 190–5.

CHAPTER 3

The Nation of Islam and Malcolm X

The Nation of Islam (NOI) became the most enduring black nationalist organisation. Like the Universal Negro Improvement Association (UNIA), the NOI developed its own businesses and parallel structures, operated hierarchically and sought to remake blacks psychologically. Although both organisations condemned white racism, violence and discrimination, they practiced self-segregation and saw no possibility of white America reforming itself. They promoted and celebrated racial pride and asserted the right of self-defence, yet both groups sought accommodation with the Ku Klux Klan and other white supremacists, and, after radical early phases, sought to avoid conflict with white authorities. Whereas the UNIA wished to liberate Africa from colonial rule and connect the black diaspora, the NOI focused on African Americans, labelling them Asiatics and, for much of its existence, largely ignored sub-Saharan Africa. While both organisations called for white reparations for racism, the UNIA envisaged selective emigration of skilled blacks to remake and lead Africa, whereas the NOI made rhetorical calls for territorial separation for African Americans.

Women formed a greater proportion of UNIA members and took a more active, although largely subordinate, role within it, and the association drew from a wider class base than the NOI which focused primarily on those at the bottom. Whereas the UNIA's initial aims included 'civilising' and Christianising Africa and later emphasised spiritual renewal and an inclusive civil religion, the NOI advocated a racially determined, eclectic form of Islam that castigated whites as devils whom Allah would soon destroy. Increasingly frustrated by the NOI's apolitical stance and dismayed by the growing moral and financial corruption of its leadership, Malcolm X, who had become its leading proselytiser, departed the NOI in 1964 and, in the months before his assassination, explored alternative means of black liberation, while avowing his commitment to black nationalism and Pan-Africanism.

The Founding of the Nation of Islam

Some enslaved Africans had brought Islamic religion with them to America and continued to practise it, although Christianity increasingly spread among the enslaved. In the second half of the nineteenth century, Edward W. Blyden regarded Islam as a positive influence that could foster nationalism in Africa, his adopted home, but it had few adherents among African Americans. Islam's modern growth among them was chiefly inaugurated by the Moorish Science Temple of America (MSTA). Founded in Chicago, probably in 1925, by North Carolina migrant Noble Drew Ali (Timothy Drew) after first taking form as the Canaanite Temple in Newark, New Jersey, in 1913, the MTSA maintained that African Americans were descendants of the Moors in Morocco, who were part of an Asiatic race that practiced Islam. The MTSA had little connection with traditional Islam, and the group's symbols were borrowed from the Black Shriners, who had appropriated Arab names and Islamic symbols from Freemasonry. Although Drew Ali taught that Marcus Garvey had prepared African Americans for his arrival as their prophet and, like Garvey, inveighed against miscegenation, the two men had significant differences. Drew Ali rejected the terms 'Negro', 'colored' and 'black'. Anxious to avoid the negative connotations of blackness and Africa in the United States, which many African Americans had internalised, he created a new identity in which all non-whites were Asiatics of divine origin and Jesus an ancestor of the Moors, whose teachings had been corrupted and misrepresented by whites to form Christianity. An advocate of racial separation, Drew Ali did not seek a return to Africa and the creation of nation states but, instead, argued that North America was an extension of Africa, while urging African Americans to embrace their true religion and be among themselves.[1]

Like the Shriners, male MTSA members wore fezzes and had El or Bey added after their last names. They also had beards. Borne of a confidence that only Muslims would be saved, some members clashed with white people and white police. Drew Ali urged his followers not to be confrontational. The MTSA advocated loyalty to the United States, displayed the American flag alongside its own, Moroccan-influenced flag and supported the Republicans in Chicago's South Side. The organisation taught a strict personal morality and emphasised personal hygiene, while eschewing many popular entertainments and the consumption of alcohol and tobacco. It also sought to build parallel institutions, such as schools and hospitals, and established several small businesses. The MTSA, which attracted many Garveyites, had several thousand members in Chicago, as well temples in several other northern cities, such as Detroit, Harlem, Philadelphia and Pittsburgh, and in the South. Women led several branches. However, the MSTA was beset by factional struggles that intensified after Drew died in 1929 in disputed circumstances, killed by rivals, the police or tuberculosis, and split into various groups.[2]

A year after Drew's death, W. D. Fard, an itinerant silk peddler in Detroit, founded the Lost-Found Nation of Islam and began attracting members from among his clientele. Apparently of mixed race and able to pass as white, Fard's background is uncertain. As a young man, Fard appears to have entered the United States illegally from Canada and married a Native American in 1914. The marriage failed and he relocated to Los Angeles, where in 1920 he had a son with a white woman, and became a petty criminal. Following his release from San Quentin jail in 1929 after serving three years, Fard may have encountered or even joined the MTSA in Chicago before moving to Detroit.[3]

Like Drew Ali, Fard argued that African Americans were Asiatic, descendants of the Earth's 'Original People' whose religion was Islam. Fard claimed to be highly educated, of royal descent and from Mecca, Saudi Arabia. He maintained that his light-skinned appearance allowed him to move freely among whites and monitor their supposed plans to destroy blacks. Fard's ideas drew from wide mix of belief systems and influences, including Judaism and Christianity, but he introduced a novel concept that whites were a devil race. The NOI taught that God was a black man who had created others in his own image who, in turn, formed thirteen tribes in Asia and ruled the planet. However, a dissident scientist created an explosion that split the planet into the Earth and the Moon, and destroyed the thirteenth tribe. One of the remaining tribes, the Tribe of Shabazz, whose members had black skin and straight hair, created the civilisations of Egypt in 'East Asia' and Mecca. Fifty thousand years ago, some members of the Tribe of Shabazz moved into the tropical forests and jungles in the interior of East Asia (Africa), which undermined their civilisation and changed their appearance to kinky hair, broad noses and thick lips. As historian Claude Andrew

Clegg III notes 'Transforming Africa into "East Asia" made the continent more palatable to those converts who harbored a deep sense of shame in having roots in Africa', but it also perpetuated negative white stereotypes about sub-Saharan Africa and its peoples.[4]

According to Fard, Yacub, a scientist born near Mecca, sought to create a new race of people to dominate the 'Original People' by separating the black and brown germs that formed them. Exiled with his followers from Arabia to Patmos, an island in the Aegean Sea, Yacub and his successors combined selective reproduction, genocide and genetic engineering that eventually over many generations produced a biologically and intellectually inferior white race of devils, whose deceitful, treacherous and murderous nature led them to try to divide and conquer Mecca. However, they were expelled to 'West Asia' (Europe) where they descended into bestiality, savagery and cave dwelling. Allah sent a 'mulatto' Musa (Moses) to bring civilisation to Europe, but, after two millennia, whites again fell into savagery. When Allah sent them the black prophet Jesus, they killed him, fearing his message of peace and justice. Whites corrupted Jesus's Islamic teachings to create Christianity, propagated in the Bible, a poisoned book that, Fard taught, contained some truths among many falsehoods that included Jesus's mother Mary's Immaculate Conception, the divinity of Christ and his physical resurrection from the dead. A third prophet, Muhammad ibn Abdullah, sought to bring whites to Islam but most ignored him, leading to conflict in which conquering Muslim armies entered Europe. In response, Europeans looked for riches in America and made slaves of the 'Original People', rendering them dependent and ignorant of their original names, religion, history and culture. Allah, who ended slavery after 400 years, allowed whites to rule for 6,000 years. When that term expired in 1914, he would destroy them to demonstrate his omnipotence. However, Allah postponed the end of white dominance to allow Fard, Allah's prophet, and the NOI to bring African Americans knowledge of their true history and redeem them from their benighted condition.[5]

Fard taught that heaven or hell were not the destiny of the dead since death ended existence, rather they were conditions experienced on earth through the observance or non-observance of Islam. Faithful Muslims would enjoy material possessions and good relationships, while the faithless would experience hell on earth. Allah would destroy the white world in a Day of Judgment, preceded by a series of natural catastrophes in which blacks were to seek territorial separation from whites, either within the United States or by emigrating to 'East Asia', to ensure their survival. Fard would build a huge circular Mother Plane containing 1,500 smaller planes that, launched from space, would bomb the white world before Allah destroyed life on earth by interfering with its atoms and producing searing heat. Black Muslims would escape the conflagration by fleeing to designated safe havens. They would build a new world of 'truth, freedom, justice and equality' when the old had cooled and could be repopulated. Inhabitants would live a millennium or more and appear to be aged sixteen, with neither disease nor want. As Clegg observes, the NOI's vision of an afterworld was akin to heaven in Judeo-Christian teachings and paradise in the Qur'an. By freeing the NOI from any obligation to challenge racial injustice, NOI theology was essentially conservative, requiring Muslims to focus their lives on the NOI and its temples and depend on God to bring justice and retribution against whites.[6]

Much of what is known about Fard's teachings either come from or were mediated by his eventual successor, Elijah Muhammad. Fard left little written material, and much of the NOI's early membership left the organisation amid factionalism. Muhammad claimed that he had recognised Fard's divinity and that when questioned Fard had confirmed it. Muhammad also claimed that Fard had consigned the leadership of the NOI to him as Allah's Last Messenger before disappearing. There is no evidence to confirm Muhammad's account, and, in August 1934, he had referred to Fard in *The Final Call to Islam*, an early NOI newspaper, as the prophet of Allah. Positioning himself subsequently as a messenger chosen by Allah incarnate certainly aided, and may well have been an effort to legitimise, Muhammad's ultimately successful claim to NOI leadership after Fard abandoned the organisation to escape conflicts with the police. As Allah's final messenger, Muhammad claimed to have been entrusted with the true teachings of the faith, making him the link between God and man and the authority on correct doctrine and religious observance.[7]

The Nation of Islam's Appeal, Growth and Nature

Fard and the NOI benefited from black nationalism's appeal that the now divided UNIA and the MTSA had responded to and helped generate, while the divisions and decline of the two organisations in the late 1920s provided an opportunity for the NOI to attract adherents. Like the MTSA and many northern branches of the UNIA, Fard appealed to African Americans who were part of the Great Migration to the urban North, and, like the two groups, he offered his followers a sense of racial pride, self-worth and empowerment denied them by a hostile white society. Like Garvey's adoption of Ethiopianism and Drew Ali's description of blacks as the 'Original People', Fard put African Americans at the centre of religion. He also renamed members, replacing what the NOI viewed as slave names given to their forbearers by their owners with their supposed original names, or an X, pending Fard's revelation to them of their original Arabic names. Like the titles of nobility Garvey gave leading UNIA officials, nomenclature conferred status. One Muslim explained, 'I wouldn't give up my righteous name. That name is my life.'[8]

Initially, Fard used the Bible, the book with which his audiences were most familiar, in his teachings, but he became increasingly critical of Christianity, arguing that white Christians had enslaved blacks and robbed them of self-knowledge. Although Fard dismissed key tenets of Christianity, there were parallels between the Bible and Fard's teachings, such as the fall of man and Armageddon, that eased acceptance of his words. Fard's contention that whites had poisoned the Bible and produced a corrupt Christianity seemed justified to converts familiar not only with slaveholders' Christianity but also that of the Ku Klux Klan and other white supremacists and segregated churches. His references to technology and mathematical formulations for different phases of the earth's history provided his teachings with an appearance of scientific justification for his mostly ill-educated adherents. Followers were completely dependent on Fard's translation and interpretation of the Qur'an as he used the Arabic text. Its usage added to the seeming credibility of his message. Fard also urged his followers to buy radios to hear the broadcasts of Joseph F. Rutherford of the Jehovah's Witnesses, a significant influence, and white Southern Baptist fundamentalist Frank Norris, which, he maintained, substantiated his claims.[9]

According to sociologist Erdmann Doane Beynon, migration north had made those who became the NOI's early converts more conscious of racial discrimination in the South when they made return visits. Fard's explanation that whites had made blacks ignorant, illiterate and dependent through 'tricknology' rang true to his followers. Life in the North had also not provided freedom from racism and economic opportunity as they had anticipated, especially after the stock market crash of 1929 turned into the Great Depression and mass unemployment. Racist welfare agents further embittered them against whites. Crowded together in northern ghettoes owned by white landlords and subject to harsh northern winters, migrants experienced unfamiliar aches, pains and chills that they subsequently blamed on whites.[10]

Fard's teachings improved the morale and the physical and material condition of his followers and so helped attract others to the NOI. Fard preached abstinence from alcohol, tobacco, narcotics and pork, and limited Muslims to one meal a day. He also warned against gluttony and extramarital sex. Fard encouraged his followers to dress well, profiting from the clothes he sold them but also affirming their sense of specialness. Although Fard did not create any businesses, his followers' purchase of good homes and furniture conveyed a message that, even in the Depression, Muslims prospered. Adoption of Fard's teachings improved the health, finances and employment prospects of members as employers recognised the disciplined qualities of Muslim workers.[11]

To manage the NOI's growing membership in Detroit, which eventually reached an estimated 8,000 people, Fard established formal organisations that reduced his direct involvement and later helped to facilitate the NOI's continuation after his departure. Instead of public school, Muslim children were to attend the University of Islam to learn 'knowledge of their own', mathematics, astronomy and about the 'ending of the spook [white] civilization'. Replicating their role in mainstream America, the NOI expected women to be subordinate to men and established the Muslim Girls' Training and General Civilization Class (MGT-GCC) to ensure females learned domestic skills. However, under Fard, and for a time Elijah Muhammad, women also served a public role as 'Mission Sisters', who, historian Ula Taylor explains, 'walked the streets disseminating their religion'. To protect Muslims from opponents and enforce its rules, the NOI established the Fruit of Islam (FOI), a male paramilitary organisation. Trained officers ran the organisations, and Fard established a hierarchy of ministers and their assistants.[12]

As the NOI grew, it experienced internal and external difficulties. Abdul Muhammad, Fard's former first minister who had once belonged to the MSTA, increasingly emphasised Moorish teachings and eventually formed a small group that pledged loyalty to the United States. According to Beynon, Fard declared that each Muslim had to kill four whites to secure transportation to Mecca, although it is unclear whether he meant this to be taken literally. In November 1932, Robert Karriem (Robert Harris) asked his lodger John J. Smith to become a human sacrifice, killing him when he resisted having first agreed. Karriem claimed membership of a small Muslim group that police mistakenly identified as the NOI. Judged insane, Karriem was incarcerated and Fard held for a month for a mental health assessment. Upon his release, following public protests by hundreds of his followers, Detroit authorities told Fard to leave the city and, finding him present in May 1933, arrested him for disturbing the peace. Forced to leave, Fard went to Chicago, by which time the NOI had an estimated 10,000 members.[13]

Some months before, according to Elijah Muhammad's account, Fard had made him his chief minister. Born Elijah Poole in Sandersville, Georgia, in 1897, Muhammad had joined the black migration north, travelling to Detroit with his family in 1923. Frequently unemployed, Poole became a habitual drunk before meeting Fard, who subsequently replaced his surname inherited from a white slaveholder with Karriem. Impressed by his devotion, Fard soon made Karriem, who believed that Fard was Allah, Supreme Minister and gave him a new name, Muhammad, to designate higher status. After Fard left for Chicago, the NOI became riven by internal conflicts and membership losses to spinoff groups. Police attention also drove members away.[14]

Escalating their campaign against black Muslims, Detroit authorities tried to close the University of Islam in April 1934, claiming that the unaccredited grade school denied children a proper education. A fight ensued between teachers and the police, leading to several arrests, although most charges were withdrawn. Muhammad was subsequently found guilty of 'contributing to the delinquency of a minor child and voodooism', fined and given probation. The school closed. In June, Muhammad saw Fard for the last time in Chicago, where he had been arrested. Fard turned over what remained of the NOI to Muhammad, headed to Los Angeles and disappeared from the historical record. Facing growing police intervention, internal dissent and a death threat, Muhammad moved to Chicago in September.[15]

In March 1935, unarmed Muslims fought with police officials inside a Chicago courtroom after one of their female members had been acquitted of assaulting a white woman and another female member had accused a court official of insulting her. In the ensuing trial, sixteen Muslim men were sentenced to six months and twenty-four Muslim women to thirty days. The resistance of these Muslim females demonstrated that not all of the NOI's women accepted passivity and reliance on men to defend them. In April, unarmed Chicago Muslims received gunshot wounds fighting with police after court officials had roughly handled Muslim women during a court case about the University of Islam, a grade school in the city. The school continued, but so did the NOI's membership losses.[16]

Seeking to control the declining membership, Muhammad banned listening to the radio and reading non-NOI publications, ordered his followers to dispense with possessions and claimed that white civilisation would soon end. With Fard gone, he became increasingly dependent on ideas gleaned from the radio broadcasts of Joseph F. Rutherford, such as condemning newly introduced federal social security numbers as 'the mark of the beast'. To distinguish the NOI from the MSTA and splinter groups, Muhammad banned fezzes. His brother Kalot helped to lead a plot to oust him, and, according to Muhammad, 75 per cent of the remaining membership turned against him. Facing death threats, Muhammad left Chicago and eventually relocated to the eastern United States, making only brief visits to Chicago.[17]

According to journalist Karl Evanzz, Muhammad told members to convert their entire families within twelve months on pain of expulsion. In January 1937, Tata Pasha [Todd McQueen], a Detroit assistant minister, instructed his brother Verlen Ali [Verlen McQueen] to convert his family or kill them. Ali's wife alerted the police. Evanzz writes that 'over five hundred families quit the Detroit and Chicago temples within weeks of the McQueen incident'. Scholar Hatim Sahib, who, like Clegg, does not mention the incident, claims that a small core of followers remained, who managed to recruit others. After the Japanese attack on Pearl Harbor in December 1941 brought an American declaration of war, over one hundred male members were, like Muhammad, arrested for draft evasion, a result of the NOI's rejection of United States citizenship and sympathy for the Japanese as Asiatics, and imprisoned.[18]

Members who had been not been arrested began meeting in private homes and recruiting others, with their numbers later bolstered by those released from prison in 1944 and 1945. Muhammad's wife Clara who had been the first teacher in Detroit's University of Islam and had helped run the NOI during Muhammad's frequent absences since the 1930s continued in that role, now formalised as Supreme Secretary. Many members left unwilling to accept her authority. Muhammad's imprisonment in 1943 afforded him a martyr status that ensured his remaining followers' loyalty and made him leery of conduct likely to cause conflict with the state. Impressed by radio as an information source in prison and by the prison farm's capacity to help feed the inmates, Muhammad now urged his followers to buy radios and decided to use agriculture in the service of Islam. Other Muslim inmates also contributed to the new focus on farming, which promised self-sufficiency. In 1945, members' contributions enabled the NOI to buy a farm in White Cloud, Minnesota, and cattle. Released in 1946, Muhammad oversaw the purchase of a restaurant, grocery store and bakery in Chicago in 1947, and instructed Muslims to buy from NOI establishments. Calls for more donations from members helped to fund both the NOI's business expansion and Muhammad's personal wealth. According to Clegg, 'In the postwar period, finance and entrepreneurship became major issues that overshadowed at least some of the [Nation's] religious and doctrinal foundations.'[19]

Another innovation was the NOI's adoption of a 'National Song' in the late 1940s The NOI had long had a flag, based on that of Turkey, but had hitherto banned singing in temple services. Whereas it had previously rented space for temples, when practical the NOI began to buy its own to free it from dependence on landlords and to escape interference from the authorities. While Muslims often had, of necessity, to work in the larger society, in so far as possible Muhammad sought to isolate them, with the NOI increasingly catering to their employment, educational and social, as well as religious, needs.[20]

In February 1950, Muhammad initiated an annual 'Saviour's Day', held over several days to mark Fard's birthday, with attendees from various temples. Held ostensibly to revere Fard and disseminate his teachings, the conventions increasingly venerated Muhammad and gave him greater freedom to interpret the NOI's message, aided by the withdrawal of lessons hitherto used by the

NOI. The convention also became another source of funds as the NOI expected attendees to contribute financially, beginning with a $50 minimum offering in 1950.[21]

The NOI's financial and institutional growth, including another eight temples by 1954, generated a managerial bureaucracy and led Muhammad to assume a more ceremonial position, while still retaining overall control of policy and direction. Assured of his followers' loyalty, in contrast to the internal conflicts of the 1930s and early 1940s, mellowed by the trappings of wealth and dogged by bronchial asthma, Muhammad increasingly delegated matters to his chief subordinates.[22]

Mostly men and migrants from the rural South with little education and menial jobs, many NOI members shared the background of their leader who understood their concerns. Muhammad's wartime imprisonment also made him more sympathetic to black prisoners. At the urging of his Muslim siblings, Malcolm Little, imprisoned in 1946 for burglary, began corresponding with Muhammad and converted. Little was born in Omaha, Nebraska, in 1925 to a dark-skinned father, Earl, from Georgia and a mother, Louise, from Grenada in the West Indies, who could have passed as white. Both parents were active in the UNIA. Earl was president of the Omaha branch and Louise its reporter. Malcolm Little grew up mostly in Lansing, Michigan, where his father died in 1931, killed, according to his son's later conflicting accounts, either by white racists who had attacked him and laid him in the path of a moving streetcar, or in an accident when he fell under a streetcar's wheels. Becoming dependent on welfare and shunned by her church for an affair resulting in pregnancy, his widowed mother had a mental breakdown and, certified insane, began a twenty-four year confinement in a state hospital in 1939. Raised by foster parents and then by his half-sister Ella in Boston after a spell in a juvenile home, Little became a petty criminal and drug user. In the NOI, he found an explanation for his and many black people's plight at the bottom of American society and a path to salvation under the name of Malcolm X.[23]

Released from jail in 1952, he began proselytising for the NOI. Muhammad made him assistant minister in Detroit in 1953, where Malcolm X displayed considerable abilities as a speaker and organiser. Soon promoted to minister, he ran temples in Boston, Philadelphia and then Harlem and played a significant role in expanding the NOI's membership, which biographer Manning Marable claims increased from 1,200 in 1953 to nearly 6,000 in 1955. While Malcolm X largely converted young men from ghettoes, by the mid-1950s the NOI had also begun recruiting from among the black middle class. Between 1956 and 1959, Muhammad contributed a column to the black newspaper the *Pittsburgh Courier* that boosted its circulation and aided the NOI's recruitment. Malcolm X also began writing for the paper and, when its new owners dropped both columns, initiated the NOI's own paper, *Islamic News*, replaced by *Muhammad Speaks* in 1960.[24]

Unlike the civil rights movement that first developed in the 1940s and 1950s in a challenge to racial discrimination, Muslims did not vote, engage in the political process, or work to overturn disenfranchisement and segregation. Despite such inaction, Malcolm X helped to develop the Muslims' reputation for militancy and an assertive masculinity. In April 1957, Harlem police badly beat Johnson X Hinton, who, along with two other Muslims, had tried to intervene during the police beating of another black man during an arrest. Alerted to the situation, Malcolm X brought a group of Muslims to the police station, where the men were being held and successfully insisted that Hinton be given hospital treatment. The Muslims later filed a successful lawsuit against the New York Police Department that brought a payout of over $70,000.[25]

Malcolm X also helped to shape the NOI by encouraging Muhammad to appoint members of his family to leading positions and severely disciplining those who infracted the organisation's rules. The NOI gained national attention in 1959 with the broadcast of a five-part documentary television series about the organisation, entitled *The Hate That Hate Produced*, in which Muhammad explained the NOI's beliefs but Malcolm X featured more prominently, displaying the charisma and articulate oratorical skills that his diminutive, soft-spoken leader lacked. The series contributed to a steep rise in the NOI's recruitment that was largely male, lower class and aged between seventeen and thirty-five, and the founding of additional temples. The NOI provided its membership, estimated as anywhere between 5,000 and 250,000 by 1960, with a sense of self-worth, identity, belonging and purpose, as well as reasons to explain their often benighted condition and a promise of redemption in their present day lives and the Armageddon they believed was coming.[26]

Malcolm X, who had contributed so much to the NOI's enrolment, missed the broadcast because he was on a short tour of Muslim countries in the Middle East, Africa and Asia to prepare the way for a visit by Muhammad and his family. Even though he encountered white Muslims who were not racist, he continued to propagate the NOI's white devils theology on his return. Anxious to assert his Muslim credentials against Sunni Islam critics in the United States, Muhammad, who had made increasing public reference to the Qur'an, visited the Middle East in November and undertook the *umra*, a minor hajj or pilgrimage to Mecca, before visiting several other countries. Keen to encourage the fledging growth of Islam among black Americans, many Muslim leaders abroad seemed willing to overlook Muhammad's divergence from traditional Islam. Although the trip led Muhammad to rename his temples mosques and implied, despite the NOI's rejection of universalistic Islam, that he had standing in the Islamic world, the poverty of 'East Asia' disappointed his expectations of paradisiacal abundance and, in Clegg's view, 'caused him to deemphasize the importance of making overtures to Arab and African Muslims and to stress traditional elements of the Nation's doctrines'.[27]

While the civil rights movement campaigned for racial integration, Muhammad called for a separate state for blacks, whether in Africa or formed from existing states in the American South, and reparations from the United States for racial injustice. Although he condemned integration, and especially miscegenation, he took no steps to realise territorial separation, or, as Garvey had unsuccessfully attempted, to facilitate black migration to Africa. However, much like Garvey four decades earlier, in January 1961 the NOI, represented by Malcolm X and local minister Jeremiah X, met with the Ku Klux Klan in Atlanta. The two groups condemned integration and reached a pragmatic agreement that the Klan would not interfere with the modest number of Muslims in the South if the NOI did not assist the southern civil rights movement. Continuing his accommodation with white supremacists, Muhammad permitted George Lincoln Rockwell, leader of the small American Nazi Party, to address NOI gatherings in 1961 and 1962, because of their shared committed to racial separatism.[28]

Compared to the 1930s and 1940s when it had clashed with civil authorities and members had gone to jail for draft evasion, the NOI had become increasingly conservative and business oriented.

Although it remained resolutely black nationalist in its emphasis on developing separate institutions and aspirations for a separate homeland, when in need of professional expertise the NOI hired non-Muslims. Its leadership, centred on Muhammad and his family members, became concerned to protect and increase the wealth that the NOI's membership growth had generated and which enabled the organisation's leaders to adopt ostentatious lifestyles, as well as fund the Muslims' growing acquisition of business and real estate. Apart from demanding frequent donations from members, the NOI compelled FOI members to sell quotas of *Muhammad Speaks*, which became a biweekly publication in 1962, and required them to absorb the losses for unsold copies. The FOI disciplined the NOI's members to ensure their obedience to its teachings and sometimes resorted to beatings.[29]

While teaching that Muslim men should love, respect and protect women, Muhammad expected Muslim women to be subordinate to men and to retreat from the public to the domestic sphere as much as possible, preferably working at home or in NOI businesses. Whereas in the 1930s Muslim women had expensive clothes, Muhammad ordered them to forgo makeup and cover their heads and bodies. He ended their role as 'Mission Sisters' and taught women to be modest in behaviour as well as dress. Although these requirements ensured that the NOI recruited far more successfully among men than women, female recruits found within it a level of respect, protection and refinement that many had not experienced before and a welcome respite from sexual exploitation by white and sometimes black men. Nevertheless, some Muslim husbands chastised and beat their wives if they challenged their authority. Just as some Muslim spouses did not obey their husbands in all matters, some Muslim women quietly demurred from the NOI's strictures by limited infractions of the dress code and eating more than the one proscribed daily meal. Muslim women also found opportunities for influence and employment in Muslim schools, mostly as teachers but sometimes in managerial roles, and in the NOI's businesses.[30]

Despite its social and economic conservatism and efforts to avoid conflict with the state, the NOI continued to attract the attention of the Federal Bureau of Investigation (FBI), headed by J. Edgar Hoover, a long-time opponent of black nationalism, that included the wire-tapping of Muhammad's telephone and paid Muslim informants. Some local authorities also targeted the NOI. In March 1961, thirty armed policemen raided a Muslim meeting in Monroe, Louisiana. After fighting back, nine Muslims were found guilty of assault and, after appeals funded by Muhammad, seven went to jail. Such external pressures exacerbated internal tensions within the NOI.[31]

Internal Conflict

Although he maintained fidelity to his leader, Malcolm X's views began to diverge from those of Elijah Muhammad in the second half of the 1950s. Influenced by movements against colonial rule in Africa and Asia and the emergence of newly independent countries on those continents, as well by the meeting of their representatives in Bandung, Indonesia, in April 1955, Malcolm X gradually began to mention them in speeches. Whereas Muhammad rejected voting and participation in what he believed was a white civilisation doomed to imminent destruction by Allah, in August 1957 Malcolm X pondered before the Detroit NOI temple how a fully enfranchised black population could, at a time when most southern blacks were denied the vote, change American politics. He warned that if established educated black leaders did not tackle discrimination effectively, 'the little man in the street will henceforth begin to take matters into his own hands'. According to biographer Bruce Perry, Malcolm X's visit to the Middle East in 1959 had already privately convinced him that colour was irrelevant in Islam and that whites were not inherently devils. The trip had also bolstered his growing Pan-Africanism.[32]

Although he had criticised national civil rights leaders as serving white interests, in May 1960 Malcolm X spoke at the Harlem Freedom Rally, jointly sponsored by the NOI and local black organisations, and appealed for a united front to secure freedom, justice and equality. While these goals were, as Marable notes, the language of the civil rights movement, they had long been incorporated in the NOI's flag, the National, symbolised by their first letters. Elsewhere, Malcolm X continued to reaffirm the NOI's apolitical stance. Nevertheless, his presence at the rally indicated a developing willingness to work with others against discrimination. Accordingly, in 1961 he joined the Emergency Committee, a black united front organisation in New York headed by veteran civil rights activist A. Philip Randolph, which focused on improving life in Harlem. Muhammad permitted Malcolm X to address colleges and universities, many of them white, to explain NOI teachings but warned him in February 1962 to avoid political statements or even 'the subject of a separate state here for us' without advance authorisation. The two men soon differed over how to respond to events on America's west coast.[33]

In April 1962, a confrontation between police and Muslims in Los Angeles left Muslim Ronald Stokes dead, another paralysed and several Muslims and police injured. Malcolm X began organising a cadre from his Harlem mosque's FOI to kill Los Angeles police officers in retaliation but was warned off by Muhammad, who sent him to the city to help its mosque and draw public attention to police violence. Malcolm X was scathing in his criticism of both the police and Los Angeles Mayor Sam Yorty, and he joined a public protest against police brutality. However, Muhammad ordered Malcolm X to end his efforts to form a united front with civil rights and religious organisations in the city. Muhammad's cautious reaction evidenced a growing conservatism that produced fissures within the NOI. On his return to New York, a frustrated Malcolm X confided to intimates 'We spout our militant revolutionary rhetoric and we preach Armageddon. [But] when our own brothers are brutalised or killed, we do nothing.' In May, Malcolm X organised a rally in Harlem against police brutality which linked the shootings of Muslims in Los Angeles with the failure of law officers to protect civil rights Freedom Riders in the South from mob attacks a year earlier when they had tested a United States Supreme Court ruling that desegregated terminals which served interstate buses.[34]

As the civil rights movement continued public protests, notably in Albany, Georgia, Elijah Muhammad tried to regain the initiative by issuing a set of demands in mid-1962 that, besides condemning police brutality and calling for religious freedom and the release of incarcerated Muslims, declared that 'As long as we are not allowed to establish a state or territory of our own, we demand not only equal justice under the laws of the United States, but equal employment opportunities, *now*!' However, Muhammad forbade Muslims to participate in civil rights protests. Malcolm X chafed against such restrictions. In July, he briefly addressed a Manhattan hospital workers' strike, and, in February 1963, he led a FOI demonstration in New York against police brutality. Conflicted by his loyalty to Muhammad and his desire to participate in the struggle against racial inequality, sometimes Malcolm X affirmed Muhammad's separatism, but, on other occasions, he departed from his leader's teachings by asserting the cultural links of black Americans with Africans, rather than with Asiatic blacks, and suggesting that the achievement of racial equality in the United States would solve its racial problems.[35]

At the same time, Malcolm X's growing public profile caused resentment and jealousy among the NOI's leaders, especially Muhammad's family, who wanted to retain control when the sickly Muhammad died and maintain the income that sustained their luxurious lifestyles. Consequently, they made efforts to limit the minister's authority and influence, such as reducing his coverage in *Muhammad Speaks*. In late 1962, Malcolm X heard rumours that Muhammad had fathered illegitimate children by several secretaries. Although he had dismissed murmurings about Muhammad's affairs in earlier years, meetings with one of Muhammad's sons, Wallace, and three of the women concerned confirmed them. In April 1963, Malcolm X met with Muhammad and suggested parallels could be found in the Qur'an and the Bible to explain the prophet's conduct, which Muhammad accepted. Malcolm X sought to prepare Muslims for the revelations should they become public by discussing them with prominent Nation officials, but rivals in the organisation, especially in its Chicago headquarters, depicted him as spreading false gossip about the leader.[36]

Despite Muhammad's violation of his own teachings against adultery, Malcolm X remained loyal, and, although Marable depicts the minister as constantly trying to push the NOI in an activist civil rights direction, leader and follower remained largely in step. In a posthumously published autobiography, Malcolm X recalled his private frustration regarding 'our general non-engagement policy', while adding that 'beyond that single personal concern, I couldn't have asked Allah to bless my efforts any more than he had'. Both men criticised civil rights leader Martin Luther King, Jr, the pursuit of integration and the movement's March on Washington that brought 250,000 people to the capitol in August 1963. On occasion, Muhammad expressed gratitude to non-Muslim African Americans who championed equality, such as New York Congressman Adam Clayton Powell, Jr, and Malcolm X expressed support for local civil rights demonstrations and also praised Powell. In September, Muhammad promoted Malcolm X to national minister and praised his fidelity.[37]

Malcolm X continued to exalt Muhammad in speeches but sometimes diverged from NOI theology. In October, he told a press conference in San Francisco that 'When you become a Muslim, you don't look at a man as being black, brown, red, or white. You look upon him as being a man' in direct contradiction of the NOI's concept of white devilry and the 'Original Man'. In an address to a meeting of black nationalists in Detroit in November, later dubbed a 'Message to the Grass Roots', he claimed that successful revolutions were based on a violent struggle for land to establish an independent nation, which he contrasted unfavourably with the nonviolent civil rights movement in America and its demand for integration. His declaration that 'you need a revolution' was at odds with the NOI's apolitical stance of waiting for Allah's expected imminent intervention to unleash the Mother Plane.[38]

When President John F. Kennedy was assassinated in November, Muhammad publicly declared his shock at 'the loss of our President' and, anxious not to risk bringing down opprobrium on the NOI, ordered his ministers to say nothing about the killing. Malcolm X obeyed the instruction when he spoke before several hundred people, mainly Muslims, in Manhattan in December, but, when asked by reports for his response to the assassination, he argued that it had been a matter of 'the chickens coming home to roost'. He claimed that Kennedy had done nothing to prevent the recent assassination of erstwhile American ally South Vietnamese president Ngo Dinh Diem and his brother in a military coup and had now suffered the same fate, maintaining that chickens returning to roost 'always made me glad'.[39]

When Muhammad swiftly chastised Malcolm X for the comments and ordered his public silence for ninety days, the minister's acceptance of the punishment and evident remorse suggested that his remarks had been spontaneous and not made in deliberate defiance of his leader. The suspension produced no backlash in the NOI, thereby strengthening Muhammad's hand. Encouraged by his advisers and members of his family, Muhammad's attitude stiffened. Concluding that Malcolm X had gained too much power and misinformed by advisors that he was spreading damaging information about the leader's young mistresses and illegitimate children, Muhammad transferred control of the Harlem mosque, which Malcolm X had continued to administer, to another Muslim.[40]

During his suspension, Malcolm X continued a friendship he had developed with Cassius Clay, a young Olympic boxing champion from Kentucky, even though the NOI disapproved of sport. However, when Clay unexpectedly won the world heavyweight title from Sonny Liston in February 1964, Muhammad proudly confirmed that Clay was a Muslim and conferred an X upon him and soon thereafter his 'original name', Muhammad Ali. Malcolm X's hopes that Ali would help him regain his place in the NOI were dashed as Ali dutifully and repeatedly declared his obedience to the messenger, who saw in the charismatic champion a symbol of black masculinity whose appeal to young male Muslims made Malcolm X dispensable.[41]

Malcolm X made repeated efforts to secure his reinstatement, which Marable attributes to Malcolm X's financial dependence on the NOI and need to provide for his young family. In March 1964, three days after receiving a letter from Muhammad that declared his suspension indefinite and signalled the conclusive failure of his efforts, Malcolm X announced his departure from the NOI. Although he affirmed that he remained a Muslim and appealed to the NOI's membership to stay within the fold, he announced his intention to establish a politically active 'black nationalist party' and also work with civil rights groups, including those in the South. Muhammad seems to have been taken aback by his departure. Unable to lure him back by contacting him through the renegade minister's brother Philbert X, Muhammad applied pressure by having the Harlem mosque demand that Malcolm X vacate his home and return any other property belonging to the NOI.[42]

Marable ascribes the rupture between Muhammad and Malcolm X to unfounded fears held by most of Muhammad's family and chief advisors that Malcolm X aspired to succeed the messenger, which would end their power and luxurious lifestyles, and, less persuasively, to Malcolm X's embrace of 'militant politics' that included 'the creation of an all-inclusive black united front against U.S. racism'. While Malcolm X had breached Muhammad's teachings and engaged with civil rights activists locally, he had retreated whenever Muhammad had ordered him to do so, and, like his leader, he had remained critical of integration and national civil rights leaders. Neither Muhammad nor Malcolm X seem to have regarded such differences as the cause of their estrangement and, whatever his frustrations at Muhammad's unwillingness to allow the NOI to participate actively in the black struggle for equality, Malcolm X had repeatedly tried to get Muhammad to reinstate him. Marable's claim that 'It was politics; not personalities, that severed Malcolm's relationship with the Nation of Islam' is unconvincing, although, in the long term, such differences might have eventually led to a split. Marable follows Perry and Clegg in arguing that Malcolm X's 1959 trip to the Middle East sowed seeds of doubt in him about the NOI's theology, but he also writes of Malcolm X that 'as late as December 1963 he agreed with Yacub's History and embraced the notion that Muhammad's contacts with Fard were with Allah in human form'. However, it would have been impossible for Malcolm X to have stayed in the NOI if he had repudiated its core religious beliefs.[43]

Remembering the NOI's bitter internal feuds in the 1930s, it seems likely that Muhammad feared Malcolm X's popularity and his knowledge of the messenger's failings. While Muhammad's chief advisors and most of his close family influenced and encouraged his distrust of the national minister, the decision to silence him was, as Malcolm X recognised, Muhammad's. Disciplining Malcolm X would, as Marable notes, demonstrate Muhammad's supremacy and authority, and silencing him and removing his ministerial responsibilities isolate him, while keeping him controlled and contained within the NOI. Muhammad does not seem to have anticipated or expected his former protégé to leave. Malcolm X took that step only after his recurrent efforts to be restored to favour had failed and, following his indefinite suspension, seemed unlikely ever to succeed. In a statement released on 12 March, he explained that 'Internal differences within the Nation of Islam forced me out of it. I did not leave of my own free will', and, in his autobiography, he claimed that his faith in Muhammad was undermined by the messenger's efforts to cover up his adultery.[44]

Malcolm X after the Nation of Islam

Only a day after he had urged Muslims to remain within the NOI while announcing his own departure, Malcolm X and a small band of supporters formed Muslim Mosque, Inc. (MMI) as an alternative. However, Marable estimates that fewer than 200 members, or below 5 per cent, of Malcolm X's former Harlem mosque left the NOI after him. Nationally, the NOI's membership seems to have held up in the months that followed, although recruitment declined. Although Malcolm X took few Muslims with him into the MMI, he continued, as before, to draw audiences from outside the NOI's ranks when he discussed the black struggle against oppression.[45]

In April, Malcolm X addressed a rally in Cleveland, Ohio, of two to three thousand people, including whites, organised by the Congress of Racial Equality (CORE), a civil rights group that was moving towards greater militancy. Entitled 'The Ballot or the Bullet', his speech avoided criticism of national civil rights leaders, declared that he would not mix his religion with his politics and called for a united black front against oppression. He stated that he was not opposed to whites but to oppression and its perpetrators and affirmed a commitment to black nationalism, which he defined as community control of politics and economic institutions in black communities, and those communities acting to solve their social problems. Fiercely critical of both major political parties, he argued that the civil rights struggle should be broadened into one for human rights as defined in international law, which would enable what he termed 'African-Americans – that's what we are – Africans who are in America' to take their case to the United Nations, where they could enlist the willing support of Africans and Asians and free themselves from dependence on largely unobtainable white support in the United States. He also argued that blacks needed to press for full voting rights in America, where they could determine the balance of power in elections. Otherwise, he suggested, they would, if denied, turn to violence, which, he implied, would take the form of guerrilla warfare. By recurrently positing a choice between 'the ballot or the bullet' and advocating the right to armed self-defence, Malcolm X imbued a speech that was mostly a call for voting rights and united black political engagement with the appearance of revolutionary militancy.[46]

However, Malcolm X left unclear who blacks should vote for and argued that both parties were instruments of their oppression. He also maintained that gerrymandering of electoral districts undermined the impact of black votes in the North. More positively, he suggested that once enfranchised southern blacks could elect African Americans to office. Black voters could also displace racist southern white Democrats from Congress and break their grip, engendered by seniority, on key congressional committees. Citing their importance in John F. Kennedy's narrow presidential victory in 1960, he argued that black votes could determine the outcome of close elections but should only be given collectively as a bloc in exchange for meaningful change, which he said the Kennedy administration had not provided. To help blacks in the United States, he argued, they needed allies abroad.[47]

Yet, just as Garvey had found the League of Nations, dominated by white colonial powers, to be unreceptive, power in the United Nations did not lie with its General Assembly, in which African and Asian counties were increasingly represented as decolonisation accelerated in the 1960s, but instead with its Security Council. The United States, like other permanent council members that included the declining western colonial powers of Britain and France, had a veto power over council decisions. Although the United States competed with the Soviet Union for the allegiance of the developing world in the Cold War, some newly emerging countries sought American aid and, like many others, did not wish to offend the United States. Prioritising the Cold War, the United States cooperated with apartheid South Africa as an ally against communism.[48]

Nevertheless, Malcolm X developed ties abroad, for both religious and political reasons. In April 1964, he departed for Cairo en route to Mecca, where he became a guest of Saudi Arabia. He completed the hajj for the first time and became a Sunni Muslim, with the name El Hajj Malik El Shabazz, although he had used the name Malcolm Shabazz since 1957. He claimed in letters home that interaction with white-skinned Muslims had convinced him that 'True Islam removes racism' and, by embracing Islam, whites could 'save America from imminent racial disaster'. He also visited several other countries in the Middle East and Africa, including Ghana, where he was impressed by the Pan-African philosophy of President Kwame Nkrumah. Malcolm X wrote to the MMI, in a break from the NOI concept of Asiatic blacks, about the 'unity between the Africans of the West and the Africans of the fatherland'. Blacks, he thought, should return to Africa culturally. Although Malcolm X may have begun to move away from NOI beliefs some years before, the trip enabled him to offer a rationale for his seemingly rapid change of direction.[49]

Immediately after leaving the NOI Malcolm X had continued to advocate the creation of a black nation separate from the United States or emigration to Africa. But by May 1964, on his return to America, he no longer called for a separate black nation and instead argued that blacks should advance their interests in the United States. He told an audience in Chicago that 'Separation is not the goal of the Afro-American, nor is integration his goal. They are merely methods toward his real end – respect as a human being.'[50]

As he sought to redefine his position, Malcolm X risked undermining his efforts to establish an institutional base. The MMI's membership never exceeded between 75 and 125 members and its activist core between 12 and 50. Many of its members had left the NOI for a variety of reasons years before Malcolm X had done so and, unlike him, many still accepted its theology. Furthermore, many of the audiences Malcolm X's speeches attracted were unwilling to becoming Muslims. His efforts to reach out to the civil rights movement threatened his efforts to appeal to black nationalists and vice versa, and, having been subject to years of his barbs, some civil rights leaders and their constituencies were understandably wary of him, especially as he tended to tailor his speeches to his audiences, alternating between courting and condemning the civil rights movement. With his ideas in flux, Malcolm X sought to make a virtue of his uncertainty about the path to follow by declaring himself flexible and committed to black liberation 'by any means necessary', a vague formulation that allowed supporters to project their wishes onto him, while relieving him of the need to develop a detailed blueprint. While he was sometimes contradictory and inconsistent, he had nevertheless abandoned the major tenets of the NOI.[51]

The NOI's leaders, ministers and publications vehemently condemned Malcolm X as a heretic and feared that he might drain its support. Elijah Muhammad and *Muhammad Speaks* made barely veiled exhortations for 'hypocrites' to be killed, and the NOI continued its legal efforts to force Malcolm X and his family from his home that was registered to the organisation. In June, Malcolm X decided to bring Muhammad's affairs to public attention. He told an MMI rally in Harlem that the NOI was prepared to kill in order to conceal its leader's adulterous behaviour, which he detailed both there and in subsequent television and radio appearances. Malcolm X subsequently arranged for two of Muhammad's former mistresses, Evelyn Williams and Lucille Rosary, who had both borne him children, to launch paternity suits and talk to the press. Malcolm X's conduct seems to have been motivated by a desire to undermine Muhammad and recruit from his organisation but also by a concern to maintain a public profile as a form of protection against FOI threats and harassment of himself and his followers.[52]

In the midst of the revelations, Malcolm X announced the formation of the Organization of Afro-American Unity (OAAU), which was designed to appeal to non-Muslim blacks and inspired by the Organization of African Unity (OAU) founded in May 1963. The OAAU's aims reiterated his call for blacks to control the institutions that served their communities and emphasised the need for 'Afro-American unity'. Concerned with black public education, it called for black-authored school textbooks, improved educational quality, employment of black teachers and principals, and black control of schools in black neighbourhoods, with the adoption, if necessary, of school boycotts to achieve these goals. The OAAU also asserted the right of armed self-defence, declared a commitment to organising a black voter registration drive and political clubs, and called for rent strikes to improve housing. It proposed establishing 'a cultural center in Harlem' and advocated a cultural revolution in which blacks regained 'our heritage and our identity' and moved 'closer to our African brothers and sisters'. However, like the MMI, the OAAU had a small membership. Of the 600 to 1,000 people who attended its inaugural rally, only 90 applied for membership and its active membership, according to its historian William W. Sales, Jr, 'never exceeded a few dozen' of the 200 who eventually joined. Rather than being complementary as Malcolm X intended, the MMI and the OAAU developed a competitive rivalry that he failed to stop, devoting much of his time to public appearances, battling the NOI and foreign travel.[53]

In July 1964, Malcolm X departed for a nineteen-week trip to the Middle East and Africa. Although he was widely feted and often treated like a high ranking leader, he was unable to gain the support he needed from his hosts for a United Nations resolution condemning the United States. The most he was able to achieve was a resolution approved by the OAU welcoming the Civil Rights Act of 1964 that outlawed segregated public accommodations in the United States, while decrying continued racial discrimination, and a resolution from the Kenyan Parliament, after he had addressed it, that expressed sympathy for the African American struggle.[54]

Whether he was inside or outside the United States, the conflict and rivalry between the NOI and Malcolm X continued unabated. His success in getting the MMI admitted to the Islamic Federation

of the United States and Canada and in being designated the
World Islamic League's representative in America undermined the
NOI's credibility in the Muslim world. Two of Muhammad's sons,
Wallace and Akbar, who was studying in Cairo, rejected their father's
teachings and met with Malcolm X. The FOI threatened Wallace
D. Muhammad with death, and NOI members both threatened
and attacked MMI members. The NOI secured a court order for
Malcolm X and his family to vacate their home by the end of January
1965. In December 1964, Louis X (born Louis Eugene Walcott
and later known as Louis Farrakhan), a thirty-one-year-old Boston
raised minister who had joined the NOI in 1955 and once been
heavily influenced by Malcolm X, wrote in *Muhammad Speaks*:

> The die is set, and Malcolm shall not escape, especially after such
> evil, foolish talk about his benefactor. Such a man as Malcolm
> is worthy of death, and would have met death if it had not
> been for Muhammad's confidence in Allah for victory over his
> enemies.

Under threats and pressure from the NOI, Williams and Rosary did
not appear in court for their paternity suits.[55]

Malcolm X continued his efforts to reach out to the civil rights
movement. In December 1964, Fannie Lou Hamer, a Mississippi
civil rights activist affiliated with the Student Nonviolent Coordinating Committee (SNCC), accepted an invitation to address an
OAAU rally, and Malcolm X later met with a group of teenagers
from McComb, Mississippi, visiting New York under SNCC auspices. In January, he joined a school desegregation vigil in Harlem.
In February, he went, at SNCC's invitation, to Selma, Alabama,
where SNCC and Martin Luther King's Southern Christian Leadership Conference were engaged in a nonviolent voter registration
campaign. Addressing a mass meeting at a chapel, he praised King's
nonviolence that he had once so vehemently criticised, while suggesting the need for armed self-defence if America rejected nonviolence. However, he did not participate in the Selma marches, just as
he refused to join civil rights demonstrations elsewhere in the South,
which would have undermined the image of uncompromising
militancy he had carefully cultivated.[56]

Malcolm X positioned himself as a Pan-Africanist, but, concerned that the term alienated North Africans and Arabs, he ceased

referring to himself as a black nationalist. Nevertheless, he continued to advocate black community control in line with his definition of black nationalism since leaving the NOI. In February, he briefly visited Britain, where he responded to an invitation from blacks and Asians in Smethwick, on the outskirts of Birmingham. He arrived in the town renowned for its racism and, with his usual flare for publicity, met up with a British Broadcasting Corporation television camera crew. His appeal for a united front against white oppression in Smethwick reflected his growing interest in and commitment to an international perspective, although it should also be remembered that the NOI had always viewed the world as divided between the 'Original People' and whites, and had regarded blacks, like all non-whites, as Asiatics.[57]

Shortly after his return to the United States, the NOI fire-bombed his house in East Elmhurst, New York, which he had still refused to give up to the NOI. He and his family escaped unharmed, but the attack was a sign of intent and days later Malcolm X was shot dead by members of the NOI as he addressed an OAAU rally in New York. Although there is no evidence of a direct order from Elijah Muhammad for the assassination, he and his inner circle had indicated for months, privately and publicly, that Malcolm X deserved to die. Three shooters and two accessories, all most likely belonging to the NOI's Newark mosque, ensured that he did. Although few had joined and fewer still had been active in the MMI or OAAU, between 22,000 and 30,000 people viewed his body, indicative of his ability to connect with and articulate the feelings of many African Americans, particularly in the nation's ghettoes.[58]

A few months later in November 1965, his autobiography, written with Alex Haley, appeared and became a bestseller. Haley, a journalist and liberal black Republican, opposed the NOI's beliefs. According to Marable, Haley regarded the autobiography as 'a cautionary tale about human waste and the tragedies produced by racial segregation' and 'misinterpreted Malcolm's last frenetic year as an effort to gain respectability as an integrationist and liberal reformer'. Begun with Muhammad's approval, while Malcolm X was still in the NOI and issued with him now unable to give final approval, much of the manuscript was an unrevised paean to Muhammad that sat awkwardly with later chapters dealing with his disillusionment with and split from his mentor. The sometimes conflicting positions in the book helped people of different persuasions claim Malcolm X as their own.[59]

The same was also true for Malcolm X's post-Nation pronouncements and activities. Marable correctly observes that 'He took different tones and attitudes depending on which group he was speaking to, and often presented contradictory opinions only days apart.' He sometimes advocated the establishment of a black political party but, at other times, denied that he had done so. Speaking at the Militant Labor Forum, a Trotskyist group, in May 1964, he suggested that capitalism, as conceived by whites, was inherently linked to racism and socialism with a commitment to racial equality. Yet, in September, he wrote 'I'm for whoever and whatever benefits humanity (human beings) as a whole whether they are capitalist, communists or socialists, all have assets as well as liabilities.' Although he often insisted that blacks had the right to self-defence when the authorities failed to protect them and denied advocating violence, on occasion he seemed to extol it, telling *Flamingo* magazine in February 1965 that 'Mau Mau I love', a reference to Kenyan guerrillas who had fought against British colonialism, and adding 'When you put a fire under a pot, you learn what's in it.' However, while he sometimes entertained the idea of armed resistance and guerrilla warfare in the United States, he did so largely for rhetorical effect and in the context of self-defence. Generally, his endorsement of revolutionary violence was limited to antiracist and anticolonial struggles abroad.[60]

Despite Marable's attempts sometimes to interpret Malcolm X's life in the NOI and after as a journey toward 'multicultural universalism' and even to becoming 'a national civil rights leader', he remained in essence a black nationalist but one whose nationalism had abandoned the territorial aspirations, however rhetorical, and theology of the NOI and embraced Pan-Africanism. Although he continued to denounce white racism and regarded it as deeply embedded, Malcolm X no longer claimed that all whites were inherently racist and conceded that some were genuinely supportive of and committed to racial equality. While he maintained the MMI and OAAU as black organisations to promote black unity, he denounced segregation laws and discrimination and moved away from doctrinal separatism. Wary of alienating supporters or potential supporters, and with his thoughts in transition, he sought to evade the divisive issue of separatism by declaring that 'I believe in a society in which people can live like human beings on the basis of equality.' The OAAU's 'Basic Unity Program', approved by Malcolm X in early 1965, rejected integration as a means by which white society siphoned off 'the best talents of non-white people' while leaving the substance of inequality intact. However, while declaring Afro-American 'unity is necessary for self-preservation', the programme also recognised that 'when the people involved have real equality and justice, ethnic intermingling can be beneficial to all' and declared that 'We are not opposed to multi-ethnic associations in any walk of life.'⁶¹

Malcolm X abandoned the NOI's teachings against miscegenation that he had once propagated, stating that 'Whoever a person wants to love, that's their business.' During, and even before joining, the NOI, Malcolm X viewed women as mostly weak, deceitful and untrustworthy. Like Muhammad, he advocated their subordination, while also calling on Muslim men to protect and respect Muslim women. Away from the NOI, Malcolm X modified his views and practices. He disavowed the negative views of women he had held and encouraged them to be active and prominent in the OAAU, which had about as many women as male members and included women in key positions. Lynn Shifflet held a leadership role as its general secretary for several months and Sara Mitchell served as secretary.⁶²

Without his charismatic presence, the OAAU and MMI, which had never been able to work together and had few active members, disintegrated. In 1965, Louis X succeeded Malcolm X as the NOI's national minister and minister of the Harlem mosque. The rapid expansion the NOI had witnessed in the late 1950s and early 1960s may have slowed with its chief recruiter, Malcolm X, gone, and the emergence of Black Power organisations, which attracted some of its members and, in part, drew support from the urban lower classes that been a mainstay of NOI recruitment since the 1950s. However, the NOI thrived in the late 1960s and the first half of the 1970s under Muhammad's continued leadership. Although Muhammad differed from Black Power organisations in some important respects (for example in his negative view of African culture, dress, languages and customs), the NOI's emphasis on racial pride, black beauty, self-help, building black institutions and black economic endeavour influenced Black Power and continued to draw adherents, especially as many Black Power groups were short-lived. In life, Malcolm X influenced many of those who were to become prominent in the Black Power era, and, in death, he remained a major influence on its development.[63]

Notes

1. Edward E. Curtis IV, *Islam in Black America: Identity, Liberation, and Difference in African-American Islamic Thought* (Albany: State University of New York Press, 2002), pp. 6–7, 16–18, 21–2, 33, 45–8, 50–1, 53–6, 61–2; E. U. Essien-Udom, *Black Nationalism: A Search for an Identity in America* (Chicago: University of Chicago Press, 1962), p. 34; Dawn-Marie Gibson, *A History of the Nation of Islam: Race, Islam, and the Quest for Freedom* (Santa Barbara, Denver and Oxford: Praeger, 2012), pp. 1–10; Sylviane A. Diouf, *Servants of Allah: African Muslims Enslaved in the Americas* (New York and London: New York University Press, 1998). Curtis notes that many scholars date the MTSA's founding to New Jersey in 1913 but, convincingly, argues that the evidence suggests a later founding. Curtis, *Islam in Black America*, pp. 47–8.

2. C. Eric Lincoln, *The Black Muslims in America*, 3rd edn (Grand Rapids: William B. Eerdmans; and Trenton: Africa World Press, 1994), pp. 48–52, 257; Essien-Udom, *Black Nationalism*, p. 35; Dean E. Robinson, *Black Nationalism in American Politics and Thought* (Cambridge: Cambridge University Press, 2001), pp. 34–5, 56; Claude Andrew Clegg III, *An Original Man: The Life and Times of Elijah Muhammad* (New York: St. Martin's Press, 1997), pp. 19–20; Karl Evanzz, *The Messenger: The Rise and Fall of Elijah Muhammad* (New York: Vintage, 1999), pp. 66–7; Rodney Carlisle, *The Roots of Black Nationalism* (Port Washington, NY and London: Kennikat Press, 1975), pp. 135–6; Curtis, *Islam in Black America*, p. 48; Ernest Allen, Jr, 'Religious Heterodoxy and Nationalist Tradition: The Continuing Evolution of the Nation of Islam', *Black Scholar* 26 (Fall–Winter 1996), p. 8.

3. Essien-Udom, *Black Nationalism*, pp. 35–6, 43; Evanzz, *Messenger*, pp. 73–4, 398–417; Karl Evanzz, 'Nation of Islam's Founder was Afghani; Suffered from Diabetes', available at <http://mxmission.blogspot.co.uk/2011/04/four-faces-of-wali-d-fard-muhammad.html> (last accessed 6 July 2016); Gibson, *A History of the Nation of Islam*, pp. 22–6; Clegg, *An Original Man*, pp. 20–1.

4. Clegg, *An Original Man*, pp. 41–8.

5. Clegg, *An Original Man*, pp. 49–62; Hatim A. Sahib, 'The Nation of Islam', *Contributions in Black Studies* 13 (1995), pp. 73–4, 96–7,

available at <http://scholarworks.umass.edu/cibs/vol13/iss1/3> (last accessed 6 July 2016).

6. Clegg, *An Original Man*, pp. 63–7, 70; Sahib, 'Nation of Islam', p. 71.

7. Clegg, *An Original Man*, pp. 22, 62–3; Sahib, 'Nation of Islam', pp. 57, 59–60, 68–72, 74, 94–5, 119 n. 7, 148, 150; Manning Marable, *Malcolm X: A Life of Reinvention* (New York: Allen Lane, 2011), p. 85; Louis A. DeCaro, Jr, *Malcolm and the Cross: The Nation of Islam, Malcolm X, and Christianity* (New York and London: New York University Press, 1998), pp. 41–2; Evanzz, *Messenger*, pp. 102–5.

8. Erdmann Doane Beynon, 'The Voodoo Cult among Negro Migrants in Detroit', *American Journal of Sociology* 43 (May 1938), pp. 897–9, 902; Clegg, *An Original Man*, pp. 27–8.

9. Beynon, 'Voodoo Cult among Negro Migrants in Detroit', pp. 895, 898–900; Clegg, *An Original Man*, pp. 72–3; Sahib, 'Nation of Islam', p. 94; DeCaro, *Malcolm and the Cross*, pp. 14–18.

10. Beynon, 'Voodoo Cult among Negro Migrants in Detroit', pp. 898–9.

11. Beynon, 'Voodoo Cult among Negro Migrants in Detroit', pp. 902, 905–6; Clegg, *An Original Man*, p. 25; Sahib, 'Nation of Islam', p. 85.

12. Beynon, 'Voodoo Cult among Negro Migrants in Detroit', pp. 897, 902; Clegg, *An Original Man*, pp. 28–9; Ula Taylor, 'As-Salaam Alaikum, My Sister, Peace Be Unto You: The Honorable Elijah Muhammad and the Women Who followed Him', *Race and Society* 1 (1998), p. 182; Sahib, 'Nation of Islam', p. 155.

13. Clegg, *An Original Man*, pp. 17, 29–34; Beynon, 'Voodoo Cult among Negro Migrants in Detroit', p. 903; Sahib, 'Nation of Islam', pp. 58, 68, 72, 75 n. 5; Evanzz, *Messenger*, pp. 83–91, 95, 105.

14. Clegg, *An Original Man*, pp. 6–17, 21–35.

15. Clegg, *An Original Man*, pp. 35–7; Evanzz, *Messenger*, pp. 96–102, 407; Rosetta E. Ross, *Witnessing and Testifying: Black Women, Religion, and Civil Rights* (Minneapolis: Fortress Press, 2003), p. 150.

16. Clegg, *An Original Man*, pp. 39–40; Taylor, 'As-Salaam Alaikum, My Sister, Peace Be Unto You', p. 181.

17. Clegg, *An Original Man*, pp. 40, 78–81; Evanzz, *Messenger*, pp. 117–21, 540 n. 19; Sahib, 'Nation of Islam', pp. 61–2. There are no reliable membership statistics for the NOI. Historian Hatim Sahib claimed that by September 1935 the NOI's 'whole membership amounted to 13 members only', a figure which Clegg repeats in his discussion of Muhammad's flight from Chicago but the figure probably only applied to the city itself. Muhammad left Chicago for a temple in Milwaukee, which suggests wider support, and established another temple in Washington, DC, in 1939. Alternatively, Karl Evanzz's claim that NOI membership had fallen 'to fewer than 5,000' by 1936 seems far too high, given splits and withdrawals from the organisation. Clegg,

An Original Man, pp. 40, 78–80; Sahib, 'Nation of Islam', pp. 61–2; Evanzz, *Messenger*, p. 121.

18. Evanzz, *Messenger*, pp. 121–2; Sahib, 'Nation of Islam', pp. 61–2; Clegg, *An Original Man*, pp. 70, 82–93; Essien-Udom, *Black Nationalism*, pp. 66–7; Zoe Colley, '"All America is a Prison": The Nation of Islam and the Politicization of African American Prisoners, 1955–1965', *Journal of American Studies* 48 (May 2014), p. 401.

19. Sahib, 'Nation of Islam', pp. 62–3; Ross, *Witnessing and Testifying*, pp. 147–9, 152–5; Clegg, *An Original Man*, pp. 96–100.

20. Sahib, 'Nation of Islam', pp. 62–3, 65, 91, 111–12; Clegg, *An Original Man*, pp. 100–4.

21. Clegg, *An Original Man*, pp. 104–5.

22. Ibid., pp. 99–100, 104.

23. Clegg, *An Original Man*, pp. 100, 105–7; Bruce Perry, *Malcolm: The Life of a Man Who Changed Black America* (Barrytown, NY: Station Hill, 1991), pp. 1–14, 24–5, 30–4, 93–135; Marable, *Malcolm X*, pp. 23, 29–47, 60–79; DeCaro, *Malcolm and the Cross*, pp. 61–74; Ted Vincent, 'The Garveyite Parents of Malcolm X', *Black Scholar* 20 (March–April 1989), pp. 10–13; Malcolm X with the assistance of Alex Haley, *The Autobiography of Malcolm X* (1965; London: Penguin, 1968), pp. 89, 470.

24. Clegg, *An Original Man*, pp. 111–12, 116, 128, 159, 251; Perry, *Malcolm*, pp. 140–63; Marable, *Malcolm X*, pp. 98–108, 110–12, 123–4; Evanzz, *Messenger*, pp. 173, 206, 221.

25. Marable, *Malcolm X*, pp. 127–9.

26. Clegg, *An Original Man*, pp. 112–23, 126, 157; Marable, *Malcolm X*, pp. 160–2; DeCaro, *Malcolm and the Cross*, p. 190; Essien-Udom, *Black Nationalism*, pp. 70–1, 83–105, 109–17; Lincoln, *Black Muslims in America*, pp. 22–3.

27. Clegg, *An Original Man*, pp. 123–5, 135–44; Marable, *Malcolm X*, pp. 165–8; Perry, *Malcolm*, pp. 205–7; Edward E. Curtis IV, 'Islamizing the Black Body: Ritual and Power in Elijah Muhammad's Nation of Islam', *Religion and American Culture* 12 (Summer 2002), p. 183; Edward E. Curtis IV, *Black Muslim Religion in the Nation of Islam, 1960–1975* (Chapel Hill: University of North Carolina Press, 2006), pp. 36, 38; Allen, 'Religious Heterodoxy and Nationalist Tradition', pp. 12–13. By contrast, Marable argues, less convincingly, that the trip led Muhammad to 'give the NOI a stronger Islamic character' by increasing 'Arabic-language instruction' and sending 'his son Akbar to study at Al-Azhar University in Cairo'. Marable, *Malcolm X*, p. 169.

28. Clegg, *An Original Man*, pp. 122, 149–55, 165–6; Evanzz, *Messenger*, pp. 465–6; Marable, *Malcolm X*, pp. 136–7, 178–9, 199–201; Lincoln, *Black Muslims in America*, pp. 91–3.

29. Clegg, *An Original Man*, pp. 152–6, 158–60, 163; Marable, *Malcolm X*, pp. 163–4; Allen, 'Religious Heterodoxy and Nationalist Tradition', pp. 13–14.
30. Taylor, 'As-Salaam Alaikum, My Sister, Peace Be Unto You', pp. 177, 180–8; Clegg, *An Original Man*, pp. 101–2, 160, 186; Marable, *Malcolm X*, pp. 142–3; Essien-Udom, *Black Nationalism*, pp. 86–90, 110, 118; Gibson, *History of the Nation of Islam*, pp. 37–8.
31. Clegg, *An Original Man*, pp. 120, 163–4, 166–7, 173–5; Marable, *Malcolm X*, p. 139.
32. Marable, *Malcolm X*, pp. 119–21, 132–3, 166–8; Perry, *Malcolm*, pp. 204–7, 264, 272.
33. Marable, *Malcolm X*, pp. 170–1, 191–3, 202; Sahib, 'Nation of Islam', p. 91.
34. Clegg, *An Original Man*, pp. 170–2; Marable, *Malcolm X*, pp. 206–8, 211.
35. Marable, *Malcolm X*, pp. 215–17, 229–30.
36. Malcolm X, *Autobiography*, pp. 396–400, 404–9; Marable, *Malcolm X*, pp. 181–3, 232–4; Clegg, *An Original Man*, pp. 180–1, 184, 188–9, 192–3; Taylor, 'As-Salaam Alaikum, My Sister, Peace Be Unto You', pp. 188–90.
37. Malcolm X, *Autobiography*, pp. 397–8, 402, Clegg, *An Original Man*, pp. 195–7; Marable, *Malcolm X*, pp. 252–9, 262, 264–5, 267; Jeffrey O. G. Ogbar, *Black Power: Radical Politics and African American Identity* (Baltimore and London: Johns Hopkins University Press, 2004), p. 43.
38. Marable, *Malcolm X*, pp. 261–2; George Breitman (ed.), *Malcolm X Speaks: Selected Speeches and Statements* (1965; New York: Pathfinder, 1992), pp. 3–17.
39. Malcolm X, *Autobiography*, pp. 409–11; Clegg, *An Original Man*, pp. 199–200; Marable, *Malcolm X*, pp. 269–73.
40. Malcolm X, *Autobiography*, pp. 411–12, Clegg, *An Original Man*, pp. 201–9; Marable, *Malcolm X*, pp. 266, 273–9.
41. Malcolm X, *Autobiography*, pp. 413–19; Clegg, *An Original Man*, pp. 210–12; Marable, *Malcolm X*, pp. 225–7, 280–1, 286–9, 292–3; Peter Goldman, *The Death and Life of Malcolm X*, 2nd edn (Urbana and Chicago: University of Illinois Press, 1979), pp. 127–9; Perry, *Malcolm*, pp. 245–9.
42. Clegg, *An Original Man*, pp. 212–14; Marable, *Malcolm X*, pp. 281–3, 293–4.
43. Marable, *Malcolm X*, pp. 166–8, 283–5; Perry, *Malcolm*, pp. 204–8, 264, 272; Clegg, *An Original Man*, p. 217. Disingenuously, in public Elijah Muhammad attributed the breach mainly to Malcolm X's advocacy of arms in violation of official NOI practice. Gibson, *History of the Nation of Islam*, pp. 64–5.

44. Breitman (ed.), *Malcolm X Speaks*, p. 20; Malcolm X, *Autobiography*, pp. 392, 416; Marable, *Malcolm X*, pp. 277–8.

45. Marable, *Malcolm X*, pp. 294–5, 299, 397; Perry, *Malcolm*, pp. 260, 294, 318; Clegg, *An Original Man*, p. 221; Allen, 'Religious Heterodoxy and Nationalist Tradition', p. 14. By contrast, Clegg claims that Malcolm X took 'as many as one-third of the three thousand New York City Muslims with him when he declared independence', but, if so, few followed him into the MMI. Clegg, *An Original Man*, p. 215.

46. Breitman (ed.), *Malcolm X Speaks*, pp. 23–44; Marable, *Malcolm X*, pp. 303–4.

47. Breitman (ed.), *Malcolm X Speaks*, pp. 26–31; Marable, *Malcolm X*, p. 307.

48. Perry, *Malcolm*, pp. 315–16; William W. Sales, Jr, *From Civil Rights to Black Liberation: Malcolm X and the Organization of Afro-American Unity* (Boston: South End Press, 1994), pp. 143–5.

49. Breitman (ed.), *Malcolm X Speaks*, pp. 58–63; Marable, *Malcolm X*, pp. 135, 193, 307–10, 314–17, 328–9, 332–3; Perry, *Malcolm*, pp. 262–72.

50. Breitman (ed.), *Malcolm X Speaks*, pp. 19–20, Marable, *Malcolm X*, pp. 332–3.

51. Marable, *Malcolm X*, pp. 295, 303, 327–8, 333–4, 391, 395; Perry, *Malcolm*, pp. 272, 317–18, 338; Malcolm X, *Autobiography*, p. 53.

52. Clegg, *An Original Man*, pp. 194, 219–21; Marable, *Malcolm X*, pp. 339–42.

53. Perry, *Malcolm*, pp. 294–6; Marable, *Malcolm X*, pp. 341–2, 350–1, 357, 374–5, 378–9; George Breitman, *The Last Year of Malcolm X: The Evolution of a Revolutionary* (New York: Pathfinder, 1967), pp. 105–11; Sales, *From Civil Rights to Black Liberation*, pp. 49, 109, 116, 148–9.

54. Marable, *Malcolm X*, pp. 360–73; Breitman (ed.), *Malcolm X Speaks*, pp. 72–77, 84–7.

55. Marable, *Malcolm X*, pp. 112–14, 363–4, 366, 370, 398, 401–2, 408–9; Clegg, *An Original Man*, pp. 222–7; Taylor, 'As-Salaam Alaikum, My Sister, Peace Be Unto You', p. 190.

56. Marable, *Malcolm X*, pp. 400, 403, 405, 411–12; Perry, *Malcolm*, pp. 253–4, 349.

57. Breitman (ed.), *Malcolm X Speaks*, pp. 212–13; Marable, *Malcolm X*, pp. 406–7, 412–15; Joe Street, 'Malcolm X, Smethwick, and the Influence of the African American Freedom Struggle on British Race Relations in the 1960s', *Journal of Black Studies* 38 (July 2008), pp. 932–50.

58. Clegg, *An Original Man*, pp. 178, 209, 219, 222, 226–7, 229–30, 234, 402; Marable, *Malcolm X*, pp. 4, 7, 416–17, 423–4, 438, 457–8,

THE NATION OF ISLAM AND MALCOLM X

465; Evanzz, *Messenger*, pp. 294, 304–5, 310; David J. Garrow, 'A Revisionist's History', *Wilson Quarterly* 35 (Spring 2011), p. 93; Malcolm X, *Autobiography*, p. 75.

59. Marable, *Malcolm X*, pp. 7, 9, 247–8, 465–7.

60. Marable, *Malcolm X*, pp. 335–7, 369, 405, 413, 485; Perry, *Malcolm*, pp. 277–85; Sales, *From Civil Rights to Black Liberation*, pp. 105–6.

61. Malcolm X, *Autobiography*, pp. 479, 484; Marable, *Malcolm X*, pp. 7–9, 12, 127, 328–9, 389–90, 405, 407, 413, 415, 421, 485; Raymond Rogers and Jimmie N. Rogers, 'The Evolution of the Attitude of Malcolm X toward Whites', *Phylon* 44 (2nd Qtr., 1983), pp. 108–15; Sales, *From Civil Rights to Black Liberation*, pp. 83–4, 92–3; Breitman, *The Last Year of Malcolm X*, pp. 115–24; William L. Van Deburg (ed.), *Modern Black Nationalism: From Marcus Garvey to Louis Farrakhan* (New York and London: New York University Press, 1997), p. 106. Marable's inconsistent analysis also denies that 'Malcolm was ultimately evolving into an integrationist, liberal reformer' and concedes that 'he never abandoned the nationalists' ideal of "self-determination"'. Marable, *Malcolm X*, pp. 466, 482, 485–6. The OAAU became interracial when Japanese-American Yuri (Mary) Nakahara Kochiyama joined it. Marable, *Malcolm X*, p. 340.

62. Perry, *Malcolm*, pp. 168–9, 188, 336–7; Marable, *Malcolm X*, pp. 47, 68–9, 142–3, 322, 348, 374, 386, 397, 427; Malcolm X, *Autobiography*, pp. 16–17, 49, 326–7; Sales, *From Civil Rights to Black Liberation*, pp. 109, 112–13, 151, 210.

63. Perry, *Malcolm*, p. 273; Breitman (ed.), *Malcolm X Speaks*, p. 43; Marable, *Malcolm X*, pp. 352–3, 397, 460–2, 468, 476, 478, 480–1; Clegg, *An Original Man*, pp. 115, 232–4, 239–41, 243–4, 250–1, 270; Curtis, *Black Muslim Religion in the Nation of Islam*, pp. 115–16; Taylor, 'As-Salaam Alaikum, My Sister, Peace Be Unto You', pp. 191–2; Sales, *From Civil Rights to Black Liberation*, pp. 127, 132, 143, 149–50, 160; Allen, 'Religious Heterodoxy and Nationalist Tradition', p. 14; Algernon Austin, *Achieving Blackness: Race, Black Nationalism, and Afrocentrism in the Twentieth Century* (New York and London: New York University Press, 2006), pp. 43–5.

CHAPTER 4

Black Nationalism, 1966–1970

The second half of the 1960s saw black nationalist organisations proliferate and a growing black nationalist orientation among African Americans unseen since the peak of the UNIA's popularity. Black nationalism took many forms, political, economic, cultural and religious, and often intersected with Marxism, Leninism and Maoism. In 1966, Stokely Carmichael of the Student Nonviolent Coordinating Committee (SNCC) helped to popularise the term 'Black Power'. The ambiguity of Black Power helped explain its appeal to many African Americans as it was claimed and interpreted according to different predilections and competing perspectives. As a result, although Black Power often took the form of black nationalism, centred on an advocacy of self-determination that ranged from calls for community control of institutions to outright statehood, it could also be reformist. Even President Richard M. Nixon claimed that he supported Black Power, by which he meant black capitalism and the development of black businesses. While not all forms of Black Power were nationalist, the impact of black nationalism was widely felt in American society and had a significant impact on African American communities.[1]

Early Manifestations of Black Power

By the late 1990s and early 2000s, some historians began to reassess Black Power, arguing that earlier scholars and the popular media had largely dismissed it as a negative, ephemeral phenomenon that brought the civil rights movement to an end and in its place advocated violence, anti-white sentiment and misogyny that divided blacks and engendered a white backlash that halted progress toward a more just society. Regarding Black Power as focused on 'self-determination, self-respect, and self-defense', historians such as Timothy B. Tyson and Komozi Woodard, found its earliest manifestations in the late 1950s and the early 1960s, with Malcolm X and Robert F. Williams among its chief progenitors. Early Black Power was profoundly influenced by anticolonial and antiracist struggles abroad, taking inspiration from Africa, Asia and the Cuba Revolution in 1959. Rather than a particular reaction to Black Power, historically white backlashes had invariably followed African Americans' assertion of their rights and humanity.[2]

In the 1950s, African American novelist Richard Wright (then living in Paris) had used the term Black Power for a passionate nonfiction work about the Gold Coast but usage of Black Power did not appear in an American context until early 1966. Adopted by New York's African American Congressman Adam Clayton Powell, Jr, Black Power was soon popularised by Stokely Carmichael and Willie Ricks of SNCC, who claimed to be unaware of prior use by Powell. However, long before the term came into vogue, the Nation of Islam (NOI) had articulated what became some of Black Power's hallmarks by rejecting the designation 'Negro' (dismissing it as a white-imposed term), fostering black self-respect and self-determination in education and business, and demanding reparations for white injustices against blacks. While usually dismissive of African culture, Elijah Muhammad had welcomed Ghanaian independence in 1957 and praised Egyptian President Abdel Nasser's Arab nationalism in North Africa. Muhammad publicly rejected armed action, but the NOI asserted the right to unarmed self-defence.[3]

While within its ranks, Malcolm X had strongly identified with the Asian and African nations who met at the Bandung Conference in 1955 and sought to chart a nonaligned course between the United States and the Soviet Union during the Cold War. Harlem, Malcolm X's base as minister of Mosque No. 7, was the unofficial capital of black America and home to leading black nationalists. In July 1958, 25,000 people had viewed Prime Minister Kwame Nkrumah of Ghana's open top car when it paraded through Harlem.[4]

Robert F. Williams of Monroe, North Carolina, also found Harlem receptive. Born in 1925, Williams, a former United States marine, had revived the National Association for the Advancement of Colored People (NAACP) in his home town by recruiting from the working class, including veterans, and tapping into a southern black self-defence tradition. In 1957, Williams's group fired upon and drove off an armed Ku Klux Klan motorcade when it attacked the home of NAACP chapter vice-president Dr Albert E. Perry, Jr. Local authorities subsequently banned Klan motorcades, and the national NAACP reaffirmed the right to self-defence.[5]

In October 1958, ten-year-old African American James Hanover Thompson and Sissy Sutton, an eight-year-old white girl, kissed in a game. After Thompson and another friend were beaten by Monroe police and sentenced to the Morrison Training School for Negroes in response, Williams addressed audiences around the country about the two black boys' plight. The case attracted global publicity. In February 1959, Governor Luther B. Hodges released the boys. Williams received strong backing from Harlem's black nationalists. 'Queen Mother' Audley Moore, founder of the Universal Association of Ethiopian Women, which called for reparations for blacks, coordinated support for him. Moore had belonged to the UNIA and then the Communist Party USA until it abandoned support for black self-determination in the Deep South, a policy the Sixth Congress of the Comintern (Communist International) had adopted in 1928.[6]

In 1959, whites lynched African American Mack Charles Parker in Mississippi and attacked two black couples in Florida, and a Monroe court acquitted two white men of attacking two black women in separate incidents. In response, Williams announced that it was imperative to 'meet violence with violence' and declared that 'if it's necessary to stop lynching with lynching, then we must resort to that method'. Although Williams explained the following day that he was not advocating retaliatory violence but self-defence, Roy Wilkins, the NAACP's executive secretary, suspended him from office. In June, the NAACP's Committee on Branches confirmed Williams's six-month suspension. Williams responded by publishing the *Crusader*, a newsletter named in honour of the African Blood Brotherhood's newspaper which had declared war on the Klan in 1921. Georgia-born Harlem black nationalist Mae Mallory set up Crusader Families as a support group for Williams. Malcolm X, who admired Williams's espousal and practice of armed self-defence, had him speak at Mosque No. 7 when in New York and helped to fundraise for him. His suspension served, the Monroe NAACP re-elected Williams as president.[7]

Williams joined black writers and intellectuals, such as Julian Mayfield, John Henrik Clarke and William Worthy, in the Fair Play for Cuba Committee (FPCC), formed when the Eisenhower administration turned against the Cuban Revolution that, led by Fidel Castro's guerrilla forces, had overturned the once American-backed dictator Fulgencio Batista in 1959. At the FPCC's invitation, Williams visited the island in June 1960, which confirmed his view that Cuba was committed to racial equality. In July, he led a second FPCC visit that included New York-based sympathisers Harold Cruse and LeRoi Jones, both of whom were to become important in the Black Arts Movement, an expression of cultural nationalism, that developed in the mid-1960s.[8]

Born in Petersburg, Virginia, in 1916, Cruse, a cultural critic and disillusioned former Communist Party member, became enamoured of Cuba. In 1962, he published an essay, 'Revolutionary Nationalism and the Afro-American', which rejected traditional western Marxist expectations that the liberation of colonies would follow from the proletariat seizing power in industrialised western countries. Instead, Cruse looked to the developing world as the agent of revolutionary change with Mao Zedong's China and Cuba at the forefront. Cruse argued that independent African nations and the Cuban Revolution were 'reaching the American Negro and arousing his nationalist impulses'. African Americans, he claimed, existed in 'a condition of domestic colonialism' and should regard their liberation as linked to the broader anticolonial struggle in which nationalism took revolutionary form. They were 'the only potentially revolutionary force in the United States' and needed to fashion a nationalism based on their own distinctive experience. Cruse's essay influenced a younger generation of black activists. The Cuban visit was also transformative for the young poet LeRoi Jones, born Everett Leroy Jones in Newark, New Jersey, in 1934. Jones increasingly identified with Africa, Asia and Latin America, and Third Word Revolution. He also became a fundraiser for Williams.[9]

In September 1960, Fidel Castro went to New York to speak at the United Nations General Assembly and stayed in Harlem's Hotel Theresa. Malcolm X met with Castro, and, favourably impressed, he downplayed Castro's whiteness. However, Elijah Muhammad, who was both anti-communist and concerned by his minister's growing popularity, disapproved. Towards the end of Castro's visit, President Nasser also visited Harlem, where 3,000 people greeted him, including 1,000 Black Muslims, who illustrated the growing identification among African Americans with the developing world.[10]

According to historian Peniel E. Joseph, 'Malcolm X and the Nation of Islam, the political activism of Robert Williams, and the Cuban revolution helped create a new generation of black nationalists.' In January 1961, the assassination of newly independent Congo's elected prime minister and Pan-African champion Patrice Lumumba, with the support of former colonial ruler Belgium and the complicity of the United States, turned America's new black nationalists into 'radicals'. In February, a contingent of them disrupted a United Nations Security Council meeting, while another group protested outside the United Nations building. Participants included LeRoi Jones, the writer and poet Maya Angelou, Trinidad-born Rosa Guy of the Harlem Writers Guild and activist Mae Mallory, leader of the Harlem Nine group of mothers who organised boycotts of de facto segregated New York schools in 1958 and filed a lawsuit that won judicial acknowledgement of inferior discriminatory education and eventually resulted in an often unimplemented 'open transfer' policy allowing parents to enrol their children in other schools. Angelou and Guy subsequently met with Malcolm X. While the minister commended their actions, in public he maintained the NOI's aloofness from demonstrations. Other protests occurred in Washington, DC, and Chicago.[11]

Aside from visits to supporters such as Malcolm X in New York, Williams remained active in Monroe, where he articulated much of what became Black Power in the mid-1960s. Tyson explains that Williams emphasised 'black economic advancement, black pride, black culture, independent black political action' and armed self-defence, and 'connected the southern freedom struggle with the anticolonialism of emerging Third World nations, especially in Africa'. In August 1961, a group of civil rights protesters, including James Forman of SNCC, came to Monroe with the intention of demonstrating the efficacy of nonviolent protest and aiding Williams, who supported nonviolent protest while maintaining the right to self-defence. A white mob beat the thirty or so demonstrators, who police then arrested. Subsequently, a married white couple, the Stegalls, drove through Monroe's black neighbourhood, where angry armed blacks threatened them. Williams rescued the couple and took them into his house for two hours. By telephone police chief A. A. Mauney told Williams that state troopers were coming, and he would be lynched. Williams escaped from Monroe on foot with his family, accompanied by Mae Mallory who had been assisting

Williams's wife Mabel, to a waiting car driven by Julian Mayfield. A grand jury charged Williams and several others, including Mallory, with kidnapping the Stegalls. The Williams family went to New York and then Canada before finding sanctuary in Cuba. Mayfield fled to Ghana. Arrested in Cleveland, Ohio, Mallory spent the next few years fighting extradition to Monroe, expounding her nationalist views from prison. She argued that blacks wanted 'to be masters of [their] fate' and sought 'liberation – the same as other oppressed peoples in Asia, Africa and Latin America'.[12]

From his Cuban haven, Williams broadcast a thrice-weekly programme, *Radio Free Dixie*, between 1962 and 1966, that was sometimes rebroadcast within the United States and available through bootleg recordings. Williams also continued to produce the *Crusader*, distributed to 40,000 people in the United States. In 1962, he published *Negroes with Guns*, in which he rejected racial separatism and supported nonviolent civil rights protest when feasible, while reaffirming his commitment to armed self-defence. Williams identified himself as an Afro-American, declared 'Our sense of national consciousness and militancy is growing', and asserted that 'We must direct our own struggle, achieve our own destiny.' Uncomfortable with the label black nationalist, he described himself as an 'inter-nationalist' because 'I am just as much against racial discrimination, in all forms, every place in the world, as I am against it in the United States.' Williams's advocacy of armed self-defence and indictment of white liberals for seeking to control the civil rights movement resonated with SNCC and Congress of Racial Equality (CORE) activists in the rural South, who increasingly found nonviolence impractical, as white racists habitually resorted to violence, and inimical to the southern black tradition of self-defence that Williams reflected. Williams's influence also extended to African Americans in the Midwest.[13]

In November 1961, the Reverend Albert B. Cleage, Jr, pastor of Central Congregational Church, formed the Group on Advanced Leadership (GOAL) in Detroit. Richard Henry served as GOAL's president and, through his brother Milton, the group forged links with Malcolm X. Cleage worked closely with James Boggs and his Chinese-American wife Grace Lee Boggs. The couple advocated black nationalism and Marxism in an anti-capitalist struggle. The Boggs hosted young radicals in their home, among them Luke Trip, who later founded Uhuru (meaning freedom in Kiswahili

[Swahili]) a black nationalist and socialist student group at Wayne State University, and Max Stanford (later Muhammad Ahmad). In 1962, Stanford, a Philadelphia native, Donald Freeman, a student at Case Western Reserve University in Cleveland, and Wanda Marshall, subsequently a student at Temple University in Philadelphia, formed the Revolutionary Action Movement (RAM), originally styled the Reform Action Movement to conceal its radical intentions, in Ohio and made Philadelphia its main base. RAM's founding was also influenced by Williams's work in Monroe and escape to Cuba, and by Cruse's advocacy of revolutionary nationalism. Its members sought advice from black former Communists, such as Cruse, Adner Berry, Harry Haywood and 'Queen Mother' Audley Moore, as well as the Boggs. Moore, who Stanford recalled, 'trained the RAM cadre in the philosophy of black nationalism and Marxism-Leninism', was particularly influential on the development of RAM on the east coast. Ethel Johnson, who had worked with Williams in Monroe and was living in Philadelphia, also helped RAM organise.[14]

'RAM', according to historians Robin D. G. Kelley and Betsy Esch, 'represented the first serious and sustained attempt in the postwar period to wed Marxism, black nationalism, and Third World internationalism into a coherent revolutionary program'. Although never a large organisation and often operating clandestinely, RAM gained adherents particularly in Philadelphia and northern California, where it mostly drew interest from the Afro-American Association, organised primarily by Donald Warden for students from the University of California, Berkeley and Merritt College. In the February 1964 edition of *Crusader*, Robert F. Williams called for guerrilla warfare and urban insurrection in the United States to bring about revolution. Influenced by Williams, named RAM's chairman in exile, and Mao Zedong, RAM, Stanford remembered, 'advocated urban guerrilla warfare, mass rebellions, and national black strikes as forms of struggle for the black national movement'. Regarding African Americans as a colonised people, it sought the establishment in the South of 'an independent black socialist republic'. Impressed by Malcolm X's emphasis on the developing world, RAM identified with anticolonial movements in Africa, Asia and Latin America. According to Stanford, Malcolm X, whom RAM helped 'radicalize', agreed to work secretly with the group during the last months of his life.[15]

Stanford also claimed that 'RAM's activities' helped to 'radical-ize' SNCC, but SNCC's move away from its founding commitment in 1960 to the 'philosophical or religious ideal of nonviolence', which, for many of its members had always been more of a tactical choice, owed much to the experience of its staff and those they sought to help. SNCC prided itself in working with local black people against disenfranchisement and segregation in some of the most repres-sive areas of the rural South, especially the Deep South, and CORE undertook similar work in rural Louisiana. Local black people often defended themselves and civil rights workers with arms in such areas as a matter of survival against violent white racists. In the early 1960s, SNCC and CORE field workers increasingly departed from the nonviolent principles of their organisations by accepting such protection for themselves and civil rights meetings. SNCC was particularly embittered because it believed that the federal govern-ment had promised protection for voter registration work. Timothy Jenkins of the National Student Association, who attended a meet-ing in June 1961 with the Justice Department along with repre-sentatives of SNCC, CORE and the Southern Christian Leadership Conference (SCLC), remembered that President John F. Kennedy's principal assistant on racial affairs had declared 'that if necessary in the course of protecting people's rights to vote, that the Kennedy Administration would fill every jail in the South'.[16]

White resistance to black voter registration in Mississippi led SNCC, in concert with other major civil rights groups, to organise the Mississippi Summer Project in 1964, designed to register black Mississippians, engage them in the political process and provide education in Freedom Schools. Prior to Freedom Summer, as the campaign became known, J. Edgar Hoover, the director of the Fed-eral Bureau of Investigation (FBI), had announced that the agency would not protect civil rights workers. Only when three civil rights activists, James Chaney, Mickey Schwerner and Andrew Goodman, disappeared in Neshoba County on the eve of Freedom Summer, did the federal government intervene. President Lyndon B. Johnson ordered the FBI to find them. Some activists suspected that the Johnson administration acted only because two of the three missing activists were white. The federal government had not intervened when racists killed blacks in earlier years as it emerged the three missing workers had been in this case. An FBI investigation later found their bodies after information supplied by an informant.

During the summer, many SNCC activists in Mississippi armed themselves.[17]

Although Johnson signed the Civil Rights Act in July 1964 that outlawed segregated public accommodations and employment discrimination, SNCC's suspicion of white liberals as unreliable and duplicitous was accentuated by the Democratic Party's National Convention in Atlantic City. As the Democratic Party in Mississippi largely excluded African Americans, SNCC had organised the Mississippi Freedom Democratic Party (MFDP) during Freedom Summer as a parallel structure that followed the national party's rules for choosing convention delegates. The MFDP asked the convention to seat its delegation in place of the regular Mississippi Democrats because, unlike the regulars, it had been open to all regardless of race and fully supported Johnson's election. Anxious not to divide the party or alienate white support in the upcoming presidential election, the Johnson administration fashioned a compromise that offered the MFDP two at-large seats, promised to seat only those regulars pledged to support the party's presidential ticket, and made a commitment that only delegations chosen without racial discrimination would be seated at future conventions. Johnson enlisted white liberals to persuade the MFDP to accept the compromise, but the delegation voted to reject it, with vice chairman Fannie Lou Hamer proclaiming 'We didn't come all this way for no two seats.'[18]

Hubert 'Rap' Brown, a Louisianan who had worked in Mississippi with SNCC, recalled that

> The [MFDP] challenge was very significant because it made us realize that the whole conspiracy was not just a conspiracy of the South. It was a conspiracy of the nation when the Democratic Party refused to seat the MFDP . . . [A]ll the liberals, our 'friends,' turned against us.

Disillusionment with white liberal allies and the federal government, as well as a belief in the necessity of armed self-defence, became key motivating factors for the emergence of Black Power among former civil rights activists, indicating that Black Power had southern as well as northern and western roots.[19]

Two weeks after the convention, a group of SNCC activists visited Guinea, a former French colony, whose president, Sékou Touré, impressed upon them the shared nature of the struggle of

blacks in Africa and the United States. Two of the SNCC delegation, John Lewis and Donald Harris, extended their tour by visiting
several other African countries and had a chance encounter with
Malcolm X in Nairobi, Kenya. Thereafter, Malcolm X worked to
establish connections with SNCC, which was moving in the direction of armed self-defence and black pride that he espoused, while
he sought to foster a united black front and press the civil rights
movement to adopt a broad-based human rights agenda.[20]

America's escalation of its involvement in the Vietnam War, with
the deployment of combat troops and large-scale bombing in 1965,
also contributed to SNCC's radicalisation as its members contrasted
the Johnson administration's failure to protect civil rights workers
and African Americans from racial violence with the federal government's foreign interventionism. In January 1966, SNCC's Executive
Committee adopted an anti-war statement that accused the United
States government of illegal aggression and endorsed draft resistance. In the same month, CORE directors James Farmer and Floyd
McKissick denounced the war and declared that 'the war which must
be escalated is the war against poverty and discrimination', a position endorsed by the organisation's national convention in July.[21]

Many of CORE's field activists also came to recognise the
necessity of armed self-defence. In 1964, armed black veterans
in Jonesboro, Louisiana, formed the Deacons for Defense and
Justice, to protect CORE workers and civil rights meetings. The
Deacons, who did not reveal their numbers or, in most cases, their
identities, spread to other areas in the Deep South, supporting an
NAACP campaign in Natchez, Mississippi, in 1964 and a CORE
campaign in Bogalusa, Louisiana, in 1965. African Americans also
formed armed self-defence groups in other communities, such as
Tuscaloosa, Alabama. However, unlike RAM or Williams, they did
not advocate urban guerrilla warfare or insurrection.[22]

RAM's hopes for a black uprising received inspiration and
encouragement from a large-scale African American riot in Watts,
Los Angeles, in 1965, which, alongside smaller riots in New York
and Philadelphia in 1964, presaged the beginning of a series of
annual urban riots in black ghettoes that would recur through 1968
and more sporadically until 1972. Often sparked by an incident
of white police violence against African Americans, the riots were
often more than wanton or random acts of destruction, although
they included looting and extensive property damage, but they were

also not organised rebellions. Although spontaneous and uncoordinated, they tended, although not exclusively, to target white-owned businesses regarded by the rioters, who were mainly working class but not the poorest in their communities or unemployed, as overcharging their customers and treating them disrespectfully. Like black nationalists, scholars of black nationalism often characterise the riots as rebellions or uprisings, implying a justified response to racial oppression, to differentiate them from mere criminal mob action suggested, for some, by the appellation riot. However, while the nearly 300 riots and tumults expressed anger and frustration at the discrimination blacks faced in their everyday lives, they did not exhibit the nationalist sentiment envisaged by RAM.[23]

Unlike RAM which, influenced by Williams, believed that an armed uprising could achieve black liberation in ninety days and regarded the black working class as inherently nationalist, black cultural nationalists argued that a successful black revolutionary struggle could not occur before the black masses had first been imbued with a nationalist identity. In the mid-1960s, LeRoi Jones and Maulana Karenga (Ron Everett) emerged as the prime exponents of cultural black nationalism.[24]

Malcolm X's assassination in February 1965 proved a turning point for Jones, who left his white Jewish wife and their daughters in Greenwich Village, New York, and moved up Harlem to focus on fomenting an African American revolution, convinced that only black nationalism could ensure liberation. Although his contact with Malcolm X had been limited, Jones increasingly followed a path influenced by Malcolm X's emphasis on self-determination, self-respect and self-defence. Jones founded the Black Arts Repertory Theater/School (BARTS) in Harlem to promote black cultural identity and production and separatism, and teach employment skills. Its participants and advisors included poets Larry Neal and Sonia Sanchez, musician Sun Ra, Max Stanford and Harold Cruse. Although BARTS was soon destroyed by young black male nihilists and Jones returned to his native Newark, as historian Daniel Matlin explains, Jones was 'the principal architect of the black arts movement, which spread to every major city in the United States from 1965 on' and saw the establishment of 800 black cultural institutions.[25]

On the West Coast, Ron Everett played the primary role in black cultural nationalism. Born in 1941, Everett had migrated to

Los Angeles from Parsonsburg, Maryland, in 1958 and eventually enrolled in the University of California, Los Angeles. Specialising in African affairs, Everett learnt Kiswahili, a language primarily spoken in parts of eastern and south-eastern Africa and championed by the continent's Pan-Africanists. In 1963, Everett joined the Afro-American Association and became strongly influenced by its focus on unity, self-help, dignity, education, racial pride and African heritage. He was also influenced by a long black nationalist tradition, embodied more recently in the teachings of the NOI and Malcolm X, that African Americans lacked culture and had to be remade culturally, psychologically and morally. Everett met frequently with Malcolm X when he visited the NOI's Los Angeles temple. Malcolm X's post-NOI emphasis on the need for a black cultural revolution, reconnection with Africa, armed self-defence and black community control also resonated with Everett.[26]

Everett, who adopted the name Karenga, Kiswahili for nationalist or keeper of tradition, regarded the Watts conflagration, like many black nationalists, as an expression of black self-determination, self-respect and self-defence. In its aftermath, he and six others, including Hakim Jamal (Allen Donaldson), a long-time collaborator with and cousin of Malcolm X, and two women, founded US, named in contradistinction to 'them', meaning whites. Cofounder Brenda Haiba Karenga and early member Dorothy Jamal, the wives of Karenga and Jamal, established the School of Afroamerican Culture for children. By the middle of 1966, Karenga had become the organisation's leader.[27]

Intentionally small, US never surpassed five or six hundred members and saw its role as fostering and working with other organisations to promote black nationalism in culture and politics. Like Malcolm X's OAAU, US sought to encourage, but not supplant, a multiplicity of independent black groups in a united front. While it regarded the dissemination of cultural nationalism, derived from its selective interpretation of African culture, as a prerequisite for a black cultural and political revolution that would prepare blacks for a guerrilla war of liberation, it also supported black electoral participation as a means toward gaining control of institutions that served the black community. In 1966, US canvassed in black neighbourhoods in support of the successful election campaign of Yvonne Braithwaite Burke for the California State Assembly.[28]

African Americans in Lowndes County, Alabama, also adopted independent political organising in an effort to exert leverage over institutions that affected their everyday lives. Influenced by the Selma voting rights campaign, they launched a voter registration drive in March 1965 and soon received SNCC's assistance. At SNCC activist Stokely Carmichael's suggestion, they established the Lowndes County Freedom Organization (LCFO) as an independent third party, which, although open to whites, was entirely black. With a black panther as its symbol, the LCFO, which endorsed armed self-defence, sought to encourage and capitalise on black voter registration made possible by federal registrars dispatched under the Voting Rights Act of 1965. In November 1966, it ran a slate of candidates for local office, who were defeated, by electoral fraud, intimidation and engrained habits of racial deference among some blacks. The Lowndes movement also challenged inequality and discrimination in educational provision, employment and the judicial system.[29]

At a staff meeting in May 1966, SNCC elected Carmichael as chairman and made local political organising, exemplified by the LCFO, its focus. A month later, Carmichael, as a leading participant in the Meredith March and assisted by Willie Ricks, popularised the term Black Power when they used it in rallies during the march. The march crossed Mississippi to complete a quixotic solo March against Fear begun by James Meredith, a native Mississippian who had desegregated the University of Mississippi in 1962 and had been shot and hospitalised on his march's second day. In a compromise, SNCC and CORE, whose black nationalist leader Floyd McKissick had been elected in January 1966, accepted Martin Luther King, Jr's insistence that the march be interracial. King, an advocate of nonviolence, conceded that the Deacons for Defense and Justice could protect the marchers. While as staffer Ivanhoe Donaldson explained 'SNCC's Alabama experience was the immediate genesis of the concept of Black Power', the idea's roots were multifaceted, its manifestations geographically varied and diverse, and its meaning contested.[30]

The Meanings of Black Power

Carmichael epitomised the strand of Black Power that emerged from civil rights activists who were disillusioned and frustrated by the slow pace of change in the South, the depth of southern white resistance and the unreliability of liberal white allies and the federal government. Born in Port of Spain in 1941, Carmichael had spent his early life in Trinidad, before joining his immigrant parents in New York when aged ten. He had participated in southern civil rights protests periodically while a student at historically black Howard University in Washington, DC, before graduating and joining SNCC full-time in 1964. After being released following an arrest for defying a police order during the Meredith March, he declared,

> This is the twenty-seventh time I have been arrested. I ain't going to jail no more. The only way we gonna stop them white men from whuppin' us is to take over. We been saying freedom for six years and we ain't got nothin'. What we got to start saying now is Black Power![31]

In a book published in 1967, Carmichael and political scientist Charles V. Hamilton defined Black Power as a call for black people to unite, 'recognize their heritage', 'define their own goals' and 'lead their own organizations'. Making an analogy with the experience of European ethnic groups in the United States, they argued that blacks should form their own organisations to 'operate effectively from a bargaining position of strength in a pluralistic society'. In areas in which African Americans formed a majority, they should seek control and in areas where they did not 'proper representation and sharing of control'. Carmichael and Hamilton endorsed armed self-defence and denied that Black Power was 'anti-white'. They lambasted integration as a one-way street that siphoned off a few token blacks into white middle class America, depriving the black community of potential leaders and assuming that it lacked anything of intrinsic worth. Carmichael and Hamilton rejected alliances with white liberals, organised labour and the Democratic Party as perpetuating black dependency and, instead, envisaged an eventual 'coalition of poor blacks and poor whites', grounded in shared economic interests.[32]

Carmichael and Hamilton's conception of Black Power seemed in some ways a form of what political scientist Dean E. Robinson terms 'ethnic pluralism'. Pluralism assumed that African Americans, like white European immigrant groups, could freely exercise their collective political strength to ensure a more favourable share of political power and resources. However, paradoxically, Carmichael and Hamilton also accepted the nationalist idea that blacks formed an internal colony in the United States, while their suggestion of a future interracial coalition of the poor was at odds with both the ethnic and the colonial paradigms they adopted. Although they made an analogy with European colonialism in Africa, they ignored Pan-Africanism and made only brief reference to the need for blacks to develop a positive self-image, 'an awareness of their cultural heritage', and an identity as 'African-Americans'. Historian James Lance Taylor notes that the book contained no explicit discussion of black nationalism, although it 'promotes elements associated with the tradition of black nationalism, such as racial solidarity, self-determination, a Manichean [regarding something as having two starkly opposed sides] notion of "us" (blacks) and "them" (whites), and a sense of "peoplehood," fueled with "black consciousness"'.[33]

Roy Wilkins and Whitney Young, the National Urban League (NUL)'s executive director, had both declined to join the Meredith March after Carmichael had insulted them and condemned the civil rights record of the Johnson administration with which Wilkins and Young worked closely. They also denounced Black Power. Wilkins called it 'the father of hate and mother of violence', and Young stated that the NUL would not countenance any organisation that 'formally adopted black power as a program'. During the march, King had repeatedly tried to counter Carmichael's calls for Black Power by championing nonviolence. Although Carmichael and the marchers adhered in practice to nonviolence, despite being attacked by state troopers and state highway patrolmen in Canton, his more strident and aggressive rhetorical utterances gained greater white press attention than his more measured comments about the need for black pride and political representation, and his disavowal of being 'anti-white'. In Greenwood, Carmichael had declared that 'Every courthouse in Mississippi ought to be burned down to get rid of the dirt' and, at the march's conclusion in Jackson, he announced that 'we have to . . . build a power base so strong in this country that it will bring them to their knees every time they mess with us!'[34]

King had counselled Carmichael and McKissick to abandon calling for Black Power, arguing that it would alienate allies and supporters, and reinforce the racism of whites who might otherwise be won over. In later writings, however, King defended Black Power in so far as it was 'a call to black people to amass the political and economic strength to achieve their legitimate goals' for 'racial justice' and to achieve psychological liberation from feelings of inferiority and shame inculcated by slavery, segregation and other forms of discrimination. He also noted 'the positive value in calling the Negro to a new sense of manhood, to a deep feeling of racial pride and to an audacious appreciation of his heritage'. Nevertheless, King concluded that Black Power was 'a nihilistic philosophy born out of the conviction that the Negro can't win. It is, at bottom, the view that American society is so hopelessly corrupt and enmeshed in evil that there is no possibility of salvation from within'.[35]

King argued that Black Power was 'unrealistic' in that it envisaged 'a separate black road to power and fulfillment' when blacks formed majorities in relatively few cities and counties, and only 10 per cent of the United States population. To achieve significant and broad-based change, King asserted that African Americans needed to form alliances with liberal whites to ensure that the Democratic and Republican parties became 'truly responsive to the needs of the poor'. While he approved of collective black action, King argued that 'the larger economic problems confronting the Negro community will only be solved by federal programs involving billions of dollars'. He contended that Black Power gave 'the impression that we are talking about black domination rather than black equality'. Although King affirmed that Carmichael and McKissick had 'declared themselves opponents of aggressive violence', he warned that 'it is dangerous to organize a movement around self-defense' because 'The line of demarcation between defensive violence and aggressive violence is very thin' and easily misinterpreted by the unsophisticated 'as an invitation to aggression'.[36]

Carmichael had sometimes rhetorically crossed the line between defensive and aggressive invocations of violence during the Meredith March, and, apt to reformulate the meaning of Black Power according to his audience, he continued to do so. In Cleveland, Ohio, he declared that 'When you talk of Black Power, you talk of building a movement that will smash everything Western civilization has created.' In 1967, Rap Brown, Carmichael's successor as SNCC chairman, proved even more prone to inflammatory rhetoric. At first, Brown reiterated SNCC's endorsement of armed self-defence, but, against the backdrop of a massive race riot in Detroit, in July 1967 he told several hundred blacks in Cambridge, Maryland, that 'If America don't come around, we going burn it down, brother', and, in reference to white-owned stores, 'You got to own some of them stores. I don't care if you have to burn him down and run him out.' A riot broke out in Cambridge that night. Police subsequently charged Brown, who denied involvement, with inciting arson, adding to a host of legal problems stemming from alleged offences in other states.[37]

Brown inherited an organisation that had voted in December 1966 to expel whites by nineteen votes to eighteen, with twenty-four abstentions. Opposed to their ejection, Carmichael had wanted white members to remain in SNCC and focus on working in white communities to counteract racism. Black nationalists in SNCC's Atlanta Project were the chief prime movers behind white expulsion, which, as Carmichael had warned, helped deter white financial donations, already dwindling following his advocacy of Black Power. Northerners formed half of the Atlanta's Project staff and some of them were or had been connected to nationalist groups, such as RAM and the NOI. CORE experienced a similar falling way of white financial support, which, as with SNCC, contributed to its rapid decline, along with state repression suffered by both groups. At its 1966 convention, CORE, like SNCC, countenanced self-defence and endorsed Black Power as 'control of economic, political, and educational institutions and resources, from top to bottom, by black people in their own areas'. Whereas SNCC advocated cooperatives, CORE championed black capitalism. The NOI's Minister Lonnie X addressed CORE's convention, attended by many Black Muslims, and lauded CORE's efforts to enhance black pride. Most whites soon left CORE, which, in 1968, excluded the few who remained from active participation and committed itself to black separatism under new national director Roy Innis. While the experience of SNCC and CORE demonstrated how Black Power intersected with the civil rights movement, Black Power continued to evolve outside, as well as within, the movement and to spawn new groups.[38]

LeRoi Jones had welcomed Carmichael's call for Black Power. Jones organised the Spirit House Movers and Players to perform the plays and poetry of the burgeoning Black Arts Movement, which in June 1966 held a Black Arts Convention, attended by 300 people in Detroit. Located in Newark's ghetto, the Spirit House staged the Black Arts Cultural Festival which included Harold Cruse and had Carmichael as its main speaker. That year, Carmichael met with Elijah Muhammad, but their meeting produced no alliance between them as each man tried to enlist the other. Carmichael declined Muhammad's invitation to join the NOI and recognise him as a prophet. Muhammad rebuffed Carmichael's appeal to attend a one-day Black Power Planning Conference in September 1966, organised by Congressman Adam Clayton Powell, Jr, who had met earlier with Carmichael and SNCC officials. In the event, SNCC declined to send representatives to the conference, fearing that Powell would seek to redefine and co-opt Black Power by using it to enlist support for the Democratic Party rather than promote independent black politics. Karenga attended the gathering, held in Washington, DC, which attracted 169 delegates from eighteen states and created a committee to plan a National Black Power Conference for the following year.[39]

Karenga also served on the planning committee, while continuing to develop US. In 1966, he devised an annual seven-day holiday, *Kwanzaa*, held between 26 December and 1 January, that he mischaracterised as being an actual African tradition, rather than, like many of his ideas, only inspired by selected African practices. Influenced by Malcolm X, African leaders Kwame Nkrumah, Sékou Touré, Léopold Senghor of Senegal and Julius Nyerere of Tanzania, and Indonesian president Sukarno, Karenga formulated *Nguzo Saba* (the Seven Principles) of *Kawaida* (tradition and reason) celebrated by *Kwanzaa* and envisaged a form of African socialism. The principles comprised *Umoja* (unity), *Kujichagulia* (self-determination), *Ujima* (collective work and responsibility), *Ujamaa* (cooperative economics), *Nia* (purpose), *Kuumba* (creativity) and *Imani* (faith). Karenga, styling himself Maulana (master teacher), ran US autocratically with himself as its presumed infallible leader.[40]

Karenga's hierarchical approach and belief that the mass of African Americans lacked culture and needed to be reformed fitted within the black nationalist tradition of the nineteenth and early twentieth centuries, as well as that of the NOI. Whereas the NOI gave its members the designation X or restored a member's supposed original name, Karenga often gave followers Kiswahili names, based on their perceived personal characteristics or contribution. Like the NOI, US became a patriarchal organisation, with women subordinate to men, although, unlike the NOI, US sanctioned polygamy in its first few years. Both US and the NOI rejected Christianity as a white man's religion. Although, unlike the NOI, US largely embraced African culture, it shared the NOI's rejection of African religion and

Christianity. US created its own religion that, historian Scott Brown explains, 'fused the creator with humanity', and rejected the idea of spirits. The organisation taught that 'We are Gods ourselves. Each Black man is God of his own house', meaning of his family. US also developed the *Simba Wachanga* (Young Lions in Kiswahili), a para-military unit that was trained in karate like the NOI's Fruit of Islam but, in contrast to the NOI, officially and heavily armed.[41]

The NOI eschewed political participation and rejected military service, with members seeking religious exemption. By contrast, US joined with the Black Congress, a group of over twenty black organisations in Los Angeles, in publicly opposing the Vietnam War. Some black marines attended US and Black Congress meetings in California. US doctrine spread sufficiently in several squadrons that they formed a *Simba* unit, the Fulani tribe, before deployment to Vietnam, where US developed chapters and sympathisers in several marine bases.[42]

Another California-based Black Power organisation, the Black Panther Party for Self-Defense (BPP) was also part of the Black Congress and gained a following among some African American troops in Vietnam. In October 1966, Huey P. Newton, who had served six months for stabbing a man, and Bobby Seale, who had been discharged from the air force in 1959 after fighting with an officer, founded the BPP in Oakland, California. Streetwise and accustomed to fighting when affronted, the two men had become politically aware as students. Newton and Seale had participated in the Afro-American Association while enrolled in Merritt College, and they had also been impressed by Malcolm X when they heard him speak at local mosques. Newton and Seale also joined the Soul Students Advisory Council, a RAM front organisation. The BPP bore the influence too of local activists Mark Comfort and Curtis Lee Baker, who, in the summer of 1965, began campaigning against police brutality and organising patrols that monitored the police and their behaviour, and later adopted black uniforms and berets. The Panthers' initial focus was an attempt to stop police misconduct by undertaking openly armed patrols in Oakland that observed police arrests and informed black suspects of their legal rights.[43]

The Party formulated a ten-point platform and programme that mixed nationalism, grounded in racial solidarity, with reform-ist demands and was largely borrowed from a ten-point NOI platform issued in 1963 and written by Malcolm X. The Panther programme's more overtly nationalist objectives sought 'power to determine the destiny of our Black community', 'an end to the robbery by the White man of our Black community', 'education that teaches us our true history', and exemption from military service for 'a racist government' that did not protect blacks at home and, in reference to Vietnam, waged war against 'people of color' abroad. The Panthers' more reformist ambitions for the black community comprised full employment, 'decent housing', the release of all incarcerated black men 'because they have not received a fair and impartial trial', all-black jury trials for black defendants, and 'land, bread, housing, education, clothing, justice and peace'. The BPP's emphasis on armed self-defence bore the influence of Robert F. Williams, its name the emblem of the LCFO and much of the ten-point programme ideas propagated by the NOI but shorn of religion. The programme did not demand the revolutionary overthrow of the United States government, although, indicative of American influence, it quoted from the Declaration of Independence on the right to replace governments that denied men their inalienable rights.[44]

Like the NOI, the Panthers recruited particularly among the unemployed, the working class, prisoners and ex-convicts. Influenced by the writings of Frantz Fanon, a psychiatrist and revolutionary from the French colony of Martinique, Newton and Seale emphasised organising among the lumpenproletariat, those at the bottom of urban black society, regarding them as a potential vanguard for change, much as Fanon had viewed peasants. The party also stressed racial unity against oppression. Like Newton, early Panther leaders argued that black men had to regain and assert their masculinity. Black women demonstrated their own agency by joining the party.[45]

The BPP first gained widespread public attention in May 1967 when a mostly armed group of twenty-four male and six female Panthers and supporters went to the California State Assembly in Sacramento to protest against the Mulford bill which prohibited public display of loaded weapons. Several Panthers entered the assembly floor and some arrests followed later. Passed overwhelmingly, the act, as intended, curtailed the Panthers' armed surveillance patrols. In October, Newton was arrested for the murder of policeman, John Frey, during a traffic stop. Newton, who had also been shot in the altercation with two officers that left the second officer wounded, denied the charge, although, according to some accounts, he later privately admitted to murder. Months earlier, Newton had gone beyond advocacy of armed self-defence by arguing that the Panthers should attack the police to demonstrate 'the correct strategic means of resistance'. Panther David Hilliard later admitted that in November a group of Panthers attacked three policemen in Hunters Point, killing one of them. However, the Panthers consistently depicted themselves as simply victims of police violence.[46]

Like RAM, which since committing itself to urban guerrilla warfare had operated clandestinely, the BPP saw black ghetto riots as uprisings that demonstrated revolutionary potential. However, unlike RAM which thought that the riots could help facilitate the overthrow of the United States government, the Panthers argued that black energy had to be channelled away from rioting into creating an effective military force.[47]

Over 100 riots occurred during the summer of 1967 when LeRoi Jones returned to Newark after teaching a Black Studies course at San Francisco State University in the spring and visiting both US and the BPP in California. He was arrested for allegedly carrying guns and badly beaten by police during the city's riot in July, in which 25 African Americans were killed by the police and National Guard and 1,200 wounded. Initially convicted, Jones was later acquitted on appeal. In the meantime, he participated in the second National Black Power Conference held in Newark soon after the riot. The conference was an important milestone in a series of large-scale black political gatherings, described by Komozi Woodard as the Modern Black Convention Movement, that endured into the early 1970s. Attended by over 1,000 people from thirty-six states, the conference attracted and reflected a broad range of black opinion that included the NAACP, the NUL and the SCLC, as well as Black Power militants, such as Rap Brown and Karenga. Jones told the meeting that the riot in Newark had been 'a rebellion of black people for self-determination'. The conference adopted resolutions advocating self-defence, black community control and a national conversation about a separate black homeland in the United States. After the conference, Jones and local black leaders founded the United Brothers, which sought to win political power in Newark.[48]

Days after the Newark riot, rioting broke out in Detroit, lasting six days. As in Newark, the state's governor ordered in the National Guard, which accounted for many of the 43 people killed and the more than 1,000 injured. In the fall of 1967, a survey of African

Americans and whites in Detroit revealed sharp differences in perceptions of Black Power, which had frequently been reported negatively by white journalists. A large majority of whites, but only about half of blacks, viewed Black Power unfavourably: 80.7 per cent of whites compared to 49.6 per cent of African Americans. Whites were also far more likely to associate Black Power with rioting, civil disorder and black rule over whites than African Americans, 22.3 per cent of whom simply dismissed it as a slogan that meant 'nothing'. Of the 42.2 per cent of blacks who took a favourable view of Black Power, compared to just 10.7 per cent of whites, 19.6 per cent regarded it as seeking a 'fair share for black people' and 22.6 per cent as a call for black unity. The survey found 'no appreciable differences in approval for black power between black respondents who endorse integration and those who did not'. Of those African Americans who favoured integration, 46 per cent endorsed Black Power, while among blacks who preferred something in between integration and separation 46 per cent also approved of Black Power. Most Black Power supporters did not equate the concept with separatism and many did not see it as incompatible with integration. In so far as Black Power adherents exhibited nationalist tendencies, they were based on a belief in black unity.[49]

In the same year, activist scholar Joyce Ladner wrote about Black Power advocates in Mississippi. She distinguished between young cosmopolitans, most of them educated and almost half of them northerners, and locals, indigenous Mississippians from a broad age range who were mostly poor and uneducated. Influenced directly by black nationalism, cosmopolitans regarded Black Power as primarily concerned with developing black consciousness and a 'common loyalty to other colored peoples of the world'. By contrast, locals viewed Black Power as a means of organising to achieve economic and political change that would improve the conditions of African Americans' everyday lives. In Ladner's estimation, both cosmopolitans and locals were motivated by frustration at the limited pace and scope of change, insufficient federal implementation of civil rights legislation and entrenched white opposition.[50]

Some historians, such as Peniel E. Joseph, refer to Black Power as a movement, but, like progressives at the turn of the twentieth century, Black Power was too diverse and even contradictory to constitute a movement, and it possessed neither a unified ideology nor a shared set of goals. Black Power encompassed nationalist demands for a separate black state in the South or elsewhere in the United States, and self-determination and control of all institutions in the black community, as well as more reformist efforts for welfare rights, fair rents and provision of basic services in the black community. Black Power advocates included Black Muslims, Christians, secularists, socialists, Marxist–Leninists, Maoists, capitalists, feminists, exponents of hypermasculinity, cultural nationalists, people who formed or rejected alliances with whites, the politically involved and politically disengaged, advocates and practitioners of self-defence, and would-be revolutionaries who called for urban guerrilla warfare. Joseph even describes Black Power as 'multiracial'. The ambiguity of Black Power enabled it to be claimed by some unlikely champions. In 1968, Whitney Young endorsed Black Power as black capitalism leading Rap Brown to lament that the concept had become 'diluted and prostituted to the point where even the most conservative negroes are now for Black Power'. Moreover, many of its advocates and organisations, including the BPP, changed significantly over time.[51]

Revolutionary Black Nationalism

The Black Panthers' original ten-point programme mixed nationalism with reformism, rather than revolution, but the party's confrontations with the police and its emphasis on guns, its uniform of powder blue shirts, black pants, leather jackets and berets, and its increasing advocacy of revolution gained it a radical reputation. With Newton in jail while awaiting trial and Seale serving six months for the Sacramento protest, Eldridge Cleaver, a former serial rapist who had joined the party a few months after his parole from jail in December 1966 for assault with intent to murder, assumed a leading role. As the party's Minister of Information, Cleaver, his future wife Kathleen Neal and Emory Douglas, Minister of Culture, orchestrated a 'Free Huey' campaign that brought the party national and international publicity and chapters in many parts of the nation. They also made the monthly *Black Panther* newspaper, begun in 1967, into a weekly. Sold by the party's chapters with sales quotas imposed by the Oakland headquarters, the paper became a major source of funds.[52]

Stokely Carmichael, Rap Brown and James Forman of SNCC participated in the 'Free Huey' campaign, addressed Panther rallies and accepted prominent positions in the BPP in 1968, marking the beginning of a short-lived alliance between the two groups. Brown's appearance at a rally in California in February violated his parole and brought him another arrest. In his first major speech since returning from a five-month international tour that had included Africa, Latin America and Europe, Carmichael, wearing a dashiki (a loose-fitting West African tunic), adopted a Pan-Africanist perspective at the rally, rooted in the interconnectedness of the black diaspora. He dismissed socialism, which increasingly informed the ideological direction of the Panthers who abandoned 'for Self-Defense' from the party's title. Carmichael's strained relations with BPP, which had formed an alliance with the white radical Peace and Freedom Party in December 1967 that significantly boosted the 'Free Huey' campaign, also arose from his opposition to allying with whites.[53]

In March 1968, Cleaver addressed the first convention of the Peace and Freedom Party, where he urged black and white radicals to collaborate in overturning capitalism and imperialism. He argued that Marxism–Leninism had to be adapted to American conditions and drew inspiration from the words of Chinese, North Korean and Cuban revolutionary leaders and Frantz Fanon on the necessity of revolutionary violence and wars of liberation. Cleaver influenced an incarcerated Newton to add a call for 'a United Nations-supervised plebiscite to be held throughout the Black colony in which only Black colonial subjects will be allowed to participate, for the purposes of determining the will of Black people as to their national destiny', to point ten of the BPP party programme, an idea Cleaver had taken from Malcolm X.[54]

Newton declared that the party was revolutionary nationalist, which he defined as combining nationalism and socialism. Aware that as a minority in the United States, African Americans were unlikely to establish a black nation state, he sought leftist allies and support among non-whites and whites at home and abroad in a common socialist struggle that he believed would end racism, colonialism and imperialism by eliminating the capitalist system that leftists believed produced them. The party opposed America's alleged domestic colonialism in solidarity with the struggle of African, Asian and Latin American peoples against European and American imperialism. Newton regarded white police in black urban communities as an occupying force akin to the United States military operating to subdue non-white people in Vietnam. The BPP's denunciation of both the police and intervention in Vietnam helped to gain it adherents.[55]

African Americans, like other Americans, had mostly supported United States' large-scale deployment of troops in Vietnam in 1965, but, by 1967, they were more inclined to view the war as a mistake and to favour swift withdrawal. Because of poverty and racial discrimination, African Americans had a greater likelihood in the mid-1960s of being drafted, fighting on the frontlines and suffering casualties than whites. Discriminated against in the draft, especially by white-dominated southern draft boards, African Americans also experienced racism from white soldiers and officers. Some resented being expected to fight ostensibly for democracy abroad when America denied them it at home and used a white-dominated National Guard to quell urban riots. Much like Muhammad Ali, who refused military induction in 1967 and paid with his world heavyweight boxing title as punishment, some African Americans regarded the Vietnamese as people of colour like themselves with whom they had no quarrel. Some black soldiers were radicalised by their experiences in Vietnam. There were others already committed or attracted to Black Power before they were drafted, especially after the massive Tet Offensive by the Viet Cong and North Vietnamese Army in January 1968 and Martin Luther King's assassination in April. Sometimes they formed or joined black nationalist groups on military bases at home before deployment abroad, as well as in Vietnam. The war also contributed to black nationalism's appeal for African Americans who were not drafted. Some returning black veterans joined black radical groups such as the BPP after completing their service and then provided members with military training.[56]

Eldridge Cleaver condemned United States involvement in Vietnam in his bestselling memoirs and reflections, *Soul on Ice*, published in 1968 and tried to make the party more confrontational. Seeking to challenge the police, in April 1968 he and nine other Panthers launched an attack on Oakland officers. Cleaver was wounded and Panther Bobby Hutton died, either killed by police deliberately or attempting to escape. Police arrested the nine survivors. While Cleaver was on bail, Newton was convicted in September of Frey's manslaughter but acquitted of wounding a second officer. When the courts ordered him back to jail to await trial, Cleaver fled to Cuba and later Algeria, where he established the BPP's international section and continued to generate publicity.[57] According to historian Akinyele Omowale Umoja, 'the BPP organized an underground from its earliest days'. Newton endorsed urban guerrilla warfare, which he believed could be inspired by small attacks undertaken by an underground vanguard. A network of independent urban cells, the black nationalist underground, which included but was not confined to BPP elements, became known as the Black Liberation Army (BLA). While in prison before he joined the Panthers, Cleaver and another inmate Alprentice 'Bunchy' Carter had envisaged creating a clandestine military wing of black nationalism. In late 1967, Carter, now free, had joined the BPP. As the party's Southern California Minister of Defense, Carter organised a secret Panther military wing in Los Angeles, with Elmer 'Geronimo' Pratt (later Geronimo ji-Jaga), a decorated special forces veteran who had served in Vietnam, playing a crucial role.[58]

The Panthers also gained a following among some black prisoners, influenced by Black Power and groundwork laid by earlier manifestations of nationalism. In the early 1960s, a small group of inmates in San California's San Quentin prison had formed the Marxist-oriented Afro-American Nationalist Organization. In the late 1960s, Huey P. Newton named long-time California inmate George Jackson as Chief Marshall. In his published prison writings, Jackson, like Newton, argued that, when politicised, prisoners could become revolutionaries. Unlike the NOI which had lost some of its support among inmates, Jackson endorsed prisoner unity across racial lines.[59]

While the Panthers gained in profile and membership, RAM foundered, undone by state repression and internal disagreements, and its failure to build black urban support, forge connections with other racial minorities and prepare for a long struggle. Kelley and Esch explain that 'RAM leaders focused on confronting the state head-on and attacking black leaders they deemed reformists.' In June 1967, police charged RAM members with conspiracy to incite riot, poison police officers and kill Roy Wilkins and Whitney Young. Targeted by the FBI's Counterintelligence Program (COINTELPRO), adopted in 1967 to disrupt and undermine radical black nationalist groups, RAM had disbanded by 1969. Some of its members joined the BLA or the BPP, or formed other organisations, such as the Afrikan Peoples Party, the Black Liberation Party and the Republic of New Africa (RNA).[60]

In March 1968, 500 black nationalists, including 'Queen Mother' Audley Moore, Betty Shabazz (Malcolm X's widow), Maulena Karenga and Amiri Baraka, gathered in Detroit for a Black Government Conference co-hosted by Gaidi Obadele (Milton Henry) and Imari Abubakari Obadele (Richard Henry), who in 1967, after GOAL had disbanded, had helped form the Malcolm X Society. One hundred of the delegates signed a 'Declaration of Independence for the Black Nation' that opposed racial and sexual inequality, called for an independent black state and reparations from the federal government for injustice against African Americans, and identified the black struggle in the United States with that of oppressed peoples in the world for freedom from white domination and capitalism. The document, signed first by Moore, signalled the establishment of the Provisional Government of the RNA, which named Robert F. Williams as president. Williams, now resident in Mao's China, had left Cuba after criticising racism there and being unwilling to subordinate black nationalism to the needs of the Communists on the island and in the United States.[61]

Like US, RNA members often took new names based on their personality and to indicate self-determination, distinctiveness from white Americans and identification with Africa. Despite the RNA's avowal of sexual equality, some members accepted patriarchal families and the organisation sanctioned polygyny, considering it an African practice. Like the BPP, the RNA advocated a plebiscite to decide the will of the 'New Afrikan population in North America', but it also sought the establishment of an independent black nation in the five Deep South states. The RNA requested negotiations with the United States government for $200 billion in reparations, contacted several African governments with the intention of establishing commercial links and also met with officials from China and the Soviet Union.[62]

The organisation combined public protests and educational programmes with buying land in Mississippi for the intended capital of the new black nation. The RNA also formed a small armed paramilitary group, the Black Legion, and elected its own government. According to historian Christian Davenport, 'members of the RNA engaged in diverse illegal and violent activities as well: robberies, shootouts with police, shooting practice, plots to bomb state and federal buildings, and even a plane hijacking'. In March 1969, police clashed with RNA members when they met at Detroit's New Bethel Church to celebrate the organisation's first anniversary. One policeman was killed and another wounded, leading to a police raid on the church and a gun battle with those inside that ended with 142 arrests, including some children. Concerned for the safety of those arrested, Judge George Crockatt, an African American, released them on bond, or on their personal recognisance. Two men were tried for the killing and wounding of the two policemen but were not convicted. The RNA became a target of the FBI's COINTELPRO programme and Robert F. Williams resigned his RNA and RAM positions after returning to the United States in 1969 and rejecting armed revolt. Disagreements between Imari Abubakari Obadele, who endorsed acquiring land in Mississippi for the putative nation and creating a large security force, and Gaidi Obadele, who envisaged blacks eventually achieving nationhood by voting for secession in areas where they were a majority, led to factional division. The RNA increasingly focused on Mississippi and, in 1970, held its national convention in Jackson, but it failed to generate a large following.[63]

As well as the RNA, Detroit also saw the founding of the Dodge Revolutionary Union Movement (DRUM), following a wildcat strike by black and white workers in May 1968 at the Hamtramck Assembly Plant in protest at an accelerated production line. DRUM, begun by nine black workers and editors from the *Inner City Voice*, a local black radical newspaper, sought to end racial discrimination in the workplace and union movement that kept blacks in the worst jobs and provide an alternative to white-led unions. DRUM organised another wildcat strike in July which inspired the creation of the Ford Revolutionary Union Movement and the Eldon Avenue Revolutionary Union Movement and other black workers' groups that coalesced in June 1969 in the League of Revolutionary Black Workers.[64]

The revolutionary union movement and black nationalism were interconnected. Stanford claimed that RAM helped found DRUM. Mike Hamlin of the *Inner City Voice* had connections with the RNA, and some of the paper's contributors and strikers were members of Uhuru. Concerned that Huey P. Newton had wrongly identified the lumpenproletariat as a revolutionary vanguard, DRUM/the League, which saw organised black workers in that role, may have been responsible for forming a Detroit BPP chapter. Like the Panthers, the League endorsed self-defence, was 'guided by the principles of Marxism-Leninism', and expressed willingness to work with other races and groups in 'waging a relentless struggle against racism, capitalism, and imperialism'. The League sought 'to secure state power' under the leadership of 'the black working class' and 'create a society free of race, sex, class, and national oppression'. However, the League never resolved a tension between regarding blacks as an internal colony and advocating a socialist solution that, because of the relatively small size of the black working class, seemed unrealistic without the white worker support that the colonial analogy and widespread white union racism suggested was unfeasible. In practice, Hamlin recalled, the League 'wrote off white workers', and confined women, none of whom sat on its executive board, to secondary, supportive roles. Nevertheless, the League gained support beyond Detroit in steel and other industries. However, beginning in 1969, declining car sales halted hiring and brought layoffs that reduced the League's core membership.[65]

The BPP rapidly expanded in Oakland and by December 1968 had established a presence in twenty American cities. In late 1968 and early 1969, BPP chapters, urged by Seale, who, like Newton, had worked in a federally funded antipoverty programme, and David Hilliard, began providing community programmes, designed to meet the immediate needs of the black community and boost the party's appeal. Free breakfasts for children, operating in twenty-three cities by late 1969, constituted the largest of these programmes that expanded to include free clothing, shoes, legal aid, health care and a host of other services. While the programmes often drew on willing and enthusiastic donations of time, resources and money by party members and sympathisers in the black and white communities, in some cases the Panthers used pressure, threats and retribution to compel merchants to donate food. So concerned did the Oakland headquarters become by an influx in the party of criminal, violent and ill-disciplined elements, it sought to purge them, along with those suspected of working with or for the authorities. Experience varied greatly across chapters, but party discipline was sometimes violent and even brutal. In New Haven, Connecticut, Panthers tortured and killed Alex Rackley, wrongly accused of being a spy.[66]

Although increasingly active in all aspects of Panther activity, women were particularly prominent in community programmes and, by the late 1960s, a time when many male Panther leaders were in jail or exile, may have constituted a majority of party membership. They contributed at all levels, with Kathleen Cleaver becoming the first woman to join the party's central committee, which nevertheless remained male dominated. In the late 1960s, Panther leaders, such as Newton, Seale and Eldridge Cleaver, began championing sexual equality, abandoning an earlier emphasis on masculinity that often cast women in supportive, subordinate roles and viewed them as complicit in or indifferent to denials of black manhood. In 1970, Newton called for alliances with revolutionaries in the women and gay liberation movements. Some Panther women challenged discrimination within the party, while others prioritised the battle against white oppression. Women exercised leadership and influence in formal positions, such as Mary Rem who founded and led a Panther chapter in Des Moines, and other ways by their participation and input in developing chapters and community programmes. Women had a diverse range of experiences in the party and some adopted the assertive, aggressive style of male Panthers. Changes in women's treatment and participation were nonlinear, but party mandates on sexual equality, however imperfectly realised, contrasted with the patriarchy of many contemporary black nationalist groups and American society.[67]

By 1968, the Panthers had become a major target for local police and the FBI, leading to police raids on chapter offices, arrests, convictions and targeted Panther deaths, and extensive, and often successful, efforts by the agency to recruit informers and promote dissension, distrust and conflict between and within black nationalist groups. In April 1969, twenty-one Panthers in New York (the New York 21) were indicted for an alleged bombing plot and other charges, which kept most of them in prison until all were eventually acquitted. In July, Hoover declared that 'the Black Panther Party, without question, represents the greatest threat to the internal security of the country', which vastly overrated the party's capabilities. In December, Chicago authorities shot local chapter leader Fred Hampton to death in bed and killed visiting Peoria, Illinois, Panther head Mark Clark. Although the campaign of repression disrupted the Panthers, deprived them of leaders and encouraged suspicion among them and toward other groups, scholars Joshua Bloom and Waldo E. Martin, Jr, claim that 'the year of greatest repression, 1969, was also the year of the Party's greatest growth' and brought it increased sympathy and support. Conversely, historian David J. Garrow contends that during 1969 party membership fell by half from a peak of 5,000 in 1968, although he agrees that repression increased black and white support for the party. It also drove chief of staff David Hilliard to declare that the party sought the overthrow of the government through armed resistance. However, as with Newton and other Panthers' earlier references to revolution, the BPP did not attempt to initiate armed revolution and, in any case, many chapters operated autonomously.[68]

Although most African Americans were unwilling to follow the Panthers down a revolutionary path, they remained widely admired. In a 1970 poll, 64 per cent of blacks surveyed agreed that the party 'gave them a sense of pride'. The *Black Panther* newspaper, instrumental in the 'Free Huey' campaign, had a circulation of 100,000. In August, a technicality unexpectedly brought Newton's freedom from prison. He soon distanced himself from armed resistance and embraced community programmes, which, he claimed, would enable the people to survive, pending revolution at some future time.[69]

Newton also adopted a new concept, intercommunalism. He contended that United States dominance had rendered international borders and nation states obsolete, leaving only oppressed communities, which should work together in a common revolutionary struggle against American capitalism and imperialism. By advocating a worldwide socialist revolution, intercommunalism appeared to mark a break with the last vestiges of BPP black nationalism, while simultaneously giving the appearance of revolutionary militancy that was, in practice, belied by the party's focus on community programmes. It is unclear how closely the party's rank and file understood or engaged with the Oakland Panthers' ideological changes. The 'Free Huey' campaign had provided an important focus and rallying point for the party that disappeared with Newton's release. Once freed, Newton proved a disappointment to many Panthers, most of whom had joined the party during his incarceration. He lacked charisma and articulacy as a public speaker and struggled to hold together a party increasingly divided between exponents of revolutionary violence and reformism.[70]

Cultural Nationalism

Newton and the Oakland Panthers had long been critical of cultural nationalism, which they dismissed derisively as 'pork-chop nationalism' that channelled energies away from focusing on revolutionary political change, and they had little interest in African cultural traditions, real or imagined. For them and other revolutionary nationalists, historian William W. Sales, Jr, explains, 'the basic cultural unity of African peoples worldwide grew not out of a common cultural heritage but out of a common history of exploitation and oppression at the hands of European racists'. Furthermore, as Panther member Linda Harrison explained 'cultural nationalism is most always based on racism'. The Panthers rejected all manifestations of racism and, unlike cultural nationalists such as US, forged alliances with whites. Nevertheless, the Panthers developed their own forms of cultural nationalism, designed to foster revolutionary consciousness, that included the Panther uniform, Afro hair styles, poetry, songs, black history in the *Black Panther* newspaper and Panther 'liberation' schools in several cities, Emory Douglas's artwork, music recorded by Elaine Brown, and Panther-approved music groups, the Lumpen, Freedom Messengers and Vanguard. While the Oakland Panthers criticised US for advocating supposedly traditional African practices, some Panther chapters exhibited interest in African culture. Some of the New York Panthers took African names and wore dashikis, and the Brooklyn chapter's liberation school included African history and dance. While West Coast Panthers took pride in enlisting 'brothers off the block' and celebrated the lumpenproletariat, some chapters sought to mould their members' behaviour and condemned excessive alcohol consumption, drug taking and promiscuity. Despite an emphasis on the lumpenproletariat, the party also recruited from the middle class.[71]

Despite the Oakland Panther leaders' contentions and historian William L. Van Deburg's claim that Black Power was 'essentially cultural', cultural black nationalism was often politically engaged. In 1968, the third annual Black Power Conference, attended by 4,000 delegates in Philadelphia, instructed Maulana Karenga of US to organise a convention to form a black political party. Already an experienced political organiser, Karenga trained LeRoi Jones, now known as Amiri Baraka and a devotee of *Kawaida*, and the United Brothers in Newark in precinct work, and oversaw their creation of a political coalition, the Committee for a Unified Newark (CFUN) that unsuccessfully contested the November elections in the city.[72]

In CFUN, Baraka envisaged women in supportive domestic roles, supposedly modelled on African practices and a presumed natural order, and established a hierarchical structure. According to Matlin, 'Baraka believed in neither the equality of the races nor that of the sexes', regarded whites as inherently evil and condemned homosexuality. He sought to develop a 'socially responsible [black] patriarchy' rooted in a reformulation of 'long-standing ideals of social and moral uplift' that in reality owed more to America than Africa. Baraka's wife, Amina (Sylvia Robinson), was the main instigator of the African Free School in Newark and headed CFUN's women's division. In practice, women ran many of CFUN's programmes, organised much of its work and undertook all secretarial duties, and many of them were unwilling to be submissive. Although he rejected polygamy, Amiri Baraka remained steadfast in his commitment to Karenga and belief in his teachings, but Karenga's attention was drawn back to the West Coast by conflict with the Black Panthers.[73]

In January 1969, growing antagonism between US and Panthers in Los Angeles, rooted in a power struggle and mutual suspicion, intensified when disagreements about their favoured candidates to head the Black Student Union at the University of California, Los Angeles and the shape of the university's Black Studies Program saw US members shoot and kill Black Panthers John Huggins and Bunchy Carter. Although Hoover had instructed the Los Angeles FBI in November 1968 to exacerbate the pre-existing conflict between US and the Panthers, and the Panthers accused US after the killings of acting for the federal government, no evidence has emerged to substantiate the claim, and historians disagree about the degree to which the FBI was responsible for fomenting discord and confrontation between the two groups. In August 1969, US members also killed Sylvester Bell, head of the San Diego Panthers. US members engaged in armed robbery and weapons theft, and prepared explosives in expectation of a black revolt against the United States government that Karenga expected to occur in 1971.[74]

While US and Baraka were the principal promoters of cultural nationalism, it also manifested itself in African American Christianity. In 1966, the National Committee of Negro (later Black) Churchmen (NCBC) published a statement on 'Black Power' that called for blacks to be included in the 'framework in which all power in America operates' and affirmed the need to 'find our way to a new self-image in which we can feel a normal sense of pride in self'. The committee, composed of Protestant clergy and laity, drew from black denominations and blacks in mostly white denominations, in which, during the late 1960s, they formed black caucuses and challenged discrimination. In July 1970, the committee issued a 'Black Declaration of Independence' that outlined historic and ongoing discrimination against African Americans and warned that 'unless we receive full Redress and Relief from these Inhumanities we will move to renounce all Allegiance to this Nation'. In November, 6,000 African Americans 'ratified' the declaration at a Black Solidarity meeting in New York. The committee also supported anticolonial and anti-apartheid struggles in Africa. African Americans formed their own organisations in the Catholic Church, among them the National Black Catholic Clergy Caucus, the National Black Sisters' Conference and the National Black Catholic Lay Caucus.[75]

Interrupting services at the Riverside Church in New York in May 1969, James Forman, formerly of SNCC, presented a 'Black Manifesto' addressed to 'the white Christian churches and Jewish synagogues' that, couched in Marxist terminology, demanded $500 million in reparations to be paid to the newly inaugurated Black Economic Development Conference (BEDC). Although the manifesto depicted African Americans as a colonised people and envisaged a revolution achieved by 'sustained guerrilla warfare' that would secure state control of the 'means of production', the money, the Manifesto indicated, would be used for more modest economic and cultural objectives, such as a black university, television station, research institute, land bank and strike fund, and publishing houses. Approved by the NCBC, the manifesto realised only a fraction of the amount it demanded and the BEDC wilted, although some religious organisations contributed money to African American causes through other channels.[76]

Influenced by Black Power, some African American theologians developed black liberation theology, notably James A. Cone of Union Theological Seminary in New York. Cone, who regarded Jesus Christ as a revolutionary, argued that Christianity had originally been, and should again be, centred on freeing the oppressed. God, he maintained, was on the side of African Americans in their liberation struggle, which involved their achieving self-determination. He added that 'if the system is evil, then revolutionary violence is both justified and necessary'. Whites, Cone argued, could participate in God's work in America by helping blacks achieve liberation.[77]

The Reverend Albert B. Cleage, Jr, went further by claiming that blacks constituted the 'chosen people' and Christ the black Messiah. The black church, he argued, should stand at the centre of bringing the black nation together in the United States by helping it to gain economic and political power through collective action, education and community organising. Focused on improving black life on earth through liberation from white oppression, Cleage endorsed *Kawaida* as essential for the realisation of a just society and accused traditional black denominations of being 'committed to the preservation of the white status quo and the pacification of black people'. In 1967, Cleage installed a painting of a black Madonna and baby Jesus in his church, which he subsequently renamed the Shrine of the Black Madonna. He founded the ecumenical Black Christian National Movement to disseminate what he regarded as an authentic Christianity religion responsive to black people's needs. Cleage gained thousands of followers in Detroit, but, despite such efforts, many young black militants regarded the church as irreparably tainted by ingrained conservatism.[78]

Militant black students, who formed black student unions and associations, also regarded colleges and universities as conservative and pressured their administrations to infuse nationalism into the curriculum. Their efforts led many leading universities and colleges to create Black Studies programmes and recruit black students and faculty. In 1969, armed students took over a campus building and helped prompt Cornell University in Ithaca, New York, to institute black studies. Fearing similar confrontations, many other universities followed suit. By 1970, two thirds of the nation's four-year colleges offered black studies courses.[79]

Concerns about co-optation brought efforts to provide alternatives to traditional education. In 1969, Malcolm X Liberation University opened in Durham, North Carolina, designed to teach technical skills required in nation building and nationalist ideology. Although a group of black independent schools, which formed the Federation of Pan-African Educational Institutions in 1970, helped to fund the university, financial shortfalls forced its closure in 1973. In 1970, black intellectuals launched the Institute of the Black World in Atlanta, led by historian Vincent Harding. Its initial aim of shaping the content and growth of Black Studies soon broadened into fostering 'a community of black scholars, artists, and organizers who are committed . . . to forward the struggles of the black community towards self-understanding, self-determination, and ultimate liberation'. Beset after the early 1970s by financial problems as support from charitable foundations declined, the Institute struggled to survive and, as historian Derrick E. White chronicles, changed in 1975 'from an activist think tank to an educational resource center'. It closed in 1983, having 'been a shell of its former self for the last six years'.[80]

Influenced by Black Power and concerned to see their interests represented, African Americans formed professional organisations that, as historian Alphonso Pinkney explains, emphasised 'black unity and solidarity' and supported black liberation. They included police organisations, such as the National Society of Afro-American Policemen, Inc., which had chapters in several states, the Afro-American Patrolmen's League in Chicago, and Officers for Justice in San Francisco. Other black professional groups founded in the late 1960s included the National Conference of Black Lawyers, the National Conference of Black Political Scientists, the Caucus (later Association) of Black Sociologists, the National Association of Black Social Workers, the Association of Black Psychologists and the Association of Black Anthropologists.[81]

Black Power reshaped black fashion and appearance, most notably in the adoption by many younger African Americans especially of natural hairstyles and African-influenced clothing. Black Power also influenced music. Some cultural nationalists, like Amiri Baraka, championed jazz avant-garde performed by artists, such as Ornette Coleman and John Coltrane, but, to Baraka's chagrin, many African Americans preferred soul music. Although soul singer James Brown recorded the affirmation 'Say It Loud – I'm Black and I'm Proud' in 1968, he used more white and Asian than black children for the song's chorus, rejected revolutionary nationalism, embraced patriotism and advocated black advancement through individual effort, thrift and accumulation. The Black Panthers dismissed Brown as a self-interested capitalist. Despite the advent of The Last Poets, a group of Harlem black nationalist and Puerto Rican poets and musicians, popular black music rarely engaged directly with black nationalism, although its artists increasingly adopted Afro hairstyles and sometimes African attire. However, in the late 1960s and early 1970s, some soul artists, such as The Impressions, The Chi-Lites and The Temptations, sang more socially conscious lyrics and, in making calls for respect and pride, echoed Black Power themes. Even if seldom overtly political, historian Brian Ward notes, soul, jazz and 'black-oriented radio and Rhythm and Blues' helped 'promote a revived sense of black identity, pride, solidarity and common consciousness'.[82]

Baraka remained at the forefront of cultural nationalism and continued his work in CFUN. Constituting 65 per cent of Newark's population, blacks and Puerto Ricans formed a political alliance that, with support from some whites, succeeded in replacing incumbent mayor, Italian-American Mayor Hugh Addonizio, with the city's first black mayor, Kenneth A. Gibson, in June 1970 and securing Newark's first Puerto Rican deputy mayor, Ramon Aneses. In September, Gibson and Baraka were among 3,000 black people, including nationalists, civil rights leaders, black elected officials and representatives from 200 community organisations, who met in Atlanta and created the Congress of African People (CAP) to foster cooperation in advancing black progress, formulating a shared political programme and supporting African liberation efforts.[83]

Karenga, a key figure in Black Power conferences, was not present. His increasing paranoia, authoritarianism and drug abuse, amidst conflict with the BPP and state repression, had led many US members to leave the group during 1969, with some relocating to Newark and CFUN. In May 1970, Karenga and three other US members tortured two women, Gail Idili-Davis and Brenda Jones, wrongly believing them to be agents seeking to kill Karenga. As leader of the *Kawaida* movement, Karenga instructed Baraka not to attend the Atlanta gathering, but Baraka refused and severed CFUN's ties with US. CFUN transformed into Newark CAP, which housed CAP's programme office and, Woodard argues, 'the headquarters of the *national* Modern Black Convention Movement'. CAP claimed to have twenty-five affiliates in major cities.[84]

The split between Baraka and Karenga, the decline of SNCC, CORE and US, the dissolution of RAM, factional divisions in the RNA, differences within the BPP, the failure of the BPP–SNCC alliance and ongoing state repression of black nationalist groups and leaders suggested that black nationalism was imploding. Yet, in other ways, black nationalism remained vibrant, evidenced by CAP, the Black Arts Movement, the founding of black professional organisations, widespread black admiration for the BPP, and the continuation of the NOI, still the most extensive black nationalist group. Black nationalism would soon reach its domestic political zenith and find renewed expression in solidarity with African liberation movements.[85]

Notes

1. William L. Van Deburg, *New Day in Babylon: The Black Power Movement and American Culture, 1965–1975* (Chicago and London: University of Chicago Press, 1992), pp. 112–91; Jeffrey O. G. Ogbar, *Black Power: Radical Politics and African American Identity* (Baltimore and London: Johns Hopkins University Press, 2004), pp. 2–3, 124, 140, 153, 191, 196.
2. Timothy B. Tyson, 'Robert F. Williams, "Black Power," and the Roots of the African American Freedom Struggle', *Journal of American History* 85 (September 1998), pp. 540–70; Komozi Woodard, *A Nation within a Nation: Amiri Baraka (LeRoi Jones) and Black Power Politics* (Chapel Hill and London: University of North Carolina Press, 1999), p. xiii; Peniel E. Joseph, *Waiting 'Til the Midnight Hour: A Narrative History of Black Power in America* (New York: Henry Holt, 2006); Peniel E. Joseph, 'The Black Power Movement: A State of the Field', *Journal of American History* 96 (December 2009), pp. 751–2.
3. Richard Wright, *Black Power: A Record of Reactions in a Land of Pathos* (New York: Harper, 1954); Joseph, 'Black Power Movement', p. 755; James Lance Taylor, *Black Nationalism in the United States: From Malcolm X to Barack Obama* (Boulder and London: Lynne Rienner, 2011), pp. 219, 256 n. 1; E. U. Essien-Udom, *Black Nationalism: A Search for an Identity in America* (Chicago: University of Chicago Press, 1962), pp. 279–81; Claude Andrew Clegg III, *An Original Man: The Life and Times of Elijah Muhammad* (New York: St. Martin's Press, 1997), pp. 58, 121–2; Ogbar, *Black Power*, pp. 2, 57, 69, 218–19 n. 2, 229 n. 12.
4. Joseph, *Waiting 'Til the Midnight Hour*, pp. 6–7, 9, 19–21.
5. Robert F. Williams, *Negroes with Guns* (1962; Detroit: Wayne State University Press, 1998), pp. 3–5, 13, 16–17, 19–20; Tyson, 'Robert F. Williams, "Black Power," and the Roots of the African American Freedom Struggle', pp. 545–6, 549–51.
6. Williams, *Negroes with Guns*, pp. 20–4; Joseph, *Waiting 'Til the Midnight Hour*, p. 28; Tyson, 'Robert F. Williams, "Black Power," and the Roots of the African American Freedom Struggle', pp. 551–6; Herb Boyd, 'Longtime Activist Queen Mother Moore, 98, Dies', *Black*

Scholar 27 (Summer 1997), n.p.; Ashley D. Farmer, 'Reframing African American Women's Grassroots Organizing: Audley Moore and the Universal Association of Ethiopian Women, 1957–1963', *Journal of African American History* 101 (Winter–Spring 2016), pp. 69–96.

7. Williams, *Negroes with Guns*, 24–30; Tyson, 'Robert F. Williams, "Black Power," and the Roots of the African American Freedom Struggle', pp. 555–9; Joseph, *Waiting 'Til the Midnight Hour*, p. 28.

8. Williams, *Negroes with Guns*, pp. 31–5; Joseph, *Waiting 'Til the Midnight Hour*, pp. 29–31; Woodard, *A Nation within a Nation*, p. 52; James Edward Smethurst, *The Black Arts Movement: Literary Nationalism in the 1960s and 1970s* (Chapel Hill: University of North Carolina Press, 2005).

9. Joseph, *Waiting 'Til the Midnight Hour*, pp. 1–4, 6, 31–4; Woodard, *A Nation within a Nation*, pp. 51–4; Harold Cruse, 'Revolutionary Nationalism and the Afro-American', *Studies on the Left* 2 (1962), in Harold Cruse, *Rebellion or Revolution?*, with a foreword by Cedric Johnson (Minneapolis and London: University of Minnesota Press, 2009), pp. 74–96; Robin D. G. Kelley and Betsy Esch, 'Black like Mao: Red China and Black Revolution', *Souls* 1 (Fall 1999), p. 12.

10. Manning Marable, *Malcolm X: A Life of Reinvention* (New York: Allen Lane, 2011), pp. 172–3; Joseph, *Waiting 'Til the Midnight Hour*, pp. 35–8; Karl Evanzz, *The Messenger: The Rise and Fall of Elijah Muhammad* (New York: Vintage, 1999), pp. 222–3; Clegg, *An Original Man*, p. 156.

11. Joseph, *Waiting 'Til the Midnight Hour*, pp. 38–44; Woodard, *A Nation within a Nation*, pp. 54–9; Adina Back, 'Exposing the "Whole Segregation Myth": The Harlem Nine and New York City's School Desegregation Battles', in Jeanne Theoharis and Komozi Woodard (eds), *Freedom North: Black Freedom Struggles Outside the South, 1940–1980* (New York: Palgrave Macmillan, 2003), pp. 65–91; Hasan Kwame Jeffries and Patrick D. Jones, 'Desegregating New York: The Case of the "Harlem Nine"', *OAH Magazine of History* 26 (January 2012), pp. 51–3.

12. Williams, *Negroes with Guns*, pp. 40–56, 63–5, 67–9; *New York Times*, 18 September 1961; Tyson, 'Robert F. Williams, "Black Power," and the Roots of the African American Freedom Struggle', pp. 559–61, 563–4; Joseph, *Waiting 'Til the Midnight Hour*, pp. 48–9; Ashley Farmer, 'Mae Mallory: Forgotten Black Power Intellectual', available at <http://www.aaihs.org/mae-mallory-forgotten-black-power-intellectual/> (last accessed 6 July 2016). Extradited to Monroe in 1964 and convicted, Mallory was freed in 1965 because African Americans had been excluded from her trial's jury selection.

13. Williams, *Negroes with Guns*, pp. 3–4, 72–86; Tyson, 'Robert F. Williams, "Black Power," and the Roots of the African American

Freedom Struggle', pp. 564–5; Brian Ward, *Just My Soul Responding: Rhythm and Blues, Black Consciousness and Race Relations* (London: UCL Press, 1998), p. 432; Ogbar, *Black Power*, p. 59.

14. Joseph, *Waiting 'Til the Midnight Hour*, pp. 54–60; Maxwell C. Stanford, 'Revolutionary Action Movement (RAM): A Case Study of an Urban Revolutionary Movement in Western Capitalist Society' (MA thesis, Atlanta University, 1986), pp. 40, 47, 63, 74–80, 82, 84–5.

15. Kelley and Esch, 'Black like Mao', pp. 14–19; Peniel E. Joseph, 'Dashikis and Democracy: Black Studies, Student Activism, and the Black Power Movement', *Journal of African American History* 88 (Spring 2003), pp. 187–8; Stanford, 'Revolutionary Action Movement', pp. 2, 59–60, 63, 66, 71, 78–9, 84, 90, 100–6, 146–7, 160-1, 169-71; Marable, *Malcolm X*, pp. 353-5, 460.

16. Stanford, 'Revolutionary Action Movement', p. 100; Ogbar, *Black Power*, pp. 57–9; Harvard Sitkoff, *The Struggle for Black Equality, 1954–1992*, 2nd edn (New York: Hill and Wang, 1993), pp. 103–4, 110–11; Clayborne Carson, *In Struggle: SNCC and the Black Awakening of the 1960s* (Cambridge, MA and London: Harvard University Press, 1981), pp. 23–4, 38–9, 70, 84–9, 97, 114–15; Mark Stern, *Calculating Visions: Kennedy, Johnson and Civil Rights* (New Brunswick, NJ: Rutgers University Press, 1992), pp. 63–6; David J. Garrow, *Bearing the Cross: Martin Luther King, Jr., and the Southern Christian Leadership Conference* (New York: William Morrow, 1986), p. 162.

17. Carson, *In Struggle*, pp. 114–15, 164; John Dittmer, *Local People: The Struggle for Civil Rights in Mississippi* (Urbana and Chicago: University of Illinois Press, 1994), pp. 242–71; Sitkoff, *Struggle for Black Equality*, p. 164.

18. Carson, *In Struggle*, pp. 108–9, 123–9; Dittmer, *Local People*, pp. 285–302.

19. H. Rap Brown, *Die Nigger Die!: A Political Autobiography*, Chapter 5, available at <http://www.historyisaweapon.com/defcon1/dnd.html#DIV11> (last accessed 30 October 2016).

20. Carson, *In Struggle*, pp. 134–5.

21. Carson, *In Struggle*, pp. 183–8; Peter B. Levy, 'Blacks and the Vietnam War', in D. Michael Shafer (ed.), *The Legacy: The Vietnam War in the American Imagination* (Boston: Beacon Press, 1990), p. 216.

22. Lance Hill, *The Deacons for Defense: Armed Resistance and the Civil Rights Movement* (Chapel Hill and London: University of North Carolina at Chapel Hill, 2004); Christopher B. Strain, 'The Deacons for Defense and Justice', in Judson L. Jeffries (ed.), *Black Power in the Belly of the Beast*, with a foreword by Tiyi M. Morris (Urbana and Chicago: University of Illinois Press, 2006), pp. 13–42; Simon Wendt, 'The Roots of Black Power?: Armed Resistance and the Radicalization of the Civil Rights Movement', in Peniel E. Joseph (ed.), *The Black*

Power Movement: Rethinking the Civil Rights-Black Power Era (New York and London: Routledge, 2006), pp. 145–65; Simon Wendt, 'Protection or Path Toward Revolution?: Black Power and Self-Defense', *Souls* 9 (October–December 2007), pp. 320–32.

23. Stanford, 'Revolutionary Action Movement', pp. 66–9, 170; Sitkoff, *Struggle for Black Equality*, pp. 185–94; Daniel Matlin, '"Lift Up Yr Self!" Reinterpreting Amiri Baraka (LeRoi Jones), Black Power, and the Uplift Tradition', *Journal of American History* 93 (June 2006), p. 103; Heather Ann Thompson, 'Urban Uprisings: Riots or Rebellions?', in David Farber and Beth Bailey (eds), *The Columbia Guide to America in the 1960s* (New York: Columbia University Press, 2001), pp. 109–17; Christopher B. Strain, *Pure Fire: Self-Defense as Activism in the Civil Rights Era* (Athens and London: University of Georgia Press, 2005), pp. 127–8; Ogbar, *Black Power*, p. 128.

24. Stanford, 'Revolutionary Action Movement', pp. 152, 163, 199.

25. Woodard, *A Nation within a Nation*, pp. 59, 62–8; Matlin, 'Lift Up Yr Self!', pp. 91, 94–9.

26. Scot Brown, *Fighting for US: Maulana Karenga, the US Organization, and Black Cultural Nationalism*, with a foreword by Clayborne Carson (New York and London: New York University Press, 2003), pp. 8–12, 17–28.

27. Ibid., pp. 2, 12, 29, 32, 38–41.

28. Ibid., pp. 1, 4, 33, 67, 79–81.

29. Hasan Kwame Jeffries, 'Organizing for More Than the Vote: The Political Radicalization of Local People in Lowndes County, Alabama, 1965–1966', in Jeanne Theoharis and Komozi Woodard (eds), *Groundwork: Local Black Freedom Movements in America*, with a foreword by Charles M. Payne (New York: New York University Press, 2005), pp. 140–63; Stokely Carmichael and Charles V. Hamilton, *Black Power: The Politics of Liberation in America* (New York: Vintage, 1967), pp. 98–120; Strain, *Pure Fire*, pp. 148–9.

30. Jeffries, 'Organizing for More Than the Vote', p. 155; Aram Goudsouzian, *Down to the Crossroads: Civil Rights, Black Power, and the Meredith March Against Fear* (New York: Farrar, Straus and Giroux, 2014), pp. 7–87.

31. Carmichael and Hamilton, *Black Power*, pp. 88–96; Peniel E. Joseph, *Stokely: A Life* (New York: Basic Civitas, 2014), pp. 5–77; Goudsouzian, *Down to the Crossroads*, pp. 142–3.

32. Carmichael and Hamilton, *Black Power*, pp. 44–6, 52–5, 58–84.

33. Carmichael and Hamilton, *Black Power*, pp. 5–32, 38–9; Dean E. Robinson, *Black Nationalism in American Politics and Thought* (Cambridge: Cambridge University Press, 2001), pp. 2, 88, 90, 93; Richard H. King, *Civil Rights and the Idea of Freedom* (Athens and

London: University of Georgia Press, 1996), pp. 154–5, 245 n. 37; Taylor, *Black Nationalism in the United States*, pp. 238–9, 260 n. 85.

34. Sitkoff, *Struggle for Black Equality*, pp. 198–200; Ogbar, *Black Power*, pp. 63–4; Carson, *In Struggle*, pp. 219–20; Goudsouzian, *Down to the Crossroads*, pp. 39–41, 150–1, 156, 180–1, 242; Joseph, *Stokely*, pp. 118–19.

35. Martin Luther King, Jr, *Where Do We Go from Here: Chaos or Community?* (1967; New York: Bantam: 1968), pp. 34–47, 51.

36. Ibid., pp. 13–14, 36, 55–61, 63, 65, 80–1.

37. Carson, *In Struggle*, pp. 221, 252–7.

38. Carson, *In Struggle*, pp. 192, 223, 236–43; August Meier and Elliott Rudwick, *CORE: A Study in the Civil Rights Movement 1942–1968* (1973; Urbana, Chicago and London: University of Illinois Press, 1975), pp. 414–20, 423–5, 429–30; Herbert H. Haines, *Black Radicals and the Civil Rights Mainstream, 1954–1970* (Knoxville: University of Tennessee Press, 1988), pp. 62–3, 194–5; Ogbar, *Black Power*, pp. 62–3, 73–5.

39. Woodard, *A Nation within a Nation*, pp. 66, 69–70, 85; Joseph, *Waiting 'Til the Midnight Hour*, pp. 154–5; Carson, *In Struggle*, pp. 223–4; Brown, *Fighting for US*, pp. 100–1.

40. Brown, *Fighting for US*, pp. 7, 12–17, 34, 43, 69–70, 163; Floyd W. Hayes III and Judson L. Jeffries, 'Us Does Not Stand for United Slaves!', in Jeffries (ed.), *Black Power in the Belly of the Beast*, pp. 76–7; Matlin, 'Lift Up Yr Self!', p. 101.

41. Brown, *Fighting for US*, pp. 17–18, 21–2, 33–5, 42–3, 45–8, 53–60, 62–7, 69–70, 72–3, 178 n 118, 199 n 78; Hayes and Jeffries, 'Us Does Not Stand for United Slaves!', pp. 83–4. Although NOI policy rejected guns, some members may have carried them. Ogbar, *Black Power*, pp. 69, 128, 229 n. 12.

42. Brown, *Fighting for US*, pp. 82–7.

43. Brown, *Fighting for US*, pp. 82–3, 84–7; Joshua Bloom and Waldo E. Martin, Jr, *Black against Empire: The History and Politics of the Black Panther Party* (Berkeley, Los Angeles and London: University of California Press, 2013), pp. 20–3, 30–5, 39, 43–4; Hugh Pearson, *The Shadow of the Panther: Huey Newton and the Price of Black Power in America* (Reading, MA: Addison-Wesley, 1994), pp. 47, 68–9; Ogbar, *Black Power*, pp. 82, 84–5.

44. Paul Alkebulan, *Survival Pending Revolution: The History of the Black Panther Party* (Tuscaloosa: University of Alabama Press, 2007), pp. xi, xiii–xiv, 4–5, 9–15; Bloom and Martin, *Black against Empire*, pp. 70–3; Evanzz, *Messenger*, pp. 465–8; Ogbar, *Black Power*, pp. 85–6; Akinyele Omowale Umoja, 'Repression Breeds Resistance: The Black Liberation Army and the Radical Legacy of the Black

Panther Party', *New Political Science* 21 (June 1999), p. 135; Walter Rucker, 'Crusader in Exile: Robert F. Williams and the International Struggle for Black Freedom in America', *Black Scholar* 36 (Fall 2006), p. 31; 'Robert F. Williams, "Black Power," and the Roots of the African American Freedom Struggle', p. 565.

45. Floyd W. Hayes, III and Francis A. Kiene, III, '"All Power to the People": The Political Thought of Huey D. Newton and the Black Panther Party', in Charles E. Jones (ed.), *The Black Panther Party Reconsidered* (Baltimore: Black Classic Press, 1998), pp. 160–3; Frantz Fanon, *The Wretched of the Earth* (1961; New York: Grove Weidenfeld, 1963); Ogbar, *Black Power*, pp. 85–6, 94–6; Zoe Colley, 'War without Terms: George Jackson, Black Power and the American Radical Prison Rights Movement, 1941–1971', *History* 101 (April 2016), pp. 270, 275–7; Robyn Ceanne Spencer, 'Inside the Panther Revolution: The Black Freedom Movement and the Black Panther Party in Oakland, California', in Theoharis and Woodard (eds), *Groundwork*, pp. 306–7; Alkebulan, *Survival Pending Revolution*, pp. 13–14. At least two Japanese Americans also joined the BPP. Ogbar, *Black Power*, pp. 168, 173.

46. Ogbar, *Black Power*, pp. 86–8; Alkebulan, *Survival Pending Revolution*, pp. 6, 15, 104; Spencer, 'Inside the Panther Revolution', pp. 307–8; Pearson, *Shadow of the Panther*, pp. 7, 145–7, 221.

47. Stanford, 'Revolutionary Action Movement', pp. 66, 170–3; Bloom and Martin, *Black against Empire*, pp. 67–70; Matlin, 'Lift Up Yr Self!', p. 104.

48. Woodard, *A Nation within a Nation*, p. 70, 84–7; Matlin, 'Lift Up Yr Self!', pp. 103–4; Joseph, *Waiting 'Til the Midnight Hour*, pp. 184, 216–18; Sitkoff, *Struggle for Black Equality*, p. 188; Simon Hall, '"On the Tail of the Panther": Black Power and the 1967 Convention of the National Conference for New Politics', *Journal of American Studies* 37 (April 2003), pp. 66–7; Alphonso Pinkney, *Black Americans*, 5th edn (Upper Saddle River, NJ: Prentice Hall, 1999), p. 46.

49. Sitkoff, *Struggle for Black Equality*, pp. 188–90; Joel D. Auerbach and Jack L. Walker, 'The Meanings of Black Power: A Comparison of White and Black Interpretations of a Political Slogan', *American Political Science Quarterly* 64 (June 1970), pp. 369–73, 383, 387. When asked what Black Power meant to them, 8.2 percent of blacks and 8.6 percent of whites responded 'Don't Know, Can't Say.'

50. Joyce Ladner, 'What Black Power Means to Negroes in Mississippi', in August Meier (ed.), *The Transformation of Activism* (Chicago: Aldine, 1970), pp. 131–54.

51. Peniel E. Joseph, 'Reinterpreting the Black Power Movement', *OAH Magazine of History* 22 (July 2008), p. 5; Joseph, 'Black

Power Movement', pp. 755, 765–6, 768–9, 775; Rhonda Y. Williams, '"We're Tired of Being Treated like Dogs": Poor Women and Power Politics in Black Baltimore', *Black Scholar* 31 (Fall 2001), pp. 31–41; Peter G. Filene, 'An Obituary for "The Progressive Movement"', *American Quarterly* 22 (Spring 1970), pp. 20–34; Carson, *In Struggle*, p. 289; Robert C. Smith, 'Black Power and the Transformation from Protest to Politics', *Political Science Quarterly* 96 (Fall 1981), p. 439. For an alternative view that stresses common themes among Black Power groups 'in one of the broadest movements in U.S. history', see Komozi Woodard, 'Amiri Baraka, the Congress of African People, and Black Power Politics from the 1961 United Nations Protest to the 1972 Gary Convention', in Joseph (ed.), *Black Power Movement*, p. 69 and Komozi Woodard, 'Imamu Baraka, the Newark Congress of African People, and Black Power Politics', in Jeffries (ed.), *Black Power in the Belly of the Beast*, p. 64. Joseph has defined Black Power in different, although not mutually exclusive, ways, such as encompassing 'cultural autonomy, racial pride, and equal citizenship', 'racial solidarity, cultural pride, and self-determination', 'armed self-defense, political and cultural self-determination, and radical internationalism', and 'self-determination and community control'. Joseph, 'Reinterpreting the Black Power Movement', p. 4; Joseph, 'Black Power Movement', pp. 755, 758, 768.

52. Alkebulan, *Survival Pending Revolution*, pp. 6, 10, 15, 49; David J. Garrow, 'Picking Up the Books: The New Historiography of the Black Panther Party', *Reviews in American History* 35 (December 2007), p. 652; Joseph, *Waiting 'Til the Midnight Hour*, pp. 209, 211–12; Eldridge Cleaver, *Soul on Ice* (1968; New York: Dell, 1970), p. 26.

53. Bloom and Martin, *Black against Empire*, pp. 111–14; Joseph, *Waiting 'Til the Midnight Hour*, pp. 191–7, 208, 221–6; Hayes and Kiene, 'All Power to the People', pp. 165–6.

54. Kelley and Esch, 'Black like Mao', pp. 22–3; Hayes and Kiene, 'All Power to the People', pp. 161–2.

55. Hayes and Kiene, 'All Power to the People', pp. 164–6; James E. Westheider, *Fighting on Two Fronts: African Americans and the Vietnam War* (New York and London: New York University Press, 1997), pp. 16, 20, 32–3, 153–4, 156; James E. Westheider, *The African American Experience in Vietnam: Brothers in Arms* (Lanham, Boulder, New York, Toronto and Plymouth: Rowman and Littlefield, 2008), pp. 64–5, 70, 135–6; Bloom and Martin, *Black against Empire*, p. 67.

56. Levy, 'Blacks and the Vietnam War', pp. 210–24; Rhodri Jeffreys-Jones, *Peace Now! American Society and the Ending of the Vietnam War* (New Haven and London: Yale University Press, 1999), pp. 94–125;

Curtis Austin, 'The Black Panthers and the Vietnam War', in Andrew Wiest, Mary Kathryn Barbier and Glenn Robins (eds), *America and the Vietnam War: Re-examining the Culture and History of a Generation* (New York and London: Routledge, 2010), pp. 101–17; Westheider, *Fighting on Two Fronts*, pp. 13–17, 19, 67, 86–9, 92, 141–5, 151; Westheider, *African American Experience in Vietnam*, pp. 25, 49, 72–9, 82–3, 95; Wallace Terry, *Bloods: An Oral History of the Vietnam Wear by Black Veterans* (New York: Ballantine, 1985), pp. 11–12.

57. Cleaver, *Soul on Ice*; Alkebulan, *Survival Pending Revolution*, pp. xiii, 15; Bloom and Martin, *Black against Empire*, pp. 78–9; Garrow, 'Picking Up the Books', pp. 652–3; Joseph, *Waiting 'Til the Midnight Hour*, p. 228.

58. Umoja, 'Repression Breeds Resistance', pp. 135–8; Austin, 'Black Panthers and the Vietnam War', pp. 109–10.

59. Colley, 'War without Terms', pp. 265–86; Zoe Colley, '"All America is a Prison": The Nation of Islam and the Politicization of African American Prisoners, 1955–1965', *Journal of American Studies* 48 (May 2014), p. 414 n. 80.

60. Kelley and Esch, 'Black like Mao', p. 20; Haines, *Black Radicals and the Civil Rights Mainstream*, pp. 68–9; Umoja, 'Repression Breeds Resistance', p. 135; Stanford, 'Revolutionary Action Movement', pp. 126, 132, 143, 163; Christian Davenport, 'Killing the Afro: State Repression, Social Movement Decline and the Death of Black Power', paper in author's possession.

61. Stanford, 'Revolutionary Action Movement', pp. 65–6, 130; Edward Onaci, 'Revolutionary Identities: New Afrikans and Name Choices in the Black Power Movement', *Souls* 17 (January–June 2015), p. 68; Donald Cunnigen, 'Bringing the Revolution Down Home: The Republic of New Africa in Mississippi', *Sociological Spectrum* 19 (January–March 1999), pp. 67, 70–1; Tyson, 'Robert F. Williams, "Black Power," and the Roots of the African American Freedom Struggle', pp. 567–8; Rucker, 'Crusader in Exile', p. 27.

62. Onaci, 'Revolutionary Identities', pp. 67–9, 73–5, 77–8, 84; Matlin, 'Lift Up Yr Self!', p. 110; Davenport, 'Killing the Afro', n.p.; Cunnigen, 'Bringing the Revolution Down Home', p. 72; Haines, *Black Radicals and the Civil Rights Mainstream*, p. 69.

63. Davenport, 'Killing the Afro'; Ahmad A. Rahman, 'Marching Blind: the Rise and Fall of the Black Panther Party in Detroit', in Yohuru Williams and Jama Lazerow (eds), *Liberated Territory: Untold Local Perspectives on the Black Panther Party* (Durham, NC and London: Duke University Press, 2008), pp. 189–90; Cunnigen, 'Bringing the

Revolution Down Home', pp. 68, 72–3, 83; Robinson, *Black Nationalism in American Politics and Thought*, p. 62.

64. James A. Geschwender and Judson Jeffries, 'The League of Revolutionary Black Workers', in Jeffries (ed.), *Black Power in the Belly of the Beast*, pp. 139–42.

65. Stanford, 'Revolutionary Action Movement', p. 134; League of Revolutionary Black Workers, 'General Program (Here's Where We're Coming From), 1970', in William L. Van Deburg (ed.), *Modern Black Nationalism: From Marcus Garvey to Louis Farrakhan* (New York and London: New York University Press, 1997), pp. 189–91; Geschwender and Jeffries, 'League of Revolutionary Black Workers', pp. 138, 144–57; Joel P. Rhodes and Judson L. Jeffries, 'Motor City Panthers', in Judson L. Jeffrie (ed.), *On the Ground: The Black Panther Party in Communities across America* (Jackson: University Press of Mississippi, 2010), pp. 138–40.

66. Bloom and Martin, *Black against Empire*, pp. 2, 13, 48, 181–93, 248–51, 342–6; Ogbar, *Black Power*, pp. 90, 121, 155.

67. Tracye Matthews, '"No One Evers Asks, What a Man's Place in the Revolution is": Gender and the Politics of the Black Panther Party 1966–1971', in Jones (ed.), *Black Panther Party Reconsidered*, pp. 267–304; Bloom and Martin, *Black against Empire*, pp. 95–8, 106, 303–8; Reynaldo Anderson, 'Practical Internationalists: The Story of the Des Moines, Iowa, Black Panther Party', in Theoharis and Woodard (eds), *Groundwork*, pp. 282–99; Ogbar, *Black Power*, pp. 100–6, 184, 224 n. 37, 225 n. 51.

68. Bloom and Martin, *Black against Empire*, pp. 4, 91–4, 210–15, 233–9; Kenneth O'Reilly, *"Racial Matters": The FBI's Secret File on Black America, 1960–1972* (New York: Free Press, 1989), pp. 293–324; Garrow, 'Picking Up the Books', pp. 655–6. There is no scholarly consensus about the size and year of the BPP's peak membership.

69. Van Deburg, *New Day in Babylon*, pp. 17, 159; Bloom and Martin, *Black against Empire*, pp. 353–5; Ogbar, *Black Power*, pp. 121, 193, 196; Alkebulan, *Survival Pending Revolution*, pp. 87, 131–2.

70. Joseph, *Waiting 'Til the Midnight Hour*, pp. 250, 252–4; Hayes and Kiene, 'All Power to the People', pp. 170–2.

71. Alphonso Pinkney, *Red, Black, and Green: Black Nationalism in the United States* (Cambridge: Cambridge University Press, 1976), pp. 123–4; William W. Sales, Jr, *From Civil Rights to Black Liberation: Malcolm X and the Organization of Afro-American Unity* (Boston: South End Press, 1994), p. 195; Bloom and Martin, *Black against Empire*, pp. 192–3; Matlin, 'Lift Up Yr Self!', p. 102; Regina Jennings, 'Poetry of the Black Panther Party: Metaphors of Militancy', *Journal of Black Studies* 29 (September 1998), pp. 110–28; Ward,

Just My Soul Responding, pp. 412–15; Brian Ward, 'Jazz and Soul, Race and Class, Cultural Nationalists and Black Panthers: A Black Power Debate Revisited', in Brian Ward (ed.), *Media, Culture, and the Modern African American Freedom Struggle* (Gainesville: University Press of Florida, 2001), pp. 161–4, 175–87; Ogbar, *Black Power*, pp. 94–100, 107–14, 116–22, 194–5, 223 n. 26; Joe Street, *The Culture War in the Civil Rights Movement* (Gainesville: University Press of Florida, 2007), pp. 144–60.

72. Van Deburg, *New Day in Babylon*, p. 9; Woodard, *A Nation within a Nation*, pp. 106–13, 120; Matlin, 'Lift Up Yr Self!', pp. 103 n. 31, 105. The Arabic words *Amiri* and *Baraka* meant 'prince' and 'blessed'. Alex Houen, 'Amira Baraka', *The Literary Encyclopedia*, available at <http://www.litencyc.com/php/speople.php?rec=true&UID=247> (last accessed 24 April 2010).

73. Woodard, *A Nation within a Nation*, p. 120; Matlin, 'Lift Up Yr Self!', pp. 93, 106–10, 115–16; Komozi Woodard, 'It's Nation Time in NewArk: Amiri Baraka and the Black Power Experiment in Newark, New Jersey', in Theoharis and Woodard (eds), *Freedom North*, pp. 299–300.

74. Bloom and Martin, *Black against Empire*, pp. 218–22; Garrow, 'Picking Up the Books', pp. 653–4; Brown, *Fighting for US*, pp. 88–99.

75. Pinkney, *Red, Black, and Green*, pp. 164–70; National Committee of Black Churchmen, 'The Black Declaration of Independence, 1970', in Van Deburg (ed.), *Modern Black Nationalism*, pp. 225–8.

76. James F. Findlay, Jr, *Church People in the Struggle: The National Council of Churches and the Black Freedom Movement, 1950–1970* (New York and Oxford: Oxford University Press, 1993), pp. 199–223.

77. Pinkney, *Red, Black, and Green*, pp. 170–1; James H. Cone, *Black Theology and Black Power* (New York: Seabury Press, 1969), p. 143.

78. Albert B. Cleage, Jr, 'The Black Messiah and the Black Revolution, 1969', in Van Deburg (ed.), *Modern Black Nationalism*, pp. 229–39; Angela D. Dillard, 'Religion and Radicalism: The Reverend Albert B. Cleage, Jr, and the Rise of Black Christian Nationalism in Detroit', in Theoharis and Woodard (eds), *Freedom North*, pp. 153–7, 170–1; 'This Far by Faith: Albert Cleage', available at <http://www.pbs.org/thisfarbyfaith/people/albert_cleage.html> (last accessed 26 March 2015); *New York Times*, 27 February 2000; Pinkney, *Red, Black, and Green*, pp. 171–3, 175.

79. Pinkney, *Red, Black, and Green*, pp. 177–90; Joseph, *Waiting 'Til the Midnight Hour*, pp. 215–16; Ogbar, *Black Power*, pp. 136–7, 140–2.

80. Pinkney, *Red, Black, and Green*, pp. 194–8; Stephen Ward, '"Scholarship in the Context of Struggle": Activist Intellectuals, the Institute of the Black World (IBB), and the Contours of Black Power

Radicalism', *Black Scholar* 31 (Fall 2001), pp. 42–53; Derrick E. White, 'An Independent Approach to Black Studies: The Institute of the Black World (IBW) and Its Evaluation and Support of Black Studies', *Journal of African American Studies* 16 (March 2012), pp. 70–80; Derrick E. White, *The Challenge of Blackness: The Institute of the Black World and Political Activism in the 1970s* (Gainesville and other cities: University Press of Florida, 2011); Joseph, *Waiting 'Til the Midnight Hour*, pp. 215–16.

81. Alex Poinsett, 'The Dilemma of the Black Policeman', *Ebony* 26 (May 1971), p. 126; Pinkney, *Red, Black, and Green*, pp. 76, 81–4, 89–93; Ogbar, *Black Power*, pp. 142–4; Smith, 'Black Power and the Transformation from Protest to Politics', pp. 436–7.

82. Woodard, *A Nation within a Nation*, p. 139; Van Deburg, *New Day in Babylon*, pp. 17–18, 192–234; Ward, *Just My Soul Responding*, pp. 389–92, 395–400, 410–12, 449; Ward, 'Jazz and Soul, Race and Class, Cultural Nationalists and Black Panthers', pp. 169–72, 176, 182, 189, 195 n. 77; Ogbar, *Black Power*, pp. 111–13; Dick Weissman, *Talkin' 'Bout a Revolution: Music and Social Change in America* (New York: Backbeat, 2010), pp. 98–103.

83. Woodard, *A Nation within a Nation*, pp. 114–15, 150–3, 162–4, 167–8.

84. Woodard, *A Nation within a Nation*, pp. 120–1, 164–8, 171; Brown, *Fighting for US*, pp. 120–6.

85. Ogbar, *Black Power*, p. 159.

CHAPTER 5

Black Nationalism, 1971–1995

The early 1970s witnessed many black nationalist organisations wane and sometimes abandon black nationalism. However, the Nation of Islam (NOI), which had influenced the development of much of Black Power and black nationalism, thrived, many African American leaders met in 1972 in a National Black Political Convention chaired by Amiri Baraka, and Black Power continued to influence black culture. Nevertheless, by the mid-1970s, black nationalism declined as an organisational entity and the Black Power era ended. Baraka moved towards Marxism–Leninism, and, after the death of Elijah Muhammad in 1975, his son and successor Wallace D. Muhammad steered the NOI toward orthodox Sunni Islam, abandoning the doctrines and business enterprises of his father. Louis Farrakhan left the reformed Nation, now known as the World Community of Al-Islam in the West (WCIW), in 1977. Eventually, he sought to restore a modified NOI. Farrakhan's NOI struggled initially before achieving growing success from the mid-1980s. In the same decade, the development of Afrocentricity, which historian Tunde Adeleke explains 'proposes Africa as the source of self-definition, self-affirmation, and identity for blacks in the United States and throughout the diaspora', brought renewed vibrancy to African American Studies programmes and reinvigorated cultural black nationalism. The emergence of musical forms such as rap and hip hop also helped disseminate black nationalist themes, especially in combination with a renewed interest in Malcolm X that was also engendered by a 1992 Hollywood film based on his autobiography, and by perceived and actual worsening social and economic conditions experienced by many African Americans. The charismatic Farrakhan benefited from and contributed to the resurgence of interest in black nationalism, but the Million Man March he called in 1995 was less of an endorsement of his ideas than his leading role implied.[1]

Black Nationalism in the Early 1970s

In the early 1970s, internal tensions wracked several black groups formed in the second half of the 1960s. In 1971, the League of Revolutionary Black Workers split amid ideological disagreements about whether to concentrate on racism and capitalism or undertake a broad-based struggle that addressed sexual discrimination and imperialism, and whether to work with white leftists. The League withered during the next few years.[2]

Factionalism in the Black Panther Party (BPP) also became increasingly public during 1971. Huey P. Newton expelled Elmer 'Geronimo' Pratt (Geronimo ji-Jaga), already under arrest for murder, most of the New York 21, Eldridge Cleaver (still in Algerian exile) and the party's international section for advocating guerrilla warfare to usher in armed revolution. Newton and the party's Central Committee focused on community programmes and dismissed dissenting calls for immediate revolutionary struggle as unrealistic. Several weeks later, the murder of two Panthers in New York, Robert Webb and Samuel Napier, who were on opposite sides of the schism, exposed the BPP's factional divide. Many members subsequently left the party. When Panther George Jackson, a Marxist revolutionary, was killed, guards claimed, trying to escape from San Quentin State Prison in California in August 1971, the *Black Panther* praised his life but made no calls for vengeance or revolution.[3]

In the same month, police and Federal Bureau of Investigation (FBI) officers raided the headquarters of the Republic of New Africa (RNA) in Jackson, Mississippi, ostensibly to arrest a fugitive suspected of murder in Detroit who was not present. When fired upon after being given only a seventy-five second warning to vacate the building, RNA members shot back. One policeman died and an FBI agent and policeman were injured in the shootout. Eleven RNA members, including three women, were arrested, with charges ranging from murder to waging war against Mississippi. Although some charges were dropped, most of the arrested received lengthy jail terms and three of them life sentences. After the raid, ten other RNA members were arrested on misdemeanour charges and most received short jail terms. In September, sixty-five Detroit police raided the RNA's House of Uhuru and, on the same day, police arrested three other RNA members in Michigan accused of murder, although two were later acquitted. In November, police also targeted three RNA members in New Mexico, but they escaped and forced a plane to take them to Cuba. Other arrests, charges, incarcerations and harassment followed, while the RNA continued to press its claims for reparations from the United States and the creation of an independent socialist republic in the Deep South. Hamstrung by raids, arrests and incarcerations, the RNA was severely undermined, and it was never able to generate significant support in the African American community. By the early 1980s, most of its imprisoned members had been released from prison. The RNA continued but made little impact.[4]

Surveying its earlier years, sociologist Donald Cunnigen argues that the RNA was unable to attract support because of competition from other black nationalist groups, such as the BPP, which were 'able to garner greater public support and attention'. Yet, he also contends that the RNA was undone by its publicity seeking, writing that 'the RNA's greatest weakness was its constant and sometimes self-defeating, manipulation of the media to promote its agenda', which brought 'unwanted attention from the White Mississippi authorities'. While state repression decimated the RNA's operating capacity, its fundamental weakness lay in its ideas' lack of appeal for the overwhelming majority of the African American population.[5]

US had lost much of its support in the African American community after organisation members killed two Black Panthers on the University of California, Los Angeles campus in 1969. Increasingly authoritarian and paranoid, in June 1971 US leader Maulana Karenga was convicted of assault and false imprisonment of two women, Gail Idili-Davis and Brenda Jones, and was sentenced to one-to-ten years in jail. Even before Karenga's imprisonment, women in US had been organised into paramilitary units, which historian Scot Brown argues, 'had a progressive impact on the organization's eventual move away from a doctrine of male supremacy to its acceptance of gender equality in the early seventies'. With Karenga in jail, US saw the fall in its membership continue and its endeavours correspondingly decline.[6]

Once mentored by Karenga, cultural nationalist Amiri Baraka of the Congress of African People (CAP) increased his political influence. During 1971, Baraka and Roy Innis of the Congress of Racial Equality (CORE) participated in a series of meetings with prominent liberal integrationist African American political and civil rights figures as they sought ways to bolster the impact of a black electorate, enlarged by the Voting Rights Act of 1965, in the upcoming federal elections. Unable to agree on a common approach, they accepted Baraka's suggestion for a national black convention. Concerns from established black leaders that radicals might take the convention over were partly assuaged by designating Congressman Charles Diggs of Michigan, chair of the Congressional Black Caucus, and Gary, Indiana, Mayor Richard Hatcher as two of its three co-convenors, alongside Baraka, who realised that calling for an independent black political party, his and CAP's preferred option, would be unacceptable to elected black politicians. Even so, before the convention met, the National Association for the Advancement of Colored People objected to what it regarded as the 'separatist' and 'radical' tone of its draft preamble that called for 'fundamental change' in America and 'an independent black political movement'.[7]

Held over three days in March 1972 in Gary, after just three months of preparation, the National Black Political Convention was too hastily organised. While each black elected official received a seat at the convention and the major civil rights groups ten delegates each, the convention allocated the remaining delegates according to the percentage size of the black population in each state but without rules for delegate selection. Some state delegations reflected democratic processes, while others were arbitrary. Without clear rules and procedures and lacking administrative support, the convention's opening session became disorderly. Amid the chaos, Baraka's personal drive enabled him, with CAP support, to replace Diggs as presiding officer.[8]

An effort to ensure that all strands of convention opinion were represented in its agenda resulted in a document that combined nationalist demands, such as reparations for slavery and discrimination and recognition of the RNA's 'right to hold a plebiscite among blacks to determine whether the United States should be divided into separate homelands for blacks and whites', with liberal reformist calls for welfare change, national health insurance and federal employment initiatives. The convention also approved two divisive resolutions, a CORE sponsored call for 'Black community control of our school system and a guarantee of an equal share of the money' and support for Palestinian self-determination that also denounced Israeli occupation of land taken in the 1967 war. To facilitate continuation of its work, the convention chose to create a National Black Political Assembly (NBPA), comprising 10 per cent of the delegates, that would hold quarterly meetings, and a National Black Political Council to attend to administrative needs.[9]

With considerable hyperbole, historian Manning Marable regards the convention as 'the zenith not only of black nationalism, but of the entire black movement during the Second Reconstruction'. Convention speakers included Bobby Seale of the BPP and the NOI's Louis Farrakhan. The Reverend Jesse Jackson, who had worked with Martin Luther King, Jr, in the Southern Christian Leadership Conference, asked the conference 'What time is it?' to elicit the response 'It's Nation Time!' Adopting a black nationalist tone, he told the delegates that 'We must form a black political party.' Historian Komozi Woodard notes that 'A number of civil rights leaders, including Coretta Scott King, raised their clenched fists in a Black Power salute during the Black National Anthem and joined the assembly as it roared, "It's Nation Time!"'[10]

However, weeks later the Congressional Black Caucus, formed in 1969, issued an alternative to the convention's agenda that reaffirmed traditional liberal goals of education, employment, health care and welfare measures and identified them as the price of black support for the two major political parties. Jesse Jackson endorsed South Dakota's white Democratic Senator George McGovern's unsuccessful campaign for the presidency, praising McGovern's economic liberalism and opposition to American involvement in the Vietnam War.[11]

Completing its transition from revolutionary nationalism to reformism, in 1972 the BPP deleted its call for a United Nations-supervised plebiscite in the black community from its ten-point programme and announced that Chairman Bobby Seale and Minister of Information Elaine Brown would stand for mayor of Oakland and a city council seat respectively in 1973. To aid their campaigns, the party subsequently called on party members to close all of its other chapters and concentrate their efforts on Oakland, which party leaders hoped would provide a blueprint for eventual electoral victories in other cities. While a few Panther chapters continued, most of them closed, and many left the Panthers' ranks unwilling to relocate to Oakland, where the BPP returned to being mostly a local group.[12]

Stokely Carmichael, who had resigned from the Black Panthers in 1969 and, amid frequent travels, eventually relocated to Guinea, established the modestly supported All-African People's

Revolutionary Party (AAPRP) in 1972. He argued that African Americans should prioritise the liberation of Africa from colonialism and make it one nation under socialism. Carmichael made frequent speaking tours of the United States and other countries on the AAPRP's behalf.[13]

Sometime Carmichael associate Owusu Sadaukai (Howard Fuller), who was originally from Milwaukee and had co-founded Malcolm X Liberation University, expressed his Pan-Africanism by organising the first African Liberation Day (ALD) in May 1972 that saw demonstrations in Washington, DC, and San Francisco, as well as in Canada and three Caribbean islands. Opposed to colonialism in Angola, Guinea-Bissau, Mozambique, Namibia and Rhodesia, ALD represented another manifestation of cooperation between Black Power advocates and black politicians. Amiri Baraka and a dashiki-wearing Charles Diggs, the chair of the House Subcommittee on Africa, spoke at the Washington, DC, demonstration, which attracted up to 30,000 people. Planning for ALD led, with the aid of CAP, to the founding of the African Liberation Support Committee (ALSC), a lobbying and organising group. Annual ALDs followed through the 1970s but none matched the attendance of the first, and by the mid-1970s, the ALSC was defunct as a result of divisions between black nationalists and Marxist–Leninists, which also appeared among the North American contingent of over 200 blacks who attended the Sixth Pan-African Congress, held in Dar es Salaam, Tanzania, in June 1974. The congress, African American Studies scholar La TaSha Levy explains, 'rejected Black Nationalism and racial Pan-Africanism in favor of a strictly class-based analysis'.[14]

Elaine Brown, who had attended the first ALD, failed, like Bobby Seale, in her Oakland election effort in 1973. Huey P. Newton and his entourage became increasingly violent and criminal in their behaviour. Whether through expulsion or resignation, by 1974 Seale and David Hilliard had left the party. Accused of murder and assault, Newton fled to Cuba in 1974 before returning to the United States in 1977 and being acquitted. During his absence, Brown ran what remained of the party. A Panther school operated in Oakland until the party's demise in 1982. While the BPP entered conventional politics in the early 1970s, some former members of the party joined others in the Black Liberation Army (BLA) committed to armed insurrection and urban guerrilla warfare. BLA members launched attacks on the police, freed imprisoned members, and robbed banks to sustain themselves and their operations. Increasingly isolated and with little support, by the mid-1970s the BLA had been largely, but not entirely, destroyed by state authorities.[15]

The NBPA also declined. In 1974, it attracted fewer black political leaders and others to its second convention in Little Rock, Arkansas. The convention rejected forming a political party, unable to agree on its function. As political scientist Robert C. Smith explains, integrationists wanted 'to mobilize the black vote as an independent force in American politics', whereas Baraka and his supporters envisaged 'a party that would combine electoral activism with community organizing and revolutionary action'. Soon after the convention, Baraka announced his rejection of cultural nationalism in favour of Marxism–Leninism–Maoism, contending that capitalism had to be overturned in order to end racism. In 1975, his political reorientation ended his role as NBPA secretary-general. CAP followed its leader's communist conversion and became the Revolutionary Communist League and, like Baraka, continued community work among Newark and New York's black populace. However, Baraka's new direction further undermined an already factionalised and diminished Black Arts Movement. A diminished NBPA lingered on for a few more years, making little impression. When Maulana Karenga was released from prison in 1975, he also championed scientific socialism and emphasised the need to address both class and racial subjugation. By contrast, disillusioned with Communism, Eldridge Cleaver returned to the United States in 1975 in a deal with the government that dropped an attempted murder charge against him. Given community service for assault, he became an evangelical Christian.[16]

While the Panthers and Baraka had moved away from nationalism, the NOI remained the largest black nationalist group. Increasingly focused on developing the NOI's business enterprises, its leader Elijah Muhammad retreated from the blanket condemnation of whites as devils that had been a cornerstone of NOI theology since its founding. In 1972, Muhammad declared that white Muslim converts would be spared from destruction in the coming Armageddon. Two years later, he told Muslims at the annual Saviour's Day to respect whites and stop calling them 'the devil'. Long in poor health, Muhammad died a year later.[17]

The Nation of Islam after Elijah Muhammad

Elijah Muhammad's son Wallace D. Muhammad, only recently returned to the NOI after periodic suspensions for deviating from NOI theology, succeeded his father as leader and swiftly moved the NOI away from black nationalism to acceptance of Sunni Islam. He abandoned the conception of whites as a devil race, closed the Fruit of Islam (FOI), encouraged voting and political involvement, and sold off the NOI's businesses. An unknown but likely small number left the NOI, which its new leader renamed the WCIW and opened to whites. Those who remained accepted the transition as a continuation of the incorporation of Sunni religious practices seen in the NOI since the 1960s and Elijah Muhammad's late softening of NOI racial orthodoxy and as God's plan. Many members also reasoned that the former Nation's teachings had been historically conditioned, and they welcomed the lifting of the NOI's more restrictive requirements.[18]

Several prominent figures left the WCIW and began their own versions of the former NOI. Sidelined in the WCIW and uncomfortable with its teachings, Louis Farrakhan, formerly Elijah Muhammad's leading minister, left in 1977 and eventually built the largest and most influential reconstituted NOI. While Farrakhan still regarded W. D. Fard as Allah and accepted the Yacub story, he recognised that African Americans were unlikely to relocate to Africa or receive territory from the United States. He also departed from the old NOI's apolitical stance by supporting Harold Washington's election as Chicago's first black mayor in 1983 and Jesse Jackson's campaign for the Democratic Party's presidential nomination in 1984. Jackson, who had apologised for calling Jews 'Hymies' and New York 'Hymie Town', condemned Farrakhan's subsequent reference to Judaism as a 'dirty religion'. Jackson finished third. His campaign boosted black voter registration and made Farrakhan a national and international figure, able to draw substantial audiences. He subsequently conducted a fourteen-city American speaking tour, secured a $5 million loan from Libyan leader Muammar Gaddafi, building on the precedent of a $3 million loan from Gaddafi to the NOI in 1973, and visited Ghana, meeting with President Jerry Rawlings. Although banned from entering the United Kingdom for anti-Semitism, Farrakhan also cultivated a following among some black British people.[19]

Furthermore, Farrakhan benefited from a comparative dearth of leadership among African Americans and the demise or decline of many prominent Black Power groups. While the NOI continued to grow, many blacks outside its ranks admired Farrakhan less for his religious views than his denunciations of what he regarded as the federal government's 'genocidal plot' to subordinate black men and his advocacy of black uplift. While Jackson called for federal government programmes to address poverty, crime, gang culture, drug use and male youth imprisonment in the black community, Farrakhan increased the NOI's prison ministry and called on black men to assume responsibility for supporting their families through hard work, discipline, thrift and strict personal morality. In doing so, he was consistent with Elijah Muhammad's approach.[20]

However, Farrakhan dispensed far more 'original' names than Muhammad and upgraded him from the Last Messenger to Christ or the Messiah. According to Vibert L. White, Jr, a disillusioned former member, '[N]ow anyone could get a name. The only requirement was that one be an officer in the Nation or be in attendance when the minister [Farrakhan] decided to rename individuals.' Despite its traditional suspicion of the federal government, the NOI had sought matching federal funding for a job training programme in 1970. Under Farrakhan, private security agencies closely connected with the NOI won federal contracts in several cities. Although he largely reiterated Muhammad's strictures on male and female conduct, Farrakhan's marked condemnations of black men's transgressions against black women and acceptance of abortion in cases of rape and incest marked a departure from the old NOI. He also made greater efforts to recruit from among Hispanic and Native Americans and sought to establish a presence in West Africa, holding Saviours' Day, as Farrakhan had renamed it to indicate that followers must save themselves and their neighbourhoods, in Accra, Ghana, in 1994.[21]

Farrakhan restored the FOI and the Muslim Girls' Training and General Civilization Class, purchased the old NOI's former Chicago headquarters and other buildings in an effort to establish his legitimacy, and oversaw the growth of NOI membership and businesses. He adopted much of the speaking style of Malcolm X and the black jeremiad nationalist tradition of castigating white America for its treatment of blacks while calling on them to uplift themselves. While Malcolm X, and less frequently Elijah Muhammad, had made anti-Semitic comments, Farrakhan did so more often and more sweepingly.[22]

Afrocentricity

While Farrakhan rebuilt the most successful of the revived NOIs, the 1980s also saw the growth of Afrocentricity, an approach with origins that dated back to the eighteenth century. Its most prominent and prolific advocate, Molefi Kete Asante, born Arthur Lee Smith in Georgia, explains that Afrocentricity puts 'African ideals at the center of any analysis that involves African culture and behavior'. Rather than originate, Asante helped to popularise the notion that Kemet (ancient Egypt) had a major influence on the development of African culture and ancient Greece that also shaped European learning and civilisation. Afrocentrists maintained that modern day Africans, whether on the continent or part of a diaspora that included African Americans, possessed shared core cultural traits, an 'African Cultural System', that were unadulterated by the passage of time, different historical experiences and geographical dispersion.[23]

Critics noted that Asante promoted a form of cultural essential ism that ignored evident cultural diversity in Africa and the black diaspora. Historian Algernon Austin also observes that if 'ancient Greek knowledge is really ancient Egyptian knowledge, there would be no need for Afrocentrism because the Western culture is already Afrocentric, and there would be no such thing as Eurocentrism'. Although Afrocentricity disclaimed any notion of cultural superiority, it made simplistic generalisations about humankind and presented African peoples more sympathetically than others. Asante claimed that 'the European seeks to conquer nature, to subdue it, the Asian flees from the illusions of the world, and the African finds coexistence with nature and a harmonious relationship with all of the elements of the universe'. Austin correctly notes that 'In Afrocentric thought, European culture is described by such negative terms as patriarchal, xenophobic, violent, criminal, and pessimistic', whereas 'African culture is the opposite of all these things'. Afrocentrists regarded African Americans as Africans, which raised the question of why did Afrocentrists focus so much on seeking to use schools and universities to teach African Americans the 'African Cultural System' that they supposedly already shared? Those who did not share such culture, Asante claimed, were 'off-center, mis-educated, de-centered, or culturally insane'.[24]

Unlike the cultural nationalists of the Black Power era, who were both culturally and politically engaged, Afrocentrists focused solely on culture. Whereas some Black Power advocates, such as Baraka, had endorsed female subordination, Afrocentrists, Austin explains, denied that 'sexism exists, or has ever existed, among blacks' and regard 'sexism as a Eurocentric tradition and feminism as an equally Eurocentric response'. Insofar as any sexism might exist among African Americans, Afrocentrists attribute it to 'internalization of Eurocentric values'.[25]

Afrocentrism was part of what Austin views as a 'resurgence of black nationalism' in the late 1980s and 1990s that resulted from African Americans' pessimism 'about their prospects in American society' based on real and perceived developments. The conservative Republican administrations of Ronald Reagan and George H. W. Bush opposed affirmative action, decried welfare and sought to weaken civil rights enforcement. Incidents of white racial violence against African Americans made more blacks inclined to view whites as racists. The spread of crack cocaine and AIDS was devastating for many poor black communities. Some African Americans believed that the federal government and/or whites were implicated in both as a means to control the black population. Influenced by popular news reporting and academic studies, many Americans, both liberal and conservative, believed that a permanent underclass had developed, largely populated by the black poor, that was reliant on 'welfare, crime, or drugs' and producing too many offspring. Although statistical evidence suggests that poverty, violent crime and teenage pregnancy were no greater in the 1980s, and sometimes less, than in the 1970s, the widespread perception of a dependent underclass helped to fuel a rightward shift in American politics. Moreover, Bush's Democratic successor, Bill Clinton, limited access to welfare, which particularly affected African Americans who comprised a disproportionate number of the poor.[26]

A popular notion that black communities were hamstrung by an underclass, low self-esteem and unsuccessful schools was also shared by Afrocentrists, who believed that exposure to Afrocentric education would raise black self-esteem and thereby increase black educational performance, entry into well-paid employment, and growth in two-parent families. Afrocentrists regarded black poverty as a product of the wrong cultural values rather than racial and economic inequalities. Afrocentrism was, Austin claims, 'fairly conservative', and, unlike the Black Power era, did not seek political goals such as African socialism, now largely discredited by economic failures. Afrocentricity made no demands on the state or whites, other than support or tolerance of Afrocentric education in, generally black, public schools, and Afrocentric programmes in colleges and universities.[27]

Austin refutes the notion that blacks lacked self-esteem or felt self-hatred, which he also dismisses as unrelated to educational achievement, noting that 'Black American students score high on self-esteem measures but have relatively low academic achievement', the reverse of Asian Americans. Furthermore, during the 1980s school educational tests indicated that 'blacks improved absolutely and in relation to whites'.[28]

The most prominent Afrocentrists, like many of their supporters, were largely middle class. Afrocentrism allowed its adherents to aspire to and live middle class lives while celebrating an African cultural identity. The black middle class, especially women, largely popularised a *Kwanzaa* observance that was no longer antithetical to Christianity, integration and capitalism. Only prosperous blacks could finance trips to Africa. Afrocentricity was in some ways akin to nineteenth-century 'civilisationism' in that it sought to uplift the black poor by changing their supposed cultural deficiencies. Maulena Karenga, who had sought to remake blacks culturally in the Black Power era, revitalised US and forged an academic career as an Afrocentrist.[29]

In the 1980s and 1990s, African American popular culture increasingly identified with Africa and iconography from the Black Power era. Many black parents gave their offspring pseudo-African, African and Muslim names, identified with blackness since the growth of Elijah Muhammad's NOI. Beginning in 1988, Jesse Jackson championed and popularised the replacement of the term black with African American. Hip-hop nationalists, including Public Enemy and Ice Cube, referenced and celebrated Black Power figures and Africa in their music and fashion. Spike Lee's 1992 film, *Malcolm X*, both reflected and stimulated renewed interest in its subject and ended with a contribution from Nelson Mandela, soon to become South Africa's first post-apartheid president.[30]

The Million Man March

Opinion polls in the 1990s suggested that a majority of African Americans favoured significant indicators of black nationalism, many more than had supported them during the late 1960s when black nationalist groups had proliferated, and that nationalism drew greater support from the middle than the lower class, with the middle class more attracted to Afrocentrist emphases on culture and racial pride. Just as in the Black Power era, black nationalists were far more likely to support black control of black community structures and services than racial separatism. With less hope for upward mobility and opportunity in America, lower class blacks were disproportionately inclined toward separatism. Support for black nationalism rose significantly after the televised police beating of black motorist Rodney King in Los Angeles in 1991, and the acquittal of four police officers for the beating in 1992 that led to a three-day riot in Los Angeles which left 52 dead and 2,500 injured. A poll of African Americans conducted in 1993 and 1994, found that 73.9 per cent of respondents thought 'blacks should control the economy in their communities' and 68.3 per cent govern there. Smaller majorities favoured 'participation in black-only organisations (56.5 percent)' and blacks forming 'their own political party (50.1 percent)', but only 14 per cent thought that 'blacks should form their own nation'.[31]

Analysing such date, political scientists Robert A. Brown and Todd C. Shaw distinguish between community nationalism, akin to Malcolm X's post-NOI nationalism, in which 'African Americans should control and support communities and institutions where they predominate' and separatist nationalism, advocated by the RNA, in which 'black independence must be territorial, juridical, and statist, or, at least a symbolic representation of each'. Nationalism of both kinds had more appeal for the young, but community nationalism received more support from the black middle and upper class and separatist nationalism from the lower class. Community nationalists were more likely than separatists to belong to black organisations and believe in 'group advancement in line with the traditional narrative of American pluralism'. By contrast, working class and poor separatists had 'not experienced dramatic improvements in quality of life during the post-civil rights era' and were more supportive of 'measures that seek to either challenge or greatly reform the present system'. While support for community nationalism was 'gender-neutral', black men were more likely than black women to support separatist nationalism. Brown and Shaw suggested that 'black women are equally attracted to community nationalist strategies [as men] because they conceive of them as more reasonable and more open to embracing a broader agenda – racism, poverty, *and* sexism – than do separatism and its primary emphasis upon race'.[32] Despite its popularity, black nationalism lacked leadership. While popular hip-hop nationalists articulated nationalist themes in their music and some like Public Enemy supported the NOI, they were not organisers or leaders and often struggled against expectations that they should be. Rap nationalists frequently referenced the NOI and many belonged to the Five-Percent Nation, an NOI derivative formed in 1964 that also held Louis Farrakhan, the most prominent nationalist leader, in esteem. Farrakhan and his NOI, the largest black nationalist group, also gained support for undertaking community programmes in black urban neighbourhoods.[33]

In October 1995, the Farrakhan-initiated Million Man March in Washington, DC, brought between 400,000 and over a million African American men to the nation's capital, where they pledged to fulfil their responsibilities to black women, children and communities, and atone for previous neglect. Feminists, such as Angela Davis and Julianne Malveaux, objected to the march's exclusion of women, but most black women supported its male focus. Women, who had the ignored the march organisers' call for them to stay at home to pray and fast in a parallel Day of Absence along with men unable to attend the march, formed 3 per cent of the attendance. The march featured several women, including Maya Angelou and Rosa Parks, among a list of speakers that ranged from integrationists to nationalists. Farrakhan emphasised self-help, self-reliance and the creation of black businesses. While he consented to a voter registration drive before the march, he did not look to government for solutions but for black men to uplift themselves and their communities by their own efforts. The march mission statement, written by Maulana Karenga, emphasised atonement, reconciliation, responsibility and the *Nguzo Saba* but also condemned government and corporate complicity in racism, demanded government reparations and proposed holding a black political convention.[34]

The march was the largest by African Americans in their history and, despite a poor speech that digressed confusingly into numerology, a triumph for Farrakhan. The NOL had worked with a range of black groups to broaden the march's appeal and Farrakhan had, accordingly, softened his separatist message in the preceding months. Surveys had consistently suggested widespread support for Farrakhan in the black community, at least in part driven by a lack of alternative leaders and a belief that whites had denounced him because of his race, with 67 per cent regarding him an 'effective leader' in a 1994 poll and 62 per cent as 'good for the black community'. A *Washington Post* survey found that 87 per cent of Million Man March participants interviewed regarded Farrakhan favourably. However, only 5 per cent said they had attended mainly to support him, the same percentage who identified themselves as members of the NOI. Twenty-nine per cent attended primarily to demonstrate support for the black family, 25 per cent mainly to endorse black men assuming greater family and community responsibility, and another 25 per cent mostly to show black unity.[35]

The march did not imply greater support for separatist than community nationalism. Brown and Shaw note 'a large majority of black men interviewed at the nationalist-led Million Man March did not identify themselves as nationalists', although the 'vast majority' endorsed 'broad ideals of black autonomy'. Although only 10.8 per cent of the marchers regarded themselves as national-ists, scholars Joseph McCormick and Sekou Franklin nevertheless detected 'a deeply rooted nationalist sentiment among those who attended this event', grounded more in community nationalism, such as 'pooling financial resources in a Black-owned bank, devel-oping more Black-owned businesses, and buying more goods and services from Black-owned businesses', than separatist ideas, such as forming an independent black political party and federal repa-rations for slavery. Perhaps reflecting the cost and difficulties of attending on a work day, the marchers were generally more pros-perous and more educated than most blacks, and so drawn from those among whom community nationalism was likely to receive greatest support. Only 7.4 per cent of participants had an income below $15,000, while 77.8 per cent had incomes above $25,000. Most of those in attendance were from Washington, DC, New York and Philadelphia and so not geographically representative of the wider black population.[36]

Farrakhan failed to build on the march's momentum and instead embarked on a series of foreign tours for the NOI, although the march likely contributed to increased black male voting turnout in the 1996 elections. However, black nationalism in America was far more extensive than the NOI's membership, and the mid-1990s saw far more African Americans supporting black nationalist ideas than had ever done during the black nationalist resurgence of the 1960s.

Black nationalism in its various forms was also stronger in the black middle and upper class than the lower class, and it mostly took cultural forms rather than politically activist ones.[37]

Notes

1. Tunde Adeleke, 'Black Americans and Africa: A Critique of the Pan-African and Identity Paradigms', *International Journal of African Historical Studies* 31 (October 1998), p. 509.
2. James A. Geschwender, 'The League of Revolutionary Black Workers: Problems Confronting Black Marxist-Leninist Organizations', *Journal of Ethnic Studies* 2 (Fall 1974), p. 12.
3. Joshua Bloom and Waldo E. Martin, Jr, *Black against Empire: The History and Politics of the Black Panther Party* (Berkeley, Los Angeles and London: University of California Press, 2013), pp. 354–80.
4. Chokwe Lumumba, 'Short History of the U.S. War on the R.N.A.', *Black Scholar* 12 (January–February 1981), pp. 72–80; 'The Repression of the RNA', *Black Scholar* 3 (October 1971), p. 57; Donald Cunnigen, 'Bringing the Revolution Down Home: The Republic of New Africa in Mississippi', *Sociological Spectrum* 19 (January–March 1999), pp. 74–6.
5. Cunnigen, 'Bringing the Revolution Down Home', pp. 79–90.
6. Scot Brown, *Fighting for US: Maulana Karenga, the US Organization, and Black Cultural Nationalism*, with a foreword by Clayborne Carson (New York and London: New York University Press, 2003), pp. 120–5.
7. Robert C. Smith, *We Have No Leaders: African Americans in the Post-Civil Rights Era*, with a foreword by Ronald C. Waters (Albany: State University of New York Press, 1996), pp. 39–44, 46–7; Komozi Woodard, *A Nation within a Nation: Amiri Baraka (LeRoi Jones) and Black Power Politics* (Chapel Hill and London: University of North Carolina Press, 1999), p. 193.
8. Smith, *We Have No Leaders*, pp. 44–6.
9. Ibid., pp. 47–52.
10. Manning Marable, *Race, Reform, and Rebellion: The Second Reconstruction in Black America, 1945–1990*, 2nd edn (Basingstoke: Macmillan, 1991), p. 123; Woodard, *A Nation within a Nation*, pp. 203, 209, 211–12.
11. Woodard, *A Nation within a Nation*, p. 209; Smith, *We Have No Leaders*, p. 53; *Chicago Tribune*, 30 April 1972.
12. Bloom and Martin, *Black against Empire*, pp. 380–1; Paul Alkebulan, *Pending Revolution: The History of the Black Panther Party* (Tuscaloosa: University of Alabama Press, 2007), pp. 53, 56, 70, 76–8, 118, 134 n. 5.

13. Peniel E. Joseph, 'Revolution in Babylon: Stokely Carmichael and America in the 1960s', *Souls* 9 (October–December 2007), pp. 295–6; Peniel E. Joseph, *Waiting 'Til the Midnight Hour: A Narrative History of Black Power in America* (New York: Henry Holt, 2006), p. 290; Peniel E. Joseph, *Stokely: A Life* (New York: Basic Civitas, 2014), pp. 280–317, 321; Smith, *We Have No Leaders*, p. 36.

14. Woodard, *A Nation within a Nation*, pp. 173–80; Komozi Woodard, 'Amiri Baraka, the Congress of African People, and Black Power Politics from the 1961 United Nations Protest to the 1972 Gary Convention', in Peniel E. Joseph (ed.), *The Black Power Movement: Rethinking the Civil Rights-Black Power Era* (New York and London: Routledge, 2006), pp. 73, 76; Marable, *Race, Reform, and Rebellion*, p. 134; Joseph, *Waiting 'Til the Midnight Hour*, pp. 283–5, 288; Joseph, *Stokely*, pp. 284, 288, 292–3, 296, 307; La TaSha Levy, Sylvia Hill and Judy Claude, 'Remembering Sixth-PAC: Interviews with Sylvia Hill and Judy Claude, Organizers of the Sixth Pan-African Congress', *Black Scholar* 37 (Winter 2008), pp. 39–40, 44.

15. Alkebulan, *Survival Pending Revolution*, pp. 119–22, 124–5, 128; Bloom and Martin, *Black against Empire*, pp. 380–9; Jeffrey O. G. Ogbar, *Black Power: Radical Politics and African American Identity* (Baltimore and London: Johns Hopkins University Press, 2004), p. 200; Ollie A. Johnson, III, 'Explaining the Demise of the Black Panther Party: The Role of Internal Factors', in Charles E. Jones (ed.), *The Black Panther Party Reconsidered* (Baltimore: Black Classic Press, 1998), pp. 391–4, 403–8; Akinyele Omowale Umoja, 'Repression Breeds Resistance: The Black Liberation Army and the Radical Legacy of the Black Panther Party', *New Political Science* 21 (June 1999), pp. 131–3, 143–55.

16. Smith, *We Have No Leaders*, pp. 56–75; Marable, *Race, Reform, and Rebellion*, pp. 133, 137; Robeson Taj P. Frazier, 'The Congress of African People: Baraka, Brother Mao, and the Year of '74', *Souls* 8 (Summer 2006), pp. 142–3, 147–56; Alex Houen, 'Amira Baraka', *The Literary Encyclopedia*, available at <http://www.litencyc.com/php/speople.php?rec=true&UID=247> (last accessed 24 April 2010); William L. Van Deburg, *New Day in Babylon: The Black Power Movement and American Culture, 1965–1975* (Chicago and London: University of Chicago Press, 1992), p. 301; Nagueyalti Warren, 'Pan-African Cultural Movements: From Baraka to Karenga', *Journal of Negro History* 75 (Winter–Spring 1990), p. 26; *New York Times*, 2 May 1998; Alkebulan, *Survival Pending Revolution*, p. 73.

17. Edward E. Curtis IV, *Black Muslim Religion in the Nation of Islam, 1960–1975* (Chapel Hill: University of North Carolina Press, 2006), p. 12; Karl Evanzz, *The Messenger: The Rise and Fall of Elijah*

Muhammad (New York: Vintage, 1999), pp. 419–22, 440–1; Ogbar, *Black Power*, pp. 201–2; Arthur J. Magida, *Prophet of Rage: A Life of Louis Farrakhan and His Nation* (New York: Basic Books, 1996), pp. 111–12; Dawn-Marie Gibson, *A History of the Nation of Islam: Race, Islam, and the Quest for Freedom* (Santa Barbara, Denver and Oxford: Praeger, 2012), pp. 67–8.

18. Gibson, *History of the Nation of Islam*, pp. 67, 71–84, 86; Curtis, *Black Muslim Religion in the Nation of Islam*, pp. 176–86; Lawrence H. Mamiya, 'From Black Muslim to Bilalian: The Evolution of a Movement', *Journal for the Scientific Study of Religion* 21 (June 1982), pp. 143–6, 148–50.

19. Magida, *Prophet of Rage*, pp. 121–4, 129–30; Gibson, *History of the Nation of Islam*, pp. 67, 81–2, 85–100, 129; Mattias Gardell, *In the Name of Elijah Muhammad: Louis Farrakhan and the Nation of Islam* (Durham, NC: Duke University Press, 1996), pp. 254–5; Ernest Allen, Jr, 'Religious Heterodoxy and Nationalist Tradition: The Continuing Evolution of the Nation of Islam', *Black Scholar* 26 (Fall–Winter 1996), pp. 15, 19; Vibert L. White, Jr, *Inside the Nation of Islam: A Historical and Personal Testimony by a Black Muslim* (Gainesville: University Press of Florida, 2001), pp. 100, 110, 150.

20. Gibson, *History of the Nation of Islam*, pp. 100–1, 105–7; Robert Singh, *The Farrakhan Phenomenon: Race, Reaction, and the Paranoid Style in American Politics* (Washington, DC: Georgetown University Press, 1997), p. 132.

21. White, *Inside the Nation of Islam*, pp. 94–5; Evanzz, *Messenger*, pp. 365, 435; Magida, *Prophet of Rage*, p. 131; Singh, *Farrakhan Phenomenon*, pp. 132–3; Gibson, *History of the Nation of Islam*, pp. 100–3, 105, 130, 135–7; Ashahed M. Muhammad, 'Saviours' Day: A Timeline and Brief History', *Final Call*, 24 February 2008, available at <http://www.finalcall.com/artman/publish/Perspectives_1/Saviours_Day_A_Timeline_and_Brief_History_4423.shtml> (last accessed 30 December 2016).

22. Gibson, *History of the Nation of Islam*, pp. 108–9, 120–3; Allen, 'Religious Heterodoxy and Nationalist Tradition', pp. 20–1, 23, 34 n. 134; Magida, *Prophet of Rage*, pp. 136–8; James Lance Taylor, *Black Nationalism in the United States: From Malcolm X to Barack Obama* (Boulder and London: Lynne Rienner, 2011), pp. 282, 298–301; Smith, *We Have No Leaders*, pp. 102–3.

23. William Jeremiah Moses, *Afrotopia: The Roots of African American Popular History* (Cambridge: Cambridge University Press, 1998); Dean E. Robinson, *Black Nationalism in American Politics and Thought* (Cambridge: Cambridge University Press, 2001), pp. 128–31; Molefi Kete Asante, *Afrocentricity: The Theory of Social Change*,

rev. edn (Chicago: African American Images, 2003), pp. 3–5, 11; Adisa
A. Alkebulan, 'Defending the Paradigm', *Journal of Black Studies* 37
(January 2007), p. 411; Austin, *Achieving Blackness*, pp. 125–6.

24. E. Frances White, 'Africa on My Mind: Gender, Counter Discourse
and African-American Nationalism', *Journal of Women's History* 2
(Spring 1990), pp. 73–97; Robinson, *Black Nationalism in American
Politics and Thought*, pp. 128–33; Austin, *Achieving Blackness*, pp.
111, 114–18, 121–6; Molefi Kete Asante, 'The Afrocentric Idea in
Education', *Journal of Negro Education* 60 (Spring 1991), pp. 171–3,
178–9; Molefi Kete Asante, 'The Ideological Significance of Afrocentricity in Intercultural Communication', *Journal of Black Studies* 14
(September 1983), pp. 4, 7; Asante, *Afrocentricity*, pp. 4–5.

25. Austin, *Achieving Blackness*, pp. 112–13, 118–19.

26. Austin, *Achieving Blackness*, pp. 130–7; Gibson, *History of the
Nation of Islam*, pp. 106–7, 111–12; Alphonso Pinkney, *Black Americans*, 5th edn (Upper Saddle River, NJ: Prentice-Hall, 1999), p. 141.

27. Austin, *Achieving Blackness*, pp. 130–41, 144–52, 191.

28. Ibid., pp. 141–4.

29. Austin, *Achieving Blackness*, pp. 156–7, 167–71, 192; Brown,
Fighting for US, pp. 160–1.

30. Austin, *Achieving Blackness*, pp. 147, 152, 157–8; Gibson, *History of
the Nation of Islam*, pp. 114–16.

31. Austin, *Achieving Blackness*, pp. 172–86, 188, 274 n. 10; Gibson,
History of the Nation of Islam, p. 113; Darren W. Davis and
Ronald E. Brown, 'The Antipathy of Black Nationalism: Behavioral
and Attitudinal Implications of an African American Ideology',
American Journal of Political Science 46 (April 2002), pp. 239–52.

32. Robert A. Brown and Todd C. Shaw, 'Separate Nations: Two Attitudinal
Dimensions of Black Nationalism', *Journal of Politics* 64 (February
2002), pp. 22–44.

33. Austin, *Achieving Blackness*, p. 158; Charise L. Cheney, *Brothers
Gonna Work It Out: Sexual Politics in the Golden Age of Rap Nation-
alism* (New York: New York University Press, 2005), pp. 149–60;
Gibson, *History of the Nation of Islam*, p. 124.

34. Gibson, *History of the Nation of Islam*, pp. 125–8; Algernon Austin,
*Achieving Blackness: Race, Black Nationalism, and Afrocentrism in
the Twentieth Century* (New York and London: New York University
Press, 2006), pp. 161–2; Michael O. West, 'Like a River: The Million
Man March and the Black Nationalist Tradition in the United States',
Journal of Historical Sociology 12 (March 1999), pp. 81–2, 92–3, 100 n.
36; Haki R. Madhubuti and Maulana Karenga (eds), *The Million Man
March/Day of Absence Mission: A Commemorative Anthology* (Chi-
cago: Third World Press; Los Angeles: University of Sankore Press, 1996).

35. Magida, *Prophet of Rage*, pp. 193–7; Gibson, *History of the Nation of Islam*, pp. 125–7; Robinson, *Black Nationalism in American Politics and Thought*, pp. 123–6; Robert Joseph Taylor and Karen D. Lincoln, 'The Million Man March: Portraits and Attitudes', available at <http://www.rcgd.isr.umich.edu/prba/perspectives/winter1997/rtaylor1.pdf> (last accessed 7 December 2016). A survey by Howard University found that 32 per cent of participants considered it 'very important' that Farrakhan initiated the march. Joseph McCormick, II, 'The Messages and the Messengers: Opinions from the Million Men Who Marched', *National Political Science Review* 6 (1997), p. 147.

36. Brown and Shaw, 'Separate Nations', pp. 32–3, 41; Joseph McCormick II and Sekou Franklin, 'Expressions of Racial Consciousness in the African American Community: Data from the Million Man March', in Yvette M. Alex-Assensoh and Lawrence J. Hanks (eds), *Black and Multiracial Politics in America* (New York and London: New York University Press, 2000), pp. 322–7, 332 n. 7; Taylor, *Black Nationalism in the United States*, pp. 271, 358 n. 35.

37. Magida, *Prophet of Rage*, pp. 199–202; Gibson, *History of the Nation of Islam*, pp. 127–9, 141, 149, 153; Allen, 'Religious Heterodoxy and Nationalist Tradition', p. 24.

Conclusion

Scholars will likely continue to contest definitions of black nationalism, with disagreement centred on whether it should be construed strictly as an aspiration for independent statehood or more broadly to include demands for self-determination focused on controlling institutions in black communities based on group solidarity. Black nationalism has roots that extend back into the colonial era and, although always manifest in some form, has experienced many periods of resurgence and decline. As Wilson Jeremiah Moses and Dean E. Robinson have argued, black nationalism was not an unchanging phenomenon, rather its shape, appeal and meaning reflected the particular circumstances of its time.

Slave revolts and maroon communities were indicative of black nationalism, grounded in a desire for independence and self-determination. African cultural survivals and the gradual formation of a shared culture among the enslaved suggested the development of some form of common identity. Illiteracy, a lack of documentation and the sheer variety of different forms of slavery over time and place make it difficult to assess the nature and extent of black nationalism among enslaved people and free blacks during slavery's long history. Much of what is known about early forms of black nationalism derives from the writings and actions of literate free blacks in the North, including some who had escaped from southern enslavement. Most of the surviving nationalist material was produced by black men, with much less known about black women's perspectives. However, the contributions of Maria W. Stewart and Mary Ann Shadd Cary, as well as the women who constituted almost a third of participants at the National Emigration Convention in 1854, immigrated with their partners and families to Africa, Canada, Haiti and Mexico, or migrated to Kansas, are indicative of black nationalism's appeal to women before the twentieth century.

In the nineteenth and twentieth centuries, black nationalism included both emigrationists and, what Lance Taylor describes as, 'stay-at-home' nationalists. Worsening conditions for blacks, such as during the period between 1850 and 1861, the end of Reconstruction and the rise Jim Crow and black disenfranchisement, and the Red Summer of 1919, produced a resurgence in black nationalism. Even Frederick Douglass contemplated immigrating to Haiti in 1861 before the outbreak of the American Civil War. Moses notes that what he calls black nationalism's golden age between 1850 and 1925 was largely hierarchical and emphasised a civilising mission, Christianity and commerce. In so doing, black nationalists were conservative in that they aspired to emulate and disseminate what they regarded as the best of western culture. Both Marcus Garvey and the Universal Negro Improvement Association (UNIA) and the Nation of Islam (NOI) under Elijah Muhammad were hierarchical, committed to a 'civilising' mission among African Americans (and for the UNIA also among Africans) and sought to develop commerce. The two organisations did not try to overturn racial discrimination in the United States, made agreements with white supremacist groups and embraced patriarchy, although challenged in that regard by some UNIA women. Unlike the more elite dominated black nationalism of the second half of the nineteenth century, the UNIA and the NOI gained mass support and appealed to the lower class, while also attracting some middle class membership.

While the UNIA and NOI viewed modern Africa negatively as benighted and requiring 'civilisation', Malcolm X and Black Power groups identified with Third World struggles against colonialism and regarded blacks in the United States as an internal colony. Many Black Power groups also embraced Pan-Africanism, a selective and sometimes invented idea of African culture, and socialism, whether Marxist–Leninist–Maoist or African. While the NOI and Malcolm X, both within and outside the NOI, were major influences on the development of Black Power, so too were Robert F. Williams, the Cuban Revolution and China. Despite turf wars between the Black Panther Party (BPP) and US, revolutionary and cultural nationalists often had much in common, with neither eschewing political change or the role of culture in moulding a revolutionary mentality, although the Panthers emphasised Third World revolutionary struggles and cultural nationalists what they perceived as distinctive African traits.

Although the post-NOI Malcolm X, Republic of New Africa (RNA), the League of Revolutionary Black Workers and, eventually, the BPP rejected female subordination, they failed to excise it from their organisations. After leaving the NOI, Malcolm X had little time to develop his ideas or the groups he founded as he was murdered less than a year afterwards. By 1970, the Panthers, who had a large and perhaps majority female membership which, despite ongoing sexual discrimination, sometimes exercised leadership, also supported gay liberation in marked contrast to the hypermasculinity that animated many nationalist groups. However, some Panther women felt compelled to adopt the assertive aggressiveness of male Panthers in order to win their respect. In the 1960s and early 1970s, Maulana Karenga and Amiri Baraka, the leading cultural nationalists, advocated female subordination in their organisations, and their emphasis, like that of the NOI, on respect and honour for women, particularly as mothers, reflected traditional white American middle class aspirations. Baraka and the NOI's ideology of racial uplift was part of a black tradition that stretched back to Garvey, Booker T. Washington and the nineteenth century and was similarly shaped by American white middle class patriarchal norms. Many black nationalist groups that arose in the 1960s, such as the BPP, the RNA, US and Baraka's Committee for a Unified Newark were hierarchical and some were violent toward members and rivals.[1]

Black Power was not always synonymous with black nationalism or understood as such by much of the black population, but it widely affected African Americans, both culturally and politically. Cultural nationalists exerted a great deal of influence in organising and directing a series of Black Power conferences that culminated in the National Black Political Convention in 1972. However, disagreements emerged among the varieties of black opinion represented at the convention, and subsequent conventions attracted fewer and mostly less influential people.

By the early 1970s, many Black Power organisations were in decline, undermined by internal disagreements and state repression. Advocates of guerrilla warfare, both rhetorical and real, found themselves no match for the vast power of the state and unable to attract black mass support. The Panthers abandoned black nationalism and, although ostensibly still committed to revolution, engaged in Oakland politics. Cultural nationalists also changed direction. By 1974, Baraka had embraced Marxism and an imprisoned Karenga scientific socialism. After the death of Elijah Muhammad in 1975, his son Wallace steered the NOI away from nationalism toward Sunni Islam.

Real and perceived deteriorating social and economic conditions helped fuel black nationalist resurgence in the late 1980s and
early 1990s. An entirely cultural approach, shorn of the revolutionary aspirations and political engagement of many Black Power
era cultural nationalists, Afrocentry sought to address perceived
deficiencies in lower class black culture, a recurrent theme in black
nationalism that had informed nineteenth-century black nationalism, the UNIA, US and the NOI. By making no demands on the
state, other than support or acquiescence in Afrocentric education,
Afrocentricity was conservative as a force. Regarding Africa as a
single cultural entity, Afrocentrists were shaped more by western
thinking than African realities. Much like Garvey and Black Power
cultural nationalists, Afrocentrists tended to celebrate ancient and
precolonial African societies, 'kingdoms' and 'empires', and ignore
their rulers' subordination of the inhabitants.[2]

Louis Farrakhan came to national and international prominence
after participating in Jesse Jackson's 1984 presidential nomination
bid, but despite breaking from Elijah Muhammad's apolitical stance,
Farrakhan's NOI was, like Muhammad himself, conservative.
Farrakhan, like Afrocentrists, placed the responsibility for uplifting blacks on black people themselves, although he, like Muhammad, endorsed government reparations for racism. The NOI also
remained largely patriarchal. Farrakhan's call for a million men to
assemble in Washington, DC, in 1995 drew the ire of some black
feminists. The Million Man March pledge stressed the conservative themes of personal morality, clean living, self-improvement
and business creation. Many of the march participants, like many
Afrocentrists, were middle class. While many marchers were black
nationalist in orientation, most were not followers of Farrakhan's
NOI or inclined toward the separatism he more usually espoused.
Many African Americans favoured community nationalism, centred
on black community control, but only a minority of nationalists
were separatists. Separatism was more attractive to lower class than
middle class nationalists.

The peaks and troughs of black nationalist support tell us much
about how African Americans have perceived their circumstances
at any given time in American history. Robinson regards black
nationalism negatively, arguing that it 'inadvertently helps to repro-
duce some of the thinking and practices that created black disad-
vantage in the first place' by identifying black 'differences from the

majority population'. He finds that black nationalism has been largely conservative by adjusting to, rather than directly challenging, racial discrimination in mainstream society. Although black nationalism has often been conservative, in some manifestations it has challenged white conceptions of black inferiority, tried to exert political influence, sought control of institutions and services in the black community, and expressed support of and solidarity with African liberation struggles. Black nationalism has also helped sustain its adherents in a hostile environment by giving them a shared sense of identity, self-worth, pride and hope for a better future. Black nationalism has often been hierarchical, authoritarian and patriarchal, and sometimes violent, but historically so has much of the wider society that influenced its development, especially in the treatment of blacks, other minorities and women.[3]

Notes

1. Paul Alkebulan, *Pending Revolution: The History of the Black Panther Party* (Tuscaloosa: University of Alabama Press, 2007), p. 100.
2. Daniel Matlin, '"Lift Up Yr Self!" Reinterpreting Amiri Baraka (LeRoi Jones), Black Power, and the Uplift Tradition', *Journal of American History* 93 (June 2006), pp. 106, 108.
3. Dean E. Robinson, *Black Nationalism in American Politics and Thought* (Cambridge: Cambridge University Press, 2001), pp. 1-2.

Suggestions for Further Reading

There is a vast and burgeoning literature about black nationalism. The reading suggestions below are necessarily very selective.

On defining black nationalism see Daryl Michael Scott, 'How Black Nationalism Became Sui Generis', *Fire!!!* 1 (Summer–Winter 2012), pp. 6–63. On key issues in black nationalist history see Dean E. Robinson, *Black Nationalism in American Politics and Thought* (Cambridge: Cambridge University Press, 2001), Akinyele Umoja, 'Searching for Place: Nationalism, Separatism and Pan-Africanism', in Alton Hornsby (ed.), *A Companion to African American History* (Malden, MA: Blackwell, 2005), pp. 529–44, James Lance Taylor, *Black Nationalism in the United States: From Malcolm X to Barack Obama* (Boulder and London: Lynne Rienner, 2011) and the editors' introductions in the document collections: John H. Bracey, Jr, August Meier and Elliott Rudwick (eds), *Black Nationalism in America* (Indianapolis and New York: Bobbs-Merrill, 1970), Wilson Jeremiah Moses (ed.), *Classical Black Nationalism: From the American Revolution to Marcus Garvey* (New York and London: New York University Press, 1996) and William L. Van Deburg (ed.), *Modern Black Nationalism: From Marcus Garvey to Louis Farrakhan* (New York and London: New York University Press, 1997).

On the development of black nationalism until the early twentieth century see Floyd J. Miller, *The Search for a Black Nationality: Black Emigration and Colonization, 1787–1863* (Urbana, Chicago and London: University of Illinois Press, 1975), Sterling Stuckey, *Slave Culture: Nationalist Theory and the Foundations of Black America* (New York: Oxford University Press, 1988), Wilson Jeremiah Moses, *The Golden Age of Black Nationalism, 1850–1925* (1978; New York and Oxford: Oxford University Press, 1988), Dexter B. Gordon, *Black Identity: Rhetoric, Ideology, and Nineteenth-Century Black Nationalism* (Carbondale: Southern Illinois University Press, 2003), Tunde

Adeleke, *UnAfrican Americans: Nineteenth-Century Black Nationalists and the Civilizing Mission* (Lexington: University Press of Kentucky, 1998), Edwin S. Redkey, *Black Exodus: Black Nationalists and Back-to-Africa Movements, 1890–1910* (New Haven: Yale University Press, 1969) and Milfred C. Fierce, *The Pan-African Idea in the United States, 1900–1919: African-American Interest in Africa and Interaction with West Africa* (New York: Garland, 1993).

Studies of key nineteenth and early twentieth-century figures include Peter P. Hinks, *To Awaken My Afflicted Brethren: David Walker and the Problem of Antebellum Slave Resistance* (University Park, PA: Pennsylvania State University Press, 1997), Valerie C. Cooper, *Word, Like Fire: Maria Stewart, the Bible, and the Rights of African Americans* (Charlottesville: University of Virginia Press, 2012), Cyril E. Griffith, *The African Dream: Martin R. Delany and the Emergence of Pan-African Thought* (University Park: Pennsylvania State University Press, 1975), Tommie Shelby, 'Two Conceptions of Black Nationalism: Martin Delany on the Meaning of Black Political Solidarity', *Political Theory* 31 (October 2003), pp. 664–92, Tunde Adeleke, *Without Regard to Race: The Other Martin Robison Delaney* (Jackson: University Press of Mississippi, 2003), Joel Schor, *Henry Highland Garnet: A Voice of Black Radicalism in the Nineteenth Century* (Westport, CT: Praeger, 1977), Jane Rhodes, *Mary Ann Shadd Cary: The Black Press and Protest in the Nineteenth Century* (Bloomington: Indiana University Press, 1998), Wilson Jeremiah Moses, *Alexander Crummell: A Study of Civilization and Discontent* (Amherst: University of Massachusetts Press, 1992), Andre E. Johnson, *The Forgotten Prophet: Bishop Henry McNeal Turner and the African American Prophetic Tradition* (New York: Lexington, 2012), Louis R. Harlan, *Booker T. Washington: The Wizard of Tuskegee, 1901–1915* (New York and Oxford: Oxford University Press, 1983) and Robert J. Norrell, *Up from History: The Life of Booker T. Washington* (Cambridge, MA and London: Belknap Press of Harvard University Press, 2009).

On Marcus Garvey and the Universal Negro Improvement Association (UNIA) see the dated but stimulating E. David Cronon, *Black Moses: The Story of Marcus Garvey and the Universal Negro Improvement Association*, with a foreword by John Hope Franklin (1955; Madison: University of Wisconsin Press, 1969), Tony Martin, *Race First: The Ideological and Organizational Struggles of Marcus Garvey and the Universal Negro Improvement Association* (Dover, MA: Majority Press, 1976), Randall K. Burkett, *Garveyism as a Religious Movement: The Institutionalization of a Black Civil Religion* (Metuchen, NJ: Scarecrow/ American Theological Library Association, 1978), Robert A. Hill (ed.), *Marcus Garvey and the Universal Negro Improvement Association Papers*, vol. I–XIII (Berkeley: University of California Press/Durham, NC: Duke University Press, 1983–2016), Mary G. Rolinson, *Grassroots Garveyism: The Universal Negro Improvement Association in the Rural South, 1920–1927* (Chapel Hill: University of North Carolina Press, 2007), Claudrena N. Harold, *The Rise and Fall of the Garvey Movement in the Urban South, 1918–1942* (New York and London: Routledge, 2007) and Adam Ewing, *The Age of Garvey: How a Jamaican Activist Created a Mass Movement and Changed Global Black Politics* (Princeton and Oxford: Princeton University Press, 2014). On the UNIA and African Blood Brotherhood see Theodore Kornweibel, Jr, *Seeing Red: Federal Campaigns against Black Militancy, 1919–1925* (Bloomington: Indiana University Press, 1994) and Winston James, *Holding Aloft the Banner of Ethiopia: Caribbean Radicalism in Early Twentieth-Century America* (New York: Verso, 1998).

On Elijah Muhammad and the Nation of Islam see Erdmann Doane Beynon, 'The Voodoo Cult Among Negro Migrants in Detroit', *American Journal of Sociology* 58 (May 1938), pp. 894–907, Hatim A. Sahib, 'The Nation of Islam', *Contributions in Black Studies* 13 (1995), pp. 48–160, C. Eric Lincoln, *The Black Muslims in America* (Boston: Beacon Press, 1961), E. U. Essien-Udom, *Black Nationalism: A Search for an Identity in America* (Chicago and London: University of Chicago Press, 1962), Claude Andrew Clegg III, *An Original Man: The Life and Times of Elijah Muhammad* (New York: St. Martin's Press, 1998), Karl Evanzz, *The Messenger: The Rise and Fall of Elijah Muhammad* (New York: Vintage, 2001), Edward E. Curtis, IV, *Islam in Black America: Identity, Liberation, and Difference in African-American Islam* (Albany: State University of New York Press, 2002), Edward E. Curtis, IV, *Black Muslim Religion in the Nation of Islam, 1960–1975* (Chapel Hill: University of North Carolina Press, 2006) and Herbert Berg, *Elijah Muhammad and Islam* (New York: New York University Press, 2009).

On Malcolm X see Malcolm X with the assistance of Alex Haley, *The Autobiography of Malcolm X* (1965; London: Penguin, 1968),

George Breitman (ed.), *Malcolm X Speaks: Selected Speeches and Statements* (New York: Pathfinder, 1992), Bruce Perry, *Malcolm: The Life of a Man Who Changed Black America* (Barrytown, NY: Station Hill Press, 1991), William W. Sales, Jr, *From Civil Rights to Black Liberation: Malcolm X and the Organization of Afro-American Unity* (Boston: South End, 1994) and Manning Marable, *Malcolm X: A Life of Reinvention* (New York: Allen Lane, 2011).

On Black Power generally see William L. Van Deburg, *New Day in Babylon: The Black Power Movement and American Culture, 1965–1975* (Chicago and London: University of Chicago Press, 1992), John T. McCartney, *Black Power Ideologies: An Essay in African-American Political Thought* (Philadelphia: Temple University Press, 1992), Eddie S. Glaude (ed.), *Is It Nation Time?: Contemporary Essays on Black Power and Black Nationalism* (Chicago: University of Chicago Press, 2002), Jeffrey O. G. Ogbar, *Black Power: Radical Politics and African American Identity* (Baltimore and London: Johns Hopkins University Press, 2004), James Edward Smethurst, *The Black Arts Movement: Literary Nationalism in the 1960s and 1970s* (Chapel Hill: University of North Carolina Press, 2005), Peniel E. Joseph, *Waiting 'Til the Midnight Hour: A Narrative History of Black Power in America* (New York: Henry Holt, 2006), Peniel E. Joseph (ed.), *The Black Power Movement: Rethinking the Civil Rights-Black Power Era* (New York and London: Routledge, 2006), Judson L. Jeffries (ed.), *Black Power in the Belly of the Beast*, with a foreword by Tiyi M. Morris (Urbana and Chicago: University of Illinois Press, 2006), Peniel E. Joseph, 'The Black Power Movement: A State of the Field', *Journal of American History* 96 (December 2009), pp. 751–76 and Ashley D. Farmer, *What You've Got is a Revolution: Black Women's Movements for Black Power* (forthcoming, Chapel Hill: University of North Carolina Press).

On Black Power advocates and organisations see Robert F. Williams, *Negroes with Guns* (1962; Detroit: Wayne State University Press, 1998), Timothy B. Tyson, *Radio Free Dixie: Robert F. Williams and the Roots of Black Power* (Chapel Hill: University of North Carolina Press, 1999), Maxwell C. Stanford, 'Revolutionary Action Movement (RAM): A Case Study of An Urban Revolutionary Movement in Western Capitalist Society' (Master's thesis, Atlanta University, 1986), Robin D. G. Kelley and Betsy Esch, 'Black like Mao: Red China and Black Revolution', *Souls* 1 (Fall

1999), pp. 6–41, Robeson Taj Frazier, *The East Is Black: Cold War China in the Black Radical Imagination* (Durham, NC: Duke University Press, 2014), Stokely Carmichael and Charles V. Hamilton, *Black Power: The Politics of Liberation in America* (New York: Vintage, 1967), Komozi Woodard, *A Nation within a Nation: Amiri Baraka (LeRoi Jones) and Black Power Politics* (Chapel Hill and London: University of North Carolina Press, 1999), Daniel Matlin, '"Lift Up Yr Self!" Reinterpreting Amiri Baraka (LeRoi Jones), Black Power, and the Uplift Tradition', *Journal of American History* 93 (June 2006), pp. 91–116, Michael Simanga, *Amiri Baraka and the Congress of African People: History and Memory* (New York: Palgrave Macmillan, 2015), Brian Ward, 'Jazz and Soul, Race and Class, Cultural Nationalists and Black Panthers: A Black Power Debate Revisited', in Brian Ward (ed.), *Media, Culture, and the Modern African-American Freedom Struggle* (Gainesville: University Press of Florida, 2001), pp. 161–96, Scot Brown, *Fighting for US: Maulana Karenga, the US Organization, and Black Cultural Nationalism*, with a foreword by Clayborne Carson (New York and London: New York University Press, 2003), Nikhil Pal Singh, *Black Is a Country: Race and the Unfinished Struggle for Democracy* (Cambridge, MA: Harvard University Press, 2004), Paul Alkebulan, *Pending Revolution: The History of the Black Panther Party* (Tuscaloosa: University of Alabama Press, 2007), Yohuru Williams and Jama Lazerow (eds), *Liberated Territory: Untold Local Perspectives on the Black Panther Party* (Durham, NC and London: Duke University Press, 2008), Donna Jean Murch, *Living for the City: Migration, Education, and the Rise of the Black Panther Party in Oakland, California* (Chapel Hill: University of North Carolina Press, 2010), Joshua Bloom and Waldo E. Martin, Jr, *Black against Empire: The History and Politics of the Black Panther Party* (Berkeley, Los Angeles and London: University of California Press, 2013), Donald Cunnigen, 'Bringing the Revolution Down Home: The Republic of New Africa in Mississippi', *Sociological Spectrum* 19 (January–March 1999), pp. 63–92 and James A. Geschwender, *Class, Race and Worker Insurgency: The League of Revolutionary Black Workers* (New York: Cambridge University Press, 1977).

On Afrocentricity see Molefi Kete Asante, *Afrocentricity: The Theory of Social Change*, rev. edn (Chicago: African American Images, 2003), E. Frances White, 'Africa on My Mind: Gender,

Counter Discourse and Africa-American Nationalism', *Journal of Women's History* 2 (Spring 1990), pp. 73–97, Robinson, *Black Nationalism in American Politics and Thought* and Algernon Austin, *Achieving Blackness: Race, Black, Nationalism, and Afrocentrism in the Twentieth Century* (New York and London: New York University Press, 2006).

On Louis Farrakhan, black nationalism in the 1990s and the Million Man March see Mattias Gardell, *In the Name of Elijah Muhammad: Louis Farrakhan and the Nation of Islam* (Durham, NC: Duke University Press, 1996), Arthur J. Magida, *Prophet of Rage: A Life of Louis Farrakhan and His Nation* (New York: Basic Books, 1996), Joseph McCormick II and Sekou Franklin, 'Expressions of Racial Consciousness in the African American Community: Data from the Million Man March', in Yvette M. Alex-Assensoh and Lawrence J. Hanks (eds), *Black and Multiracial Politics in America* (New York and London: New York University Press, 2000), pp. 315–36, Robinson, *Black Nationalism in American Politics and Thought*, Robert A. Brown and Todd C. Shaw, 'Separate Nations: Two Attitudinal Dimensions of Black Nationalism', *Journal of Politics* 64 (February 2002), pp. 22–44, Austin, *Achieving Blackness* and Dawn-Marie Gibson, *A History of the Nation of Islam: Race, Islam, and the Quest for Freedom* (Santa Barbara, Denver and Oxford: Praeger, 2012).

Index

BRITISH ASSOCIATION
ᶠᴼᴿAMERICAN STUDIES

Series Editors: Martin Halliwell, Professor of American Studies at the University of Leicester; and Emily West, Professor of American History at the University of Reading.

The British Association for American Studies (BAAS)

The British Association for American Studies was founded in 1955 to promote the study of the United States of America. It welcomes applications for membership from anyone interested in the history, society, government and politics, economics, geography, literature, creative arts, culture and thought of the USA.

The Association publishes a newsletter twice yearly, holds an annual national conference, supports regional branches and provides other membership services, including preferential subscription rates to the *Journal of American Studies*.

Membership enquiries may be addressed to the BAAS Secretary. For contact details visit our website: www.baas.ac.uk